Question Time 5

150 More Questions and Answers on the Catholic Faith

QuestionTime 5

150 Questions and Answers on the Catholic Faith

FR JOHN FLADER

Foreword by Peter Rosengren

Published in 2020 by Connor Court Publishing Pty Ltd

Copyright © John Flader 2020

ALL RIGHTS RESERVED. This book contains material protected under International and Federal Copyright Laws and Treaties. Any unauthorised reprint or use of this material is prohibited. No part of this book may be reproduced or transmitted in any form or by any means, electronic or mechanical, including photocopying, recording, or by any information storage and retrieval system without express written permission from the publisher.

Connor court Publishing Pty Ltd
PO Box 7257
Redland Bay QLD 4165
sales@connorcourt.com
www.connorcourt.com

Nihil obstat: Rev. Peter Joseph, STD
Imprimatur: +Most Reverend Anthony Fisher OP, Archbishop of Sydney
Date: 10 September 2020

The *Nihil obstat* and *Imprimatur* are a declaration that a book or pamphlet is considered to be free from doctrinal or moral error. It is not necessarily implied that those who have granted them agree with the contents, opinions or statements expressed.

ISBN: 9781922449320

Scripture quotations are from the Revised Standard Version, Second Catholic Edition, Ignatius Edition, of the Bible, copyrighted 2006, by the Division of Christian Education of the National Council of Churches in the United States of America, and are used by permission. All rights reserved.

Cover design by Ian James

Printed in Australia

*In memory of St Josemaría Escrivá
who taught me love for the Church*

CONTENTS

Foreword to Question Time 1 xv

Introduction xvii

Abbreviations xix

I. CATHOLIC DOCTRINE 1

God 1
   601 A gender-neutral God? 1
   602 Are the bushfires God's punishment? 3

Sacred Scripture 6
   603 Old Testament Jewish feasts 6
   604 More Jewish feasts 8
   605 Still more Jewish feasts 10
   606 The accuracy of the New Testament text 12
   607 Archaeological evidence for the New Testament 14
   608 The Dead Sea Scrolls 17
   609 The Pharisees and Sadducees 19
   610 Who were the scribes? 21
   611 Does Christ bring peace? 23
   612 St Paul making up "what is lacking" 25

Jesus Christ 28
   613 Historical evidence for Christ 28
   614 Did Jesus know he was God? 30
   615 Did Jesus behave like God? 32
   616 Jesus the Messiah 34

617 More prophecies of the Messiah 36
618 Proof of the Resurrection of Christ 38

The Church 41
619 The Church is one 41
620 The Church is holy 43
621 The Church is catholic 45
622 The Church is apostolic 47
623 Fathers of the Church 49
624 Eastern Fathers of the Church 51
625 Western Fathers of the Church 53
626 More Western Fathers of the Church 55
627 The Fathers of the Church and conversions 58
628 Dogmas and doctrines 60
629 The Leuven Project 62
630 Plenary Councils 64
631 The Church is hierarchical 66
632 Decision-making in the universal Church 68
633 Decision-making in the local Church 70
634 The *sensus fidei* 72
635 A Vatican document on the *sensus fidei* 74
636 Practical consequences of the *sensus fidei* 77
637 Seventh-Day Adventists and the Church 79
638 Faith in the Church 81
639 Prayer for the Church 83
640 Prayer for the Pope 85

The Last Things 88
641 Predestination 88
642 Pope Francis and hell 90

II. LITURGY AND THE SACRAMENTS 93

Liturgy in general 95
    643 A new Sign of the Cross 95
    644 What can be blessed 97
    645 Incense in the liturgy 99

Baptism 102
    646 Baptism in the early Church 102
    647 More ceremonies of Baptism in the early Church 104

The Eucharist 107
    648 Candles in the Mass 107
    649 Has the Pope changed the Our Father? 109
    650 Receiving Communion kneeling 111
    651 Communion for Protestants 113
    652 Communion in a nursing home 115
    653 The Eucharistic miracle of Santarem 117
    654 The Eucharistic miracle of Amsterdam 119
    655 A Eucharistic miracle in Mexico 121

Penance 124
    656 The seal of confession 124
    657 Would priests violate the seal of confession? 126
    658 The consequences of state legislation on the seal of
           confession 128

Holy Orders 130
    659 Voluntary priestly celibacy 130
    660 The effects of laicisation 132
    661 The ordination of women and the Plenary Council 134

Marriage 137
   662 Weddings not celebrated in a church 137
   663 Convalidation of a marriage 139
   664 The internal forum solution 141
   665 Is divorce on the decline? 143
   666 A right to same-sex marriage? 145
   667 Same-sex marriage: why not? 147
   668 Children in same-sex relationships 149
   669 Blessings for gay couples 151

III. MORAL LIFE IN CHRIST 155

General Moral Issues 157
   670 Can freedom be diminished? 157
   671 Freedom and responsibility 159
   672 The emotions and responsibility 161
   673 The principle of double effect 163
   674 Mortal sin and salvation 165
   675 The indirect voluntary 167
   676 Good and bad fruit 169

Specific moral issues 172
   677 The Sunday Mass obligation 172
   678 Embryo adoption 174
   679 When does the soul enter the body? 176
   680 Abortion and a woman's body 178
   681 Abortion and the death penalty 181
   682 The Pope and the death penalty 183
   683 What is euthanasia? 185
   684 Arguments against euthanasia 187

CONTENTS

685 More arguments against euthanasia 189
686 The slippery slope of euthanasia 191
687 Involuntary euthanasia 193
688 Euthanasia in Australia 195
689 Attending a person dying by assisted suicide 197
690 The origins of gender theory 200
691 Gender theory and the Yogyakarta Principles 202
692 The power of the gender movement 204
693 The European Union and the gender ideology movement .. 206
694 Safe Schools and Gender Dysphoria 208
695 Pope Francis and gender ideology 210
696 Vatican document on gender theory 212
697 More on the Vatican document on gender theory 214
698 The attack on the family 216
699 More on the attack on the family 218
700 Still more on the attack on the family 221
701 Defending family values 223
702 Safe Schools and same-sex marriage 225
703 More about Safe Schools 227
704 Attending same-sex "weddings" 229
705 *Humanae Vitae* revisited 231
706 Why is contraception not permitted? 233
707 Condoms and HIV 235
708 Politicians and legislation against the moral law 237
709 Voting for a "less bad" law 240
710 Politicians and excommunication 242
711 Yoga and Christianity 244
712 Tai Chi and Christianity 246

IV. CHRISTIAN PRAYER 249

Prayer and Devotions 251
- 713 The value of the rosary 251
- 714 The rosary and the battle of Lepanto 253
- 715 The rosary and more battles 255
- 716 The Infant of Prague 257
- 717 Our Lady of Good Success 259
- 718 Our Lady of Good Success and prophecies about our times 261

Seasons and Feasts 264
- 719 Advent and penance 264
- 720 Advent in the Eastern tradition 266
- 721 History of the celebration of Christmas 267
- 722 Christmas Names and Masses 269
- 723 History of the feast of Epiphany 271
- 724 Generosity in Lent 274
- 725 Sackcloth and ashes 276
- 726 Passiontide 278
- 727 The history of Holy Week 280
- 728 The Easter Vigil 281
- 729 The Octave of Easter 283
- 730 Easter water 285
- 731 The Easter Season 286
- 732 Feast of the Ascension 288
- 733 Feast of Pentecost 290
- 734 Feast of Mary, Mother of the Church 292
- 735 Feast of the Annunciation 295
- 736 Feast of the Transfiguration 297

CONTENTS

737 Feast of the Holy Name of Mary 299
738 Holy days of obligation 301

Our Lady and the Saints 304
739 Why devotion to Mary? 304
740 Do Catholics worship Mary? 306
741 Is Our Lady Co-redemptrix? 308
742 Blessed Imelda Lambertini 310
743 St Rose of Lima 312
744 St Nunzio Sulprizio 314
745 St Giuseppe Moscati 316
746 St Josephine Bakhita 318
747 St Padre Pio 321
748 Pope St Paul VI 323

Apparitions 326
749 Our Lady of Guadalupe 326
750 Our Lady of Zeitoun 328

Index 331

Foreword to *Question Time 1*

Contrary to some stereotypes in our society, the life of the Christian is one of constant reflection and questioning. The more we learn about God, the more we read the Bible, the more we puzzle over problems in our daily lives and in our societies which seem to challenge Christian beliefs and Catholic teachings, the more questions we have. Praying and meditating regularly also gives rise to many questions as we ponder God's mercy and love, his promises to us, and the evil and suffering that frequently confront us in our daily lives.

Father John Flader's book *Question Time 1 - 150 Questions and Answers on the Catholic Faith* is a wonderful resource for every Catholic who has ever had questions about the faith or about our life together with God. This book brings together answers from Fr Flader's popular column in *The Catholic Weekly* and reflects the timelessness and fascination that different questions have for Christians of all ages and across all generations. The ground covered in this book is nothing if not wide ranging. Can we hurt God? What does the Church think about Evolution? Did the children of Adam and Eve commit incest? Is everyone saved? What does infallibility mean? Does limbo exist? What is an indulgence?

Fr Flader also covers important questions about the life and teaching of Jesus, the sacraments of the Church, the Mass, Mary, and prayer. Moral problems such as suicide, the death penalty, homosexuality, and gambling are also discussed.

Question Time 1 will be a much referenced resource for everyone who uses it. Different questions at different times of the year and at different times in our lives will bring readers back to it again and again. In its succinct and elegant explanations of Catholic teaching and belief, Catholics will find information, encouragement, reassurance, and clarity. They will probably also find some new questions to ask.

Fr Flader has done us all an enormous service in collating his columns and in bringing them to print in this book. I have enjoyed reading it and learnt much from it and I hope you do too.

+George Cardinal Pell
ARCHBISHOP OF SYDNEY
7 March, 2008

Introduction

Now that fifteen years have passed since I began writing the *Question Time* column for *The Catholic Weekly* and this fifth volume of questions and answers sees the light of day, it is time to write a new Introduction.

How did this whole project begin? It started in 2004 when I was Director of the Catholic Adult Education Centre of the Archdiocese of Sydney and was receiving occasional questions about the Catholic faith. I duly answered them and filed the answers in a folder on my office computer. In December of that year I was sitting with the editor of *The Catholic Weekly* at a lunch and offered to use this material to write a question-and-answer column for the paper. His eyes lit up because the Archbishop had asked him to find someone to write such a column and now here was someone offering to do so.

I began writing the column in January 2005 and have done so every week since then. Soon I was receiving reports of people who were cutting out the columns and pasting them on paper for future reference, or photocopying them for others. Over those first years numerous people asked if there was any plan to publish the columns as a book.

Although I hadn't thought of doing so, it seemed more and more appropriate to satisfy the desires of those people. Thus was born *Question Time 1*, the first 150 columns, published by Connor Court in 2008. To be honest, the first volume was simply titled *Question Time*, since it was not certain there would be a second or subsequent volumes.

That first book came to be published in Spanish and Indonesian, and there was another English edition published in the Philippines. Also, the column was soon being used by Catholic newspapers in Perth and Brisbane.

INTRODUCTION

As regards the structure of the book, it seemed appropriate to arrange the questions and answers systematically by topic, following the general structure of the *Catechism of the Catholic Church*. Thus, in all the volumes Chapter 1 deals with matters of Catholic doctrine, Chapter 2 with questions relating to the sacraments and the liturgy in general, Chapter 3 with matters of morals and Chapter 4 with questions relating to prayer and Christian devotions.

People sometimes ask if I am running out of questions. The answer is an emphatic no. I receive an envelope from *The Catholic Weekly* from time to time containing questions sent in by readers and from that source alone I have more questions than I can answer. But questions also come directly by email from around the country, and even from abroad, and many others come from personal conversations and from classes I give. So there is no shortage of questions.

How long can I keep this up? God only knows. I continue to write the column and all the new ones go into a folder on my computer titled *Question Time 6*. So my intention at present is to write long enough at least to bring that book to light. After that, we shall see.

I want to pay special tribute and a note of heartfelt thanks to Anthony Cappello of Connor Court Publishing, who courageously undertook the risk of publishing the first volume and has continued to publish all the others.

And to Fr Peter Joseph, who appears as the censor of all the books but who, in reality, is much more than that. He makes numerous helpful suggestions to add to the text itself and he points out editorial corrections to be made. His help has been invaluable.

I pray that *Question Time 5* will help those who read it to understand their faith better and to come to a deeper love for Jesus Christ, Our Lady and the Church.

Deo omnis gloria!

Fr John Flader

Abbreviations

AG	Second Vatican Council, Decree *Ad gentes* on the Church's Missionary Activity (1965)
AL	Pope Francis, Apostolic Exhortation *Amoris Laetitia* (2015)
CC	Pope Pius XI, Encyclical *Casti connubii* (1930)
CCC	*Catechism of the Catholic Church* (1992)
CCL	*Code of Canon Law* (1983)
CDF	Congregation for the Doctrine of the Faith
CL	Pope John Paul II, Apostolic Exhortation *Christifideles Laici* (1988)
CPG	Pope Paul VI, *Credo of the People of God* (1968)
DPA	Congregation for the Doctrine of the Faith, *Declaration on Procured Abortion* (1974)
DV	Congregation for the Doctrine of the Faith, Instruction *Donum vitae* (1987)
EG	Pope Francis, Apostolic Exhortation *Evangelii Gaudium* (2013)
EN	Pope Paul VI, Apostolic Exhortation *Evangelii Nuntiandum* (1975)
EV	Pope John Paul II, Encyclical *Evangelium vitae* (1995)
FC	Pope John Paul II, Apostolic Exhortation *Famliaris consortio* (1981)
GE	Pope Francis, Apostolic Exhortation *Gaudete et Exsultate* (2018)

GS	Second Vatican Council, Pastoral Constitution *Gaudium et spes* on the Church in the Modern World (1965)
HV	Pope Paul VI, Encyclical *Humanae vitae* (1968)
LG	Second Vatican Council, Dogmatic Constitution on the Church *Lumen gentium* (1964)
RP	Pope John Paul II, Apostolic Exhortation *Reconciliatio et Paenitentia* (1984)
SBB	*Shorter Book of Blessings*
SC	Second Vatican Council, Constitution on the Liturgy, *Sacrosanctum Concilium* (1963)
STh	St Thomas Aquinas, *Summa Theologiae*
UR	Second Vatican Council, Decree *Unitatis redintegratio* on Ecumenism (1964)

I. CATHOLIC DOCTRINE

God

601 A gender-neutral God?

I understand some Catholic schools are opting to describe God with gender-neutral terms, not wanting to use the masculine as we are accustomed to doing. I don't understand this. Can you please give me your thoughts on it?

I don't understand it either. It's another example, in the Catholic sphere, of political correctness taken to the extreme, beginning with the noble goal of wanting to be inclusive, of not discriminating against women in our language. But frankly, you who ask the question are a woman yourself and I am sure there are many other women like you who find no problem in calling God "he".

But where does the issue arise? A spokesperson for an Australian Catholic girls' school recently told a newspaper that as they believe God is neither male nor female, they will use gender-neutral terms in their prayers. In other words, God is no longer to be "he". Other Catholic schools in that city, including at least one for boys, will do the same, using more inclusive language such as "Godself" instead of "himself."

The principal of one of the schools told the newspaper that the school "has a commitment to using inclusive language. Prayers written specifically for use within our college do not refer to God as male or female. There are occasions where gendered language may be appropriate, including references to specific religious and biblical figures."

What can we say about this? To begin with, as eternal pure spirit, God is of course neither male nor female in the human sense. He is simply God, transcending all human categories of gender. At the same time, in creating humans male and female in his image and likeness (cf. *Gen* 1:26), God seems to suggest that in some way maleness and femaleness together reflect the fullness of his divinity.

The *Catechism of the Catholic Church* deals with this question in its section on God the Father. It says: "In Israel, God is called 'Father' inasmuch as he is Creator of the world. Even more, God is Father because of the covenant and the gift of the law to Israel, 'his first-born son.' God is also called the Father of the king of Israel. Most especially he is 'the Father of the poor,' of the orphaned and the widowed, who are under his loving protection" (*CCC* 238).

The *Catechism* goes on to clarify that by calling God "Father", "the language of faith indicates two main things: that God is the first origin of everything and transcendent authority; and that he is at the same time goodness and loving care for all his children" (*CCC* 239). That is, just as in the conception of a child the father takes the initiative and is in a sense the "first origin" of the child along with the mother, so God as creator is the first origin of everything and can rightly be called "Father".

At the same time, within the family the father is the figure of authority, even though he has equal dignity with the mother. In this sense too, God, who is "transcendent authority", can rightly be called "Father". And just as the father of a family has goodness and loving care for his children, God has this in an eminent way and for this reason too is called "Father".

The *Catechism* concludes its teaching on the fatherhood of God saying: "We ought therefore to recall that God transcends the human distinction between the sexes. He is neither man nor woman: he is God. He also transcends human fatherhood and motherhood, although he is their origin and standard: no one is father as God is Father" (*CCC* 239). Note that we are talking here not about the first person of the Blessed Trinity, God the Father, but about the one God in his unity.

Given that God is rightly called Father, it has been traditional to use male terms in speaking of him, terms such as "he", "himself", "him", etc. The Catechism does this. If we were to abandon these terms, we would end up in hopeless confusion. If God is not "he", is he "it"? We could not demean God more than by using such a term, making him out to be not a person but a thing. And, as we have seen, we end up with such cumbersome words as "Godself".

No, we cannot go down that path without degrading God. God is Father, as Jesus taught us to pray: "Our Father who art in heaven." And as Father he is "he". Amen.

602 Are the bushfires God's punishment?

Regarding the recent bushfires in Australia, I wonder if God has removed his protection from us in light of the secular and inhumane country that we have become; e.g. abortion of defenceless unborn babies, euthanasia, religious freedom being challenged, etc.

Your question reflects a thought many have had and some have expressed publicly with regard to the bushfires ravaging the country. Is God punishing us for our sins? Before answering your particular question, we should bear in mind a number of truths.

First, it is of the very nature of the universe that there should be natural "disasters". Asteroids and comets collide with planets; the shifting of tectonic plates far beneath the earth's surface gives rise to earthquakes, which in turn may trigger tsunamis; lightning strikes trees, giving rise to bush fires; torrential rains cause floods, etc. In addition, the cycle of global warming and cooling which has been going on from the beginning gives rise to periodic ice ages and times of greater warmth, etc.

Second, added to the very nature of the planet is human sin, beginning with the original sin of our first parents. The book of Genesis speaks of it as having an effect even on nature, with thorns and thistles making life harder for man (cf. *Gen* 3:18). St Paul describes nature as "subjected to futility" and "groaning in travail" (*Rom* 8:20-22).

Third, in the midst of everything going on in nature and in human affairs, God's fatherly providence is always present. Nothing happens that he is unaware of or that he could not prevent if he so desired. His providence reaches from end to end, extending to the birds of the air and the lilies of the field (cf. *Mt* 6:26, 28) and even to the hairs on our head (cf. *Mt* 10:30).

But aren't there instances in which God has used natural disasters to punish people for their sins? Yes, there are. At the time of Noah, the Lord "saw that the wickedness of man was great in the earth, and that every imagination of the thoughts of his heart was only evil" and he sent the great flood to destroy everyone except Noah and his family (cf. *Gen* 6:5-7:24). Likewise, he destroyed Sodom and Gomorrah with fire and brimstone because their sin was "very grave" (cf. *Gen* 18:20-19:25). Like the good Father he is, God sometimes punishes men for their sins to show them the malice of their ways, discourage them from doing it again and bring them to repentance.

In the second book of Chronicles God explains: "When I shut up the heavens so that there is no rain, or command the locust to devour the land, or send pestilence among my people, if my people who are called by my name will humble themselves, and pray and seek my face, and turn from their wicked ways, then I will hear from heaven, and will forgive their sin and heal their land" (*2 Chron* 7:13-14).

At the same time God draws great good from natural disasters. People are led to realise how fragile their life is, how uncertain their days on earth are, and they are often moved to repent of their sins and draw closer to God in trustful prayer. Also, when they see that families have lost loved ones and property, they are moved to overlook the petty grievances they harboured in their own families and to cling more tightly to each other. People are moved to pray more and to attend Mass for those who are suffering, and this contributes immensely to their own sanctification. Then too, thousands of people put themselves out as volunteers to fight bushfires or to help in the aftermath, and many more donate money, clothes, blankets or food. These disasters bring out the very best in everyone and they unite nations and communities in solidarity with each other.

As regards whether we can say that the present fires are punishment for Australia's sinful ways, we can never know. But it is something I would not encourage. There have been devastating fires throughout our history and there is no reason to attribute them to particular patterns of human sinfulness at the time. Hardly a week goes by without some natural disaster – earthquakes, floods, volcanic eruptions, cyclones, fires, etc. – occurring somewhere in the world and, again, we cannot say that any one of them is divine retribution.

When these events occur we should pray hard for all those affected and do all we can to help out materially, but not blame our sins for what was going to happen anyway from time to time. And, of course, we should strive to make our own lives and our country more Christian.

Sacred Scripture

603 Old Testament Jewish feasts

In the Bible we often read about Jewish feasts like the Passover, Feast of Unleavened Bread, Pentecost, etc. Can you tell me something about them?

You ask a very interesting question and it is important for all of us to know something about these feasts as they are mentioned in the New Testament and they feature in the life of Our Lord.

The most important feast for the Jews was of course the Passover. It was the principal feast of the whole year and it commemorated the deliverance of the Jewish people from over four hundred years of increasing hardship in Egypt. As we remember, Joseph, the son of Jacob, had been sold into slavery in Egypt by his brothers and had risen to become the administrator of the Pharaoh's realm. His brothers later went to Egypt to seek bread during a famine in Israel and, at Joseph's request, his family moved there and over the next four centuries increased in number until they were working as virtual slaves.

They were brought out of Egypt by Moses, when the angel of death came at night and killed the first-born of the Egyptians' sons and animals, passing over the houses of the Israelites, who had sprinkled the blood of a lamb on their doorposts and lintels, moving the Pharaoh to let them leave (cf. *Ex* 12:1-32).

Thereafter the Jews were to celebrate this feast on this same day of the month each year: the evening of the fourteenth day of the month of Nisan, the day of the Spring full moon. Each family was to eat a lamb that had been sacrificed earlier in the day, along with unleavened bread and bitter herbs, and they were to drink cups of wine and say certain prayers, following a prescribed ritual. All men were to go up to Jerusalem for the feast and we know that Mary and Joseph went there each year (cf. *Lk* 2:41; *Ex* 23:14-17). The celebration of Passover lasted a week, during which only unleavened bread was eaten.

According to the Gospels of Matthew, Mark and Luke, Jesus celebrated the Last Supper in the Passover ritual meal (cf. *Mt* 26:17). In so doing he transformed the Passover into its definitive meaning of the Eucharist, the celebration of the deliverance of mankind from slavery to sin, death and the devil by the death of the Lamb of God on the Cross.

Another Jewish feast closely associated with the Passover was that of Unleavened Bread, or Azymes, the festival at which the first fruits of the harvest were dedicated to God (cf. *Lev* 23;15; *Deut* 16:9). Given that the Israelites were not able to grow crops and have a harvest until they entered the promised land forty years after leaving Egypt, it is clear that this feast was instituted only after that. Over time it came to be celebrated together with the Passover since both involved unleavened bread and both were celebrated at the same time of the year.

According to the official rite laid down in later times, both feasts were to be celebrated in Jerusalem. The celebration began with the Passover meal on the night before 14 Nisan. The festival lasted for a week, during which it was forbidden to eat leavened bread or even keep leaven in the house. The most solemn days were the first and last days, along with the sabbath which fell between 14 and 21 Nisan.

Another important feast for the Jews was the Festival of Weeks, or Pentecost. It was instituted to thank God for the completion of the harvest of grain, including wheat, barley and rye. It was celebrated seven weeks, or fifty days, after the feast of Unleavened Bread, whence its Greek name of Pentecost. The feast was closely related to that of Unleavened Bread, celebrating respectively the beginning and the end of the harvest. Also celebrated on this day was the giving of the Torah, or Covenant, to Moses on Mount Sinai (cf. J. Flader, *Question Time 3*, q. 434).

As with the Passover, every Israelite man was to present himself in the temple in Jerusalem for the feast of Pentecost. This explains why there were Jews from all over that part of the world in Jerusalem for the feast when the Holy Spirit came down on the apostles on the day of Pentecost (cf. *Acts* 2:5-11).

The atmosphere surrounding the feast was one of great joy. Banquets were held with the whole family, servants and invited guests taking part.

604 More Jewish feasts

In the Bible we often read about Jewish feasts like the Feast of Tabernacles, Day of Atonement, etc. Can you tell me something about them?

The Feast of Tabernacles is mentioned in chapter seven of St John's gospel, where in spite of the threats to kill him Jesus went up to Jerusalem for the feast "not publicly but in private" (*Jn* 7:10).

After the feasts of the Passover and Pentecost, the Feast of Tabernacles was the third of the great festivals of the year. As with the other two, all Jewish men were to go up to Jerusalem for it. It celebrated the happy end of the harvest of all agricultural produce and for this reason was also called the feast of "ingathering".

It took place from the fifteenth to the twenty-second day of the seventh month of the Jewish calendar, hence in September or October, and it was a time of rejoicing and thanksgiving for the fruits of the land which God had given his people. The name probably originated in the tents, or tabernacles, which the people used to put up in the fields and vineyards as living quarters during the harvest.

As the years passed this custom was given a religious and historical meaning with reference to the tents in which the Hebrews lived during their forty years in the desert after the exodus from Egypt. Also, during the seven days of the festival the Israelites would live in tents in the open fields around Jerusalem.

On the first night the entire city was lit up by four huge lamps in the women's court, a reminder of the bright cloud of the Exodus (cf. *Jn* 7:37-39; 8:12). This background explains Our Lord's referring to himself as the "light of the world".

On each of the eight days of the festival the high priest would sprinkle the altar of holocausts with water taken in a large cup from the Pool of Siloam in remembrance of the water which sprang up miraculously in the desert and he would beg God for the gift of rain (cf. *Ex* 17:1-7). Jesus referred to this water when, on the last day of the festival, he proclaimed: "If any one thirst, let him come to me and drink. He who believes in me, as the Scripture has said, 'Out of his heart shall flow rivers of living water.'" (*Jn* 7:37-38).

Another very important feast in the Jewish calendar was the Day of Atonement. There are references in the Letter to the Hebrews to this day, on which the high priest entered the Holy of Holies (cf. *Heb* 9:3-7). Its Hebrew name is Yom Kippur and it is celebrated on the tenth day of the month Tishri, the same month in which the Feast of Tabernacles is held.

The Day of Atonement was the day on which Israel was reconciled with God, with all their sins forgiven, restoring the nation to its status of a holy people. The feast was also the occasion for cleansing the sanctuary of any contamination caused by the presence of sinners. The ceremonies in the temple were conducted by the high priest, dressed in simple linen vestments, who only on this day could enter the Holy of Holies.

The high priest first sacrificed a young bull for his own sins and those of the priestly line, and then entered the Holy of Holies, sprinkling some of the bull's blood on the mercy seat (cf. *Lev* 16:11-14). Upon coming out he sacrificed a goat, chosen by lot from a pair, for the sins of the people and then entered the Holy of Holies and sprinkled the blood on the mercy seat. Then he came out and sprinkled some of the blood of the bull and the goat on the altar (cf. *Lev* 16:15-19, 33). Coming out of the temple he laid his hands on the second goat, symbolically burdening the animal with the sins and faults of the people, and then sent the goat out into the wilderness.

After biblical readings relevant to the feast and the recitation of prayers, the high priest put on solemn priestly garments and sacrificed two rams as a burnt offering, one for himself and the other for the people. He then offered the rest of the normal sacrifices and lastly blessed the people and dismissed them.

Today Yom Kippur is regarded as the holiest day in the Jewish calendar.

605 Still more Jewish feasts
In the Bible we read about Jewish feasts like the Dedication of the Temple, Purim, the Sabbath and the Day of the New Moon. Can you tell me something about them?

The feast of the Dedication of the Temple, known more popularly by Jews as Hanukkah, commemorated the day on which Judas Maccabeus cleansed the temple of Jerusalem in 165 BC after it had been defiled in 167 BC by Antiochus IV Epiphanes (cf. *1 Mac* 1:54; 4:58). The word Hanukkah, by the way, means "dedication". We recall that the temple had been built by King Solomon, son of King David, in the tenth century BC. Judas determined that the great event of the cleansing should be commemorated each year on the twenty-fifth day of the month Chislev, corresponding to our December. The festival lasted eight days.

On the first day sacrifices were offered in the temple and processions were held with the singing of hymns and psalms. The temple, synagogues and houses were lit up with so many lights that the festival became known also as the Festival of Lights. A family tradition was to light one additional candle each night on a nine-branched candlestick, using the ninth candle to light the others, until on the last day all nine candles were alight. In Our Lord's time the festival was also known by the Greek name of Encaenia, from the word for "inauguration".

The annual celebration of the dedication of a cathedral in the Catholic Church today undoubtedly owes much to this Jewish feast of the second century BC.

A lesser Jewish feast was that of Purim. It commemorated the deliverance of the Jews in exile in Persia at the time of King Ahasuerus in the sixth century BC. The event is recorded in the book of Esther, chapters 8-10. As we recall from that book, Haman, the minister of the king, had convinced the king to have all the Jews in Persia put to death and their property confiscated. Queen Esther, a Jewess, begged the king for the order not to be carried out and, following much prayer and penance by the Jews, the king spared the Jews and put Haman to death instead.

The name Purim, from the Hebrew word for "lot", derives from the fact that Haman had cast lots to determine the day on which the Jews were to be killed (cf. *Esther* 3:7). This was the least religious of the Jewish feasts and it does not seem to have had any special importance at the time of Our Lord.

A very important feast day for the Jews from the beginning until now is the weekly celebration of the Sabbath, the seventh day of the week, the day of rest. The word Sabbath in fact means "rest". It was on the seventh day of creation that God rested and so all Jews were to rest from work that day (cf. *Gen* 2:3). The observance of the Sabbath is spelled out in the third commandment: Remember to keep holy the Sabbath (cf. *Ex* 20:8-11). The Sabbath also commemorated the Israelites' deliverance from slavery in Egypt (cf. *Deut* 5:15).

Jews celebrated the Sabbath beginning at sundown on Friday and ending at sundown on Saturday. On that day they were forbidden to perform many tasks and they could only travel a short distance, some 2000 cubits or about a kilometre. For example, Mount Olivet, just outside Jerusalem, was a "Sabbath day's journey" away (*Acts* 1:12).

In addition to being a day of rest, the Sabbath was also a day of special worship of God. Already during the forty years in the desert after leaving Egypt, on the Sabbath the priests were to offer two sacrifices in the morning and two in the afternoon rather than the usual one at each of these times.

Finally, the Day of the New Moon, the first day of the month in the lunar calendar, was to be celebrated with a solemn burnt offering of bulls and lambs along with a goat as a sin offering, plus offerings of flour and wine (cf. *Num* 28:11-15). No work was to be done on that day, which was to be dedicated to worshipping God and thanking him for his blessings. The feast is mentioned by St Paul (cf. *Col* 2:16).

606 The accuracy of the New Testament text

I have always wondered how we can be sure that our texts of the New Testament bear any resemblance to the originals written two thousand years ago. Can you help me?

You ask a very important question. Most of us accept without questioning that the texts we use today are a faithful rendering of the originals, which of course are no longer in existence. Naturally, if we don't have the originals we cannot be absolutely sure that our texts match them perfectly, but that is the case with all ancient writings. In the case of the New Testament, we are on very solid ground, much more solid than with practically any other ancient writing.

When a document was written thousands of years ago it was copied successively many times, with the first copies being copied again, and all this was done of course by hand. It is only natural that when copies are made of other copies errors can creep in. But when the extant copies are numerous, and they come from widely differing geographical regions, and moreover they date back to a time close to when the original was written, we can be more confident that they are a faithful copy of the original. That is the case with the New Testament.

Added to this, when there are translations of the documents made relatively early on, the translations can be compared with each other and so it is possible to work back to the original, even if there are no extant copies in the original language. In the case of the New Testament, practically all of which was written in Greek, in addition to numerous Greek manuscripts we also have early translations in such languages as Latin, Syriac and Coptic, and then secondary translations made from these in languages like Armenian, Gothic, Georgian and Ethiopic.

But that is not all. In the case of the New Testament, even if we didn't have any of these manuscripts, there are still numerous quotations of New Testament writings in the many commentaries on Scripture, sermons, letters and other writings of the early Church Fathers, so that we could reproduce a great part of the New Testament from them. When all of these writings are compared with each other, it is possible to establish with great accuracy the original text.

If we look at other ancient writings, we see how blessed we are with the New Testament. For example, of the Roman historian Tacitus' *Annals of Imperial Rome*, written around 116 AD, there is only one extant manuscript of the first six books and it was copied around 850 AD. Of books eleven to sixteen there is another manuscript dating from the eleventh century, while books seven to ten are lost altogether.

And of Josephus' *The Jewish War*, written around 75 AD in Aramaic or Hebrew, there are only nine Greek manuscripts in existence, dating from the tenth, eleventh and twelfth centuries, plus a Latin translation from the fourth century.

By comparison, we have over five thousand manuscripts of the New Testament in Greek alone. The earliest of these were written on papyrus, which grew in the Nile delta in Egypt. The most significant are the Chester Beatty Biblical Papyri, which date back to the beginning of the third century and were discovered in 1930. They contain portions of the four Gospels, the Acts of the Apostles, the letters of St Paul, the letter to the Hebrews and the book of Revelation. Moreover, there are other papyrus manuscripts which date back to the beginning of the third century as well.

The very earliest fragment of a papyrus manuscript, containing five verses of chapter eighteen of St John's Gospel, is dated between 100 and 150 AD, judging from the style of the script. Considering that the Gospel itself was probably written towards the end of the first century in Ephesus in Asia Minor, that is a very early copy indeed and it was made in Egypt, a long way from where the Gospel itself was written.

As regards the number of extant manuscripts of other ancient works, next after the New Testament comes Homer's *Iliad*, of which there are fewer than 650 manuscripts, some of them quite fragmentary. The work was written around 800 BC and the earliest partial manuscripts are from the second and third centuries AD, a long time after the original was written. The earliest complete manuscript is from the tenth century AD.

So we are on very solid ground indeed in knowing the original text of the New Testament.

607 Archaeological evidence for the New Testament

A friend says she has read that archaeological findings in Israel bear out the truth of some statements in the New Testament that had been contested by scholars. Is this true?

This is an important question. If there is archaeological or other scientific evidence which contradicts statements in the New Testament, or the Old Testament for that matter, we will be inclined to doubt the veracity of the Bible. But if these findings consistently confirm what is stated in the Bible they confirm the credibility of the inspired text. There are a number of biblical statements which have been challenged by critics, only to be confirmed later by archaeological discoveries. What follows is taken largely from Lee Strobel's excellent book *The Case for Christ* (Zondervan, Grand Rapids 2016).

For example, St Luke says in the second chapter of his gospel that when Jesus was born Joseph and Mary went to Bethlehem because the census decreed by Caesar Augustus required all to go to their own city. It has been questioned whether there was any evidence for a census at that time which made this demand. In fact an official government census order from a Roman Prefect of Egypt dated AD 104 has been found which states that "it is necessary to compel all those who for any cause whatsoever are residing out of their provinces to return to their own homes, that they may both carry out the regular order of the census and may also attend diligently to the cultivation of their allotments."

Likewise, Luke says that the census was conducted when Quirinius was governor of Syria during the reign of Herod the Great (cf. *Lk* 1:5, 2:2). But Herod died in 4 BC and Quirinius began to rule Syria in 6 AD. An archaeologist has recently found writing on coins which state that Quirinius was a ruler in Syria and Cilicia from 11 BC until after Herod's death. It seems there were two officials named Quirinius and the census Luke describes took place at the time of the first one.

Although this finding has been disputed by some, Sir William Ramsay (1851-1939), archaeologist and professor at Oxford and Aberdeen Universities, believed that Quirinius was a ruler in Syria on two separate occasions, one of which was during the time of an earlier census dated around 8-7 BC. Harold Hoehner, who earned his doctorate at Cambridge, says that Herod was ill and came into conflict with the emperor Augustus in 8-7 BC, so that it would have been reasonable for Augustus to order a census to assess the situation before Herod died. For more on the year of the census and of Christ's birth see my book *Question Time 3*, q. 317.

Another controverted statement of Luke is in the third chapter of his gospel where he says that Lysanias was tetrarch of Abilene when Our Lord was born. But scholars have challenged this, saying that Lysanias was not a tetrarch but rather ruler of Chalcis some fifty years earlier. A tetrarch, by the way, is one of four joint rulers at a given time. But an inscription was found from the time of Tiberius, who was emperor from 14 to 37 AD, which names Lysanias as tetrarch in Abila near Damascus at that time, confirming what Luke had written. In fact, there were two officials named Lysanias.

Another example is St Luke's use of the term *politarchs* for city officials in Thessalonica in Acts 17:6. Many historians have said there was no evidence for that term being used in any ancient Roman documents. Yet an inscription was found on a first-century arch which reads, "In the time of the *politarchs*...", confirming the use of the term at the time of St Luke. Archaeologists have since found more than thirty-five inscriptions that use the term, several of them in Thessalonica itself dating from the time at which Luke was writing.

One prominent archaeologist examined carefully Luke's references to thirty-two countries, fifty-four cities and nine islands and found not one mistake on the part of Luke. The inference may be drawn that if Luke was so meticulous about geographical and other historical matters, he would have been equally meticulous and accurate in reporting events in the life of Jesus and the apostles.

Similarly, St John in the fifth chapter of his gospel speaks of Jesus healing an invalid by the Pool of Bethesda with its five porticoes. Scholars have questioned this statement since no such place had ever been found. But beginning in the late nineteenth century the pool was found by excavating some thirteen metres beneath the ground, and indeed it had five porticoes or porches lined with columns.

Other archaeological discoveries that confirm St John's writings are the Pool of Siloam (cf. *Jn* 9:7), Jacob's well (*Jn* 4:12) and the Stone Pavement near the Jaffa Gate where Jesus appeared before Pilate (*Jn* 19:13).

As regards St Mark, Michael Martin, an atheist, accuses him of being ignorant of the geography of Palestine since Mark says that "Jesus left the vicinity of Tyre and went through Sidon, down to the Sea of Galilee and into the region of the Decapolis" (*Mk* 7:31). Martin alleges that given these directions Jesus would have been travelling away from the Sea of Galilee, not towards it. But a study of ancient maps and the probable roads between them through mountainous terrain reveals that Mark was correct.

The very existence of the town of Nazareth is another fact mentioned by the New Testament but questioned by historians, who say there is no mention of the town in the Old Testament, in other ancient Jewish writings or by any historian or geographer before the beginning of the fourth century. In 2006 the Nazareth Archaeological Project began excavating beneath the Sisters of Nazareth convent, a location known since 1880, and they found the remains of a first-century house which conformed to the plan of a so-called courtyard house, typical of early Roman-period settlements in Galilee. Archaeologists found doors and windows, cooking pottery and a spindle used in spinning thread. The presence of limestone vessels, which Jews believed could not become impure, suggests that a Jewish family lived there. Another first-century house was discovered nearby in 2009, all of which confirms the presence of a small Jewish town on the site of Nazareth.

So once again, we have external proof for many controverted statements in the New Testament.

608 The Dead Sea Scrolls

I have often heard about the Dead Sea Scrolls and was wondering what they are and whether they have any significance for Christians.

The Dead Sea Scrolls are ancient Jewish manuscripts which were discovered in Israel in the caves of Qumran, in the West Bank near the Dead Sea between 1946 and 1956 by Bedouin shepherds and archaeologists. The scrolls were found in earthenware jars in eleven caves which contained the manuscripts and other artefacts. Scholars date them between the last three centuries before Christ and the first century after Christ. Bronze coins found at the same sites range from one of John Hyrcanus, who was high priest from 135 to 104 BC, through to the first Jewish-Roman War from 66 to 73 AD.

The scrolls have great significance, both because of their antiquity and because they contain numerous texts of the Old Testament which corroborate those found in other manuscripts. The scrolls are in fact the second-oldest known manuscripts of the Hebrew Bible. The oldest, discovered in Jerusalem in two silver scroll-shaped amulets, date back to around 600 BC and contain portions of the Book of Numbers.

Before the discovery of the Dead Sea Scrolls, the oldest known Hebrew-language manuscripts of the Bible were the Masoretic texts dating to the tenth century AD. The scrolls are from a thousand years earlier and they demonstrate the unusual accuracy of transmission of the original Bible texts to the Masoretic texts.

What is more, the scrolls contain parts of all the books of the

Hebrew Bible except the Book of Esther. There are no fragments from the New Testament. The Dead Sea Scrolls also contain non-biblical manuscripts which show the diversity of religious thought at the time.

The thousands of written fragments discovered in the Dead Sea area are pieces of larger manuscripts damaged by natural causes or human interference. The great majority have only small scraps of text, although some, fewer than a dozen, are almost intact. Most of the texts are written in Hebrew, with some in Aramaic and others in Greek. Most are written on parchment, some on papyrus and one on copper.

Some seventy per cent of the identified texts are religious, mostly from the Old Testament, while the remainder relate to secular matters, including the Community Rule and beliefs of a Jewish sect.

Archaeologists have generally associated the scrolls with the Essenes, an ancient Jewish sect along with the Pharisees and Sadducees, which flourished from the second century BC to the first century AD. The Essenes followed an ascetical life including voluntary poverty, daily ablutions by immersion in water, prayer, a strict observance of the Sabbath and works of charity. Their priests practised celibacy.

The understanding is that the Essenes wrote the scrolls and hid them in the nearby caves during the Jewish Revolt sometime between 66 and 68 AD. The site of Qumran was destroyed during the revolt and the caves containing the scrolls were not discovered until 1946. The association of the scrolls with the Essenes is borne out by such facts as the striking similarity between the description of an initiation ceremony found in the Community Rule in the scrolls and the description of a similar ceremony of the Essenes mentioned by the historian Flavius Josephus, the sharing of property mentioned both in the Community Rule and in the work of Flavius Josephus, the discovery of ritual baths in Qumran which correspond to the practice of daily ablutions described in the Community Rule, and the discovery in Qumran of inkwells and tables on which writing could be done.

Moreover, Pliny the Elder, a Roman historian writing after the fall of Jerusalem in 70 AD, describes a group of Essenes living in a desert community on the northwest shore of the Dead Sea, where Qumran was located.

The Dead Sea Scrolls are indeed fascinating and significant for containing so many texts of the Old Testament from such an early period.

609 The Pharisees and Sadducees

In the Scriptures we often read about the Pharisees and the Sadducees. Can you tell me who these people were?

Within the Jewish people at the time of Christ, the Pharisees and Sadducees formed two major groups who had different backgrounds and different views on a number of topics.

The Pharisees were variously a political party, a social movement and a school of thought at the time of Our Lord. The word "Pharisee" actually means "set apart" or "separated".

The Pharisees emerged around the middle of the second century BC after Judas Maccabeus, a Hasmonean, defeated the Seleucid forces under King Antiochus Epiphanes (cf. *2 Mac*). The Seleucids had desecrated the Temple and forced Jews to violate their law by following Seleucid customs, including eating pork. Judas' nephew John Hyrcanus established a new monarchy ruled by Hasmonean priests. In this new dynasty the priests had both political and spiritual power. The Pharisees taught that Jews must retain their ritual purity by setting themselves apart from the beliefs and customs of the Greek and Seleucid Gentiles against whom the Maccabees had fought, whence their name Pharisees, or separatists.

The Sadducees too became active around the middle of the second century BC, but they came rather from the upper social and economic classes, constituting an elite within Jewish society. Their name seems to have derived from Zadok, the first high priest to serve in the Temple built by Solomon. The Sadducees fulfilled various political, social and religious roles, including serving as high priests and maintaining the Temple. This gave them great prestige among the people since the priesthood was often considered the highest class in Jewish society. They are believed to have died out sometime after the destruction of the Temple in 70 AD.

One of the big differences between the Pharisees and the Sadducees was in their attitude toward the Law of Moses. The Sadducees saw only the written Law, or Torah, as the source of divine authority and they interpreted it literally, whereas the Pharisees held to both the Torah and the oral tradition that had grown up around it. This tradition included a host of laws and customs that the rabbis, or teachers, had added over the centuries. The Pharisees and their sages, or rabbis, maintained that this oral tradition, the Talmud, had originated on Mount Sinai alongside the Torah. For the Pharisees, therefore, the Torah in its totality was not a fixed text but rather an ongoing process of interpretation and application in which God was actively involved.

Stemming from this, one of the tenets of the Pharisees that distinguished them from other groups, including the Sadducees, was that all Jews were to observe meticulously in their daily lives the laws regarding ritual purity which applied strictly only to service in the Temple. For example, when Jesus went to eat at the house of a Pharisee, the latter was astonished that he did not first wash before eating. Jesus then admonished the Pharisees for cleansing the outside of the cup and dish while inside being full of extortion and wickedness, and for levying a tithe on mint and rue and every kind of herb while neglecting justice and the love of God (cf. *Lk* 11:37-42). For this reason today we use the word "pharisee" for someone who is meticulous about outward religious observances but whose heart is not in the right place.

One of the more obvious differences between the Pharisees and Sadducees that we find in the New Testament regarded belief in life after death and in the existence of angels or spirits. The Sadducees did not believe there was any life after death while the Pharisees believed there was. St Paul exploited this difference when he was brought before the Roman tribune and called to defend himself before the Sanhedrin, or council, of the Jews (cf. *Acts* 23:1-10). When he perceived that some members of the council were Pharisees and others Sadducees, he said: "I am a Pharisee, a son of Pharisees; with respect to the hope and the resurrection of the dead I am on trial" (*Acts* 23:6).

This gave rise to a dispute between the two groups, as St Luke explains: "For the Sadducees say that there is no resurrection, nor angel, nor spirit; but the Pharisees acknowledge them all" (v. 8).

610 Who were the scribes?

In the New Testament we often read about the scribes, sometimes in connection with the Pharisees. Can you tell me who they were and what they did?

The word" scribe" in English refers to someone who writes and this was one of the scribes' original functions. The Hebrew word *sopherim* which is usually translated as scribe came from a root word meaning variously to write, to set in order and to count. In fact the scribes did all of this, especially with respect to the law revealed by God through Moses. The scribes would write down the law and copy it, arrange its precepts in logical order and even count carefully the number of words.

Scribes also served kings and other rulers as what today we would call secretaries, writing their letters, drawing up decrees and managing their finances. For example, in King David's time Jehoshaphat fulfilled the function of recorder and Seraiah that of secretary (cf. *2 Sam* 8:16-17). Among King Solomon's "high officials" were Elihoreph and Ahijah, who served as secretaries, and Jehoshaphat as recorder (cf. *1 Kings* 4:3). As high officials, scribes had great authority and prestige among the people.

There was a lesser class of scribes, most of whom were Levites, whose role was limited to writing. For example, Baruch "wrote upon a scroll at the dictation of Jeremiah all the words of the Lord which he had spoken to him" (*Jer* 36:4).

After the Babylonian captivity, when the Jews returned to Israel, the scribes had great authority in their role of copying the law and teaching it to the people. Among them was Ezra, a descendant of Moses' brother Aaron and thus a Levite, who is described as "a scribe skilled in the law of Moses which the Lord the God of Israel had given; and the king granted him all that he asked, for the hand of the Lord his God was upon him" (*Ezra* 7:6).

At the time of Christ, the scribes could draft legal documents such as contracts for marriage and divorce, loans, inheritance, mortgages, the sale of land, etc. But their most important function was to study the law, interpret it and teach it to others. Thus they were sometimes called lawyers or doctors, that is teachers, of the law. They were generally among the most educated men in society and as such they enjoyed great prestige and influence. They were eligible to be elected to the supreme council of the Jews, the Sanhedrin.

We see the equivalence between the terms scribe and lawyer, for example, when the Pharisee who asked Jesus which was the greatest commandment of the law was called a lawyer by Matthew (cf. *Mt* 22:34-35) and a scribe by Mark (cf. *Mk* 12:28).

Many of the scribes were also Pharisees, who supplemented the written law with their oral traditions, which the scribes would interpret and teach. The scribes for this reason were often rabbis, or teachers, since they taught the law to the Jewish people and to the youth in particular.

Because both the scribes and the Pharisees were zealous about the law and its interpretation, they were often the ones to challenge Jesus about his interpretation (cf. *Mk* 2:6, 16; 3:22; *Mt* 9:11, 12:2). And since they flaunted their authority and prestige, Jesus was often very critical of them. For example, he says: "The scribes and the Pharisees sit on Moses' seat; so practise and observe whatever they tell you, but not what they do; for they preach but do not practise… They do all their deeds to be seen by men; for they make their phylacteries broad and their fringes long, and they love the place of honour at feasts and the best seats in the synagogues, and salutations in the market places, and being called rabbi by men" (*Mt* 23:1-3, 5-7). We see here how the scribes were indeed highly regarded by the people.

Later in the same discourse Jesus criticises their lack of integrity: "But woe to you, scribes and Pharisees, hypocrites! because you shut the kingdom of heaven against men; for you neither enter yourselves, nor allow those who would enter to go in" (*Mt* 23:13). Woe to you, scribes and Pharisees, hypocrites! for you traverse sea and land to make a single proselyte, and when he becomes a proselyte, you make him twice as much a child of hell as yourselves" (*Mt* 23:15).

As is clear, knowing who the scribes were helps us greatly to understand the Scriptures.

611 Does Christ bring peace?

In the Gospel of a recent weekday Mass Jesus said he had come not to bring peace but a sword, and to set parents against their children. I have never understood this passage. Can you enlighten me?

The passage to which you refer is in the Gospel of Matthew: "Do not think that I have come to bring peace on earth; I have not come to bring peace, but a sword. For I have come to set a man against his father, and a daughter against her mother, and a daughter-in-law against her mother-in-law; and a man's foes will be those of his own household" (*Mt* 10:34-36).

These words are indeed disturbing and difficult to understand. If this were the only time Christ spoke of peace, we would be understandably troubled and inclined not to follow him at all. How are we meant to interpret these words?

The first thing to remember is that a troublesome passage like this must interpreted not on its own but in light of the whole of Scripture. Quoting the Second Vatican Council, the *Catechism of the Catholic Church* gives this as one of three principles for interpreting the Bible: "Be especially attentive 'to the content and unity of the whole Scripture.' Different as the books which comprise it may be,

Scripture is a unity by reason of the unity of God's plan, of which Christ Jesus is the centre and heart, open since his Passover" (cf. *DV* 12 §4; *CCC* 112).

We should begin then by looking for other passages in which Christ speaks of peace. Fortunately there are a good number. For example, he says: "Peace I leave with you; my peace I give to you; not as the world gives do I give to you" (*Jn* 14:27). "I have said this to you, that in me you may have peace" (*Jn* 16:33). "Blessed are the peacemakers, for they shall be called sons of God" (*Mt* 5:9).

Besides Christ himself, others too say that he came to bring peace. At his birth the angels praise God and say, "Glory to God in the highest, and on earth peace among men with whom he is pleased!" (*Lk* 2:14). St Paul too says that Christ came to bring peace: "Therefore, since we are justified by faith, we have peace with God through our Lord Jesus Christ" (*Rom* 5:1). He also says that Christ "is our peace" and that "he came and preached peace to you who were far off and peace to those who were near" (*Eph* 2:14, 17).

So it is clear from the whole of the New Testament that Christ indeed came to bring peace. This is an example of what a scripture scholar friend of mine likes to say: "If you take the text out of the context, all you are left with is a con."

Then why does Christ say he has come not to bring peace, but a sword? We see a glimpse of the answer in the Gospel of Luke, where Christ says he has come to bring "division" (cf. *Lk* 12:51). He goes on to say in the Gospel passage we have quoted above, as in the other synoptic Gospels, that he has come to set a man against his father, a daughter against her mother and that a man's foes will be those of his own household (cf. *Mt* 10:35-36).

He does not want division but he knows that it may result when one member of a family takes his word seriously and others do not. For example, a son may tell his father that he wants to follow God's call to the priesthood or the religious life, and his father rejects him because he wanted him to take over the family business. Or a Muslim girl tells her parents that she is becoming a Christian and the family rejects her and may even threaten to kill her.

These are not outcomes Christ wants but he knows they may result when someone follows him rather than following the wishes of his or her parents. For this reason he goes on to say: "He who loves father or mother more than me is not worthy of me; and he who loves son or daughter more than me is not worthy of me, and he who does not take his cross and follow me is not worthy of me" (*Mt* 10:37-38).

The apostles followed this exhortation when they were threatened by the Jewish council and told not to preach in the name of Christ anymore. They replied: "We must obey God rather than men" (*Acts* 5:29). We too must be prepared to incur the anger or rejection of our family or friends if God is calling us to follow him more closely.

612 St Paul making up "what is lacking"

I have always wondered what St Paul meant when he said in his letter to the Colossians that he makes up what is lacking in the sufferings of Christ. Since Christ surely left nothing unfinished, what does St Paul mean?

The text to which you refer is the following: "Now I rejoice in my sufferings for your sake, and in my flesh I complete what is lacking in Christ's afflictions for the sake of his body, that is, the Church..." (*Col* 1:24).

All commentaries on this passage agree that Christ left nothing undone, nothing lacking in his suffering for the Church. His suffering was sufficient to atone for all the sins of mankind of all time. This is implied in his last words from the cross: "It is finished" (*Jn* 19:30). Then what does St Paul mean by saying he is completing what is lacking in Christ's afflictions?

One can distinguish here between objective redemption and subjective redemption. Objective redemption is the making up by Christ for all the sins of mankind by his suffering and death on the cross. It was brought about in a completely sufficient way on Calvary. In that sense we say that mankind was redeemed or saved by Christ's death and resurrection.

But that does not mean that every individual will in fact be saved and go to heaven. Subjective redemption is the application of the merits of Christ's Passion to individual souls down the ages. That is an ongoing task and it will last until the end of time. Without it an individual will not go to heaven. It is here that we can say something is lacking in Christ's affliction.

St Alphonsus Liguori comments: "Can it be that Christ's Passion alone was insufficient to save us? It left nothing more to be done, it was entirely sufficient to save all men. However, for the merits of the Passion to be applied to us, according to St Thomas (*STh*, 3, 49, 3), we need to cooperate (subjective redemption) by patiently bearing the trials God sends us, so as to become like our head, Christ" (*Thoughts on the Passion,* 10).

St Paul is applying this truth to himself. He seeks to follow in Christ's footsteps by taking up his cross to continue the task of bringing salvation to all. St John Paul II writes that sharing in the sufferings of Christ gives a person "the certainty that in the spiritual dimension of the work of Redemption he is serving, like Christ, the salvation of his brothers and sisters... It is suffering, more than anything else, which clears the way for the grace which transforms human souls. Suffering, more than anything else, makes present in the history of humanity the force of the Redemption" (*Salvifici doloris,* 27).

Another way to look at this is to consider that Christ can be understood both in the sense of his physical person but also in the sense of his Mystical Body the Church, of which he is the head. The head has already suffered so as to redeem us, but now it is up to us, the members of his body, to share in his suffering so as to make up for our sins and be worthy of salvation. We can also offer our suffering for others, so that they may be converted and begin their own process of working out their salvation.

St Augustine writes: "You [a member of Christ's Body] suffer so much as was to be contributed out of your sufferings to the whole sufferings of Christ, who has suffered in our Head, and suffers in his members, that is, in our own selves" (*Exposition on Ps* 62:4). Here the "sufferings of Christ" are the sufferings of the members of his Mystical Body to be undergone until the end of time.

In this sense St Paul looks at his prison chains and sees his own suffering as the way he can convey the sufferings of Christ to the souls of others and so bring completion to the Passion in an external way. Thus, we understand his words that he rejoices in his own sufferings for the sake of the Colossians, and in his flesh he completes what is lacking in the afflictions of the Mystical Body of Christ for the sake of the Church.

Jesus Christ

613 Historical evidence for Christ

I have a sceptical friend who doubts that Jesus ever existed and he doesn't accept anything in the Bible. Is there any evidence for Jesus in texts outside the Bible?

There are a number of very early extra-biblical texts that corroborate what the Bible says about Jesus.

Some of the earliest are the writings of the first-century Jewish historian Flavius Josephus. Born in 37 AD, Josephus was a priest and a Pharisee who wrote his four works towards the end of the first century. His most ambitious work, completed around the year 93, was *The Antiquities,* a history of the Jewish people from creation to his own time. In it he describes how a high priest named Ananias took advantage of the death of the Roman governor Festus – both of whom are mentioned in the New Testament – to have the apostle James put to death: "He convened a meeting of the Sanhedrin and brought before them a man named James, the brother of Jesus, who was called the Christ, and certain others. He accused them of having transgressed the law and delivered them up to be stoned" (*The Antiquities* 20.200).

All the details in this account from a Jewish historian are consistent with what the New Testament tells us. Indeed, James the Less was referred to as "the brother of the Lord" (*Mt* 13:55) since he was a relative of Jesus, and the historians Eusebius and Hegesippus said that he was put to death by the Jews in Spring of the year 62.

Another more extensive reference to Jesus by Josephus in *The Antiquities* reads: "About this time there lived Jesus, a wise man, if indeed one ought to call him a man. For he was one who wrought surprising feats and was a teacher of such people as accept the truth gladly. He won over many Jews and many of the Greeks. He was the

Christ. When Pilate, upon hearing him accused by men of the highest standing among us, had condemned him to be crucified, those who had in the first place come to love him did not give up their affection for him. On the third day he appeared to them restored to life, for the prophets of God had prophesied these and countless other marvellous things about him. And the tribe of Christians, so called after him, has still to this day not disappeared" (*ibid.* 18.63-64).

The authenticity of the text was questioned by some during the Enlightenment but today there is substantial agreement among Jewish and Christian scholars that it is authentic, although there may have been some interpolations added by copyists. For example, the statement "He was the Christ" could very well have been added by Christians. Nonetheless, we have here a very complete reference to Jesus from a first-century extra-biblical source.

Another exceedingly important text is that of the Roman historian Tacitus. In his *Annals,* written in 115 AD, he describes how Nero persecuted the Christians in order to divert suspicion from himself for the fire that destroyed Rome in the year 64: "Nero fastened the guilt and inflicted the most exquisite tortures on a class hated for their abominations, called Christians by the populace. Christus, from whom the name had its origin, suffered the extreme penalty during the reign of Tiberius at the hands of one of our procurators, Pontius Pilatus, and a most mischievous superstition, thus checked for the moment, again broke out not only in Judaea, the first source of the evil, but even in Rome" (*Annals* 15.44). Here again we have a very clear and unquestionable reference to Christ and his death, from the most important Roman historian of the first century.

Another important early reference comes from Pliny the Younger, the Roman governor of Bithynia, in modern-day in Turkey. Pliny was the nephew of Pliny the Elder, an encyclopedist who died in the eruption of Vesuvius in the year 79. In a letter to the emperor Trajan around the year 111 seeking advice as to whether his way of dealing with Christians was correct, he said that Christians "also declared that the sum total of their guilt or error amounted to no more than this: they met regularly before dawn on a fixed day to chant verses alternately amongst themselves in honour of Christ as if to a god, and also to bind themselves by oath, not for any criminal purpose, but to abstain from theft, robbery, and adultery" (*Letters*, 10.96).

On the basis of these texts, among others, there can be no question about Jesus' existence.

614 Did Jesus know he was God?

Over the years I have heard or read several times that Jesus didn't know he was God but came to realise it later in life. Is this true?

This is nonsense. It is nothing short of an oxymoron. If Jesus came to realise later in life that he was truly God, then he was God all along. But how could God, who knows all things, not know at any time that he was God? While the matter is clear to believers, the statement that Jesus didn't know he was God has been made frequently and so it bears examination.

It is clear that Jesus didn't often say forthrightly that he was God and there is a good reason for this. We must remember that the Jews of his time believed that God was Yahweh, who had revealed himself and his name to Moses on Mount Horeb (cf. *Ex* 3:1-15). The Jews held that name in such reverence that they didn't dare to pronounce it. If Jesus had claimed to be God they would have accused him of claiming to be Yahweh, and therefore of blaspheming, as in fact they did later.

Before we look at texts which reveal Christ's self-awareness that he was God we should remind ourselves of what the angel had told Our Lady about the child she was to bear: "He will be great and will be called the Son of the Most High; and the Lord God will give to him the throne of his father David, and he will reign over the house of Jacob for ever; and of his kingdom there will be no end" (*Lk* 1:32-33). The Son of the Most High is clearly God, and a kingdom that lasts forever is no earthly kingdom but one in which God himself reigns. In other words, the child to be born of Mary would be God. Later the angel tells Mary that "the child to be born will be called holy, the Son of God" (*Lk* 1:35). So we know that Jesus is truly God, the Son of God.

What is more, Jesus' whole behaviour reveals that he was God and that he was aware of it. Already at the age of twelve when he remained behind in Jerusalem, he was found in the temple "sitting among the teachers, listening to them and asking them questions; and all who heard him were amazed at his understanding and his answers" (*Lk* 2:46-47). We see here that Jesus at the age of twelve was already extraordinary in his understanding, to the point that even the teachers, or rabbis, were amazed. In that moment too Jesus said to Mary and Joseph, "Did you not know that I must be in my Father's house?" (*Lk* 2:49) His reference to his "Father" suggests that he knew he had a special relationship with his Father God and even Mary and Joseph "did not understand the saying which he spoke to them" (*Lk* 2:50).

Several times in his conversations Jesus made the distinction between the apostles' relationship with God the Father and his own. For example, after his Resurrection when he appeared to Mary Magdalene he told her to "go to my brethren and say to them, I am ascending to my Father and your Father, to my God and your God" (*Jn* 20:17). Jesus knew that he was the eternal Son of the Father while the apostles and other disciples were in a sense adopted sons, so that there was an essential difference between them. Jesus never spoke of "our Father" when including both himself and his followers. It was always "my Father and your Father".

When in answer to Jesus' question "But who do you say that I am?", St Peter professed, "You are the Christ, the Son of the living God" (*Mt* 16:16), Jesus did not correct him but rather told him: "Blessed are you, Simon Bar-Jona! For flesh and blood has not revealed this to you, but my Father who is in heaven" (*Mt* 16:17). What Peter could not know by human means, that Jesus was the very Son of God, he knew because the Father in heaven had revealed it to him.

Moreover, Jesus knew that he was not just one more son of God like the apostles. He was the eternal Son who shared the Father's divine nature. He affirmed this when he said in the temple of Jerusalem, "I and the Father are one" (*Jn* 10:30). Because this meant that Jesus was claiming to be God, the Jews took up stones to put him to death, saying: "We stone you for no good work but for blasphemy; because you, being a man, make yourself God" (*Jn* 10:33). Here Jesus is claiming explicitly to be God and he will later be put to death for it.

He goes on to tell the Jews that if they did not believe him they should at least believe his works, or miracles, "that you may know and understand that the Father is in me and I am in the Father" (*Jn* 10:38). Again, he is claiming to be God, one with the Father.

In conclusion, of course Jesus knew he was God.

615 Did Jesus behave like God?

We know that Jesus claimed to be God and showed he was God by his miracles. But other people have done miracles, including the apostles. Did Jesus do anything else that showed he was indeed God?

You ask a good question. A person can claim to be God and yet be stark raving mad. Mental hospitals are full of patients suffering from delusions of grandeur. And as you say, even the apostles did miracles, including raising people from the dead (cf. *Acts* 9:36-41; 20:7-12). The fact that Jesus was well balanced and not suffering from delusions and that he did numerous miracles should be enough for us to believe in his divinity. But it is helpful to know that he also said and did other things that only someone who was in fact God would dare to do.

First, Jesus dared to forgive sins. We can forgive someone who has offended us, but no one dares to forgive someone who has offended someone else, let alone someone who has offended God. Only God can forgive sins. Yet Jesus does. St Luke relates how Jesus said to a paralytic who had been lowered through the roof on a stretcher, "Man, your sins are forgiven you" (*Lk* 5:20). The scribes and Pharisees naturally asked, "Who is this that speaks blasphemies? Who can forgive sins but God only?" Then to show that he had authority to forgive sins, Jesus said to the paralytic, "I say to you, rise, take up your bed and go home." The man rose up and went home glorifying God (*Lk* 5:21-24). While the apostles did miracles, they didn't dare to forgive sins because they weren't God. But Jesus did because he was God, and then he worked a miracle to prove it. Of course, when the apostles later began to forgive sins as priests it was only because Jesus had given them the power to do so.

Second, Jesus claimed to be without sin, something no human person would dare do. We know that even good, holy, people have no pretensions of being without sin. Rather they are very aware of their sinfulness and they don't try to hide it. With Jesus it was different. One day, speaking in the temple in Jerusalem he said to the Jews, "Which of you convicts me of sin?" (*Jn* 8:46) If Jesus, now in his thirties, can claim to be without sin, it can only be because he is God.

Third, a short time later in the same discourse in the temple Jesus claimed to have pre-existed Abraham, who lived some 1800 years before him. He said to the Jews, "Your father Abraham rejoiced that he was to see my day; he saw it and was glad." The Jews then said to him, "You are not yet fifty years old, and have you seen Abraham?" Jesus replied, "Truly, truly, I say to you, before Abraham was, I am" (*Jn* 8:56-58). This was truly an extraordinary statement, one no human being could make. What is more, in saying "I am", Jesus was using the divine name Yahweh, thereby claiming to be God himself. This enraged the Jews "So they took up stones to throw at him; but Jesus hid himself, and went out of the temple" (*Jn* 8:59).

Fourth, in the Last Supper with his disciples Jesus prayed to the Father in terms no human being would use, speaking of his eternal existence with the Father. He said: "And now, Father, glorify me in your own presence with the glory which I had with you before the world was made" (*Jn* 17:5). Once again, we see how Jesus is not afraid to affirm his eternal existence with the Father, and with it his divinity.

Someone might object that there are also passages in Scripture in which Jesus appears to say that he is not God. For example, on one occasion a man asked him, "Good Teacher, what must I do to inherit eternal life?" Jesus said, "Why do you call me good? No one is good but God alone" (*Mk* 10:17-18). Jesus' reply need not be understood to mean that he is denying he is God. Rather it should be understood along the lines of "If you knew who I am you would realise how appropriate it is to call me good, since only God is truly good."

Also, in the Last Supper Jesus told his disciples that he was going to the Father and they should rejoice because "the Father is greater than I" (*Jn* 14:28). This can be understood in the sense that the Father in his divinity is greater than Jesus in his humanity, and the disciples should rejoice because Jesus will be returning to heaven where he is equal to the Father in his divinity. It can also be understood in the sense that the Father is greater than Jesus because Jesus was begotten by the Father and has his origin in the Father. In any case, Jesus is equal to the Father in his divinity, as he affirms when he says "I and the Father are one" (*Jn* 10:30).

So yes, Jesus said and did many things apart from his miracles to show his divinity.

616 Jesus the Messiah

I know that the Jews in the Old Testament were awaiting a Messiah, someone to lead them in the future, and that Christians believe that the Messiah was Jesus. But what exactly does the Old Testament say about what sort of person the Messiah was to be?

There are numerous Old Testament texts that speak of a Messiah to come. The Hebrew word Messiah, by the way, means "anointed one", as does the name Christ. So it is correct to say that Jesus was "the Christ", the anointed one, the Messiah.

In general, the Old Testament Jews believed that a Messiah would come who would be a king-like figure from the line of King David, who would deliver the people of Israel from their oppressors, return Jerusalem to the Jewish people and usher in an age of peace (cf. *2 Sam* 7:12-13; *Is* 11; *Jer* 23:5-8, 30-31; *Hos* 3:5).

More particularly, Moses himself, the great prophet and leader of the Israelites, spoke of a prophet to come who would be a leader like him: "The Lord your God will raise up for you a prophet like me from among you, from your brethren – him you shall heed..." (*Deut* 18:15). A few lines later God himself says to Moses: "I will raise up for them a prophet like you from among their brethren; and I will put my words in his mouth, and he shall speak to them all that I command him" (*Deut* 18:18). Jesus himself, the Word of God who passes on what the Father tells him (cf. *Jn* 15:15), is the prophet mentioned in these texts.

The Messiah would come from the tribe of Judah, as the patriarch Jacob prophesies: "The sceptre shall not depart from Judah, nor the ruler's staff from between his feet, until he comes to whom it belongs; and to him shall be the obedience of the peoples" (*Gen* 49:10). Jesus was of the tribe of Judah, he was King of the Jews as indicated by the sceptre, the symbol of kingly authority, and all peoples are subject to his authority, both Jews and Gentiles.

Then too the Messiah would be born in Bethlehem: "But you, O Bethlehem Ephrathah, who are little to be among the clans of Judah, from you shall come forth for me one who is to be ruler in Israel, whose origin is from of old, from ancient days" (*Mic* 5:2). Jesus was born in Bethlehem and his origin is from of old, from all eternity.

The Messiah would come from the family of King David, he would sit on his throne, his kingdom would last forever and he would be God's very Son. God tells King David through the prophet Nathan: "When your days are fulfilled and you lie down with your fathers, I will raise up your offspring after you, who shall come forth from your body, and I will establish his kingdom. He shall build a house for my name, and I will establish the throne of his kingdom for ever. I will be his father, and he shall be my son" (*2 Sam* 7:12-14).

This prophecy is fulfilled perfectly in Jesus, as the angel tells Our Lady in the Annunciation: "He will be great, and will be called the Son of the Most High; and the Lord God will give to him the throne of his father David, and he will reign over the house of Jacob for ever; and of his kingdom there will be no end" (*Lk* 1:32-33).

The Messiah would be born of a virgin and would be God. Isaiah prophesies: "Behold, a virgin shall conceive and bear a son, and shall call his name Immanuel" (*Is* 7:14). Once again, this prophecy is fulfilled in Jesus. An angel tells Joseph in a dream that the child Mary is carrying "is of the Holy Spirit" (*Mt* 1:20), and St Matthew goes on to explain: "All this took place to fulfil what the Lord had spoken by the prophet: 'Behold, a virgin shall conceive and bear a son, and his name shall be called Emmanuel' (which means, God with us)" (*Mt* 1:22-23).

Also, the prophet Daniel tells us that the Messiah would be called "son of man" and his kingdom would last forever: "I saw in the night visions, and behold, with the clouds of heaven there came one like a son of man... And to him was given dominion and glory and kingdom, that all peoples, nations, and languages should serve him; his dominion is an everlasting dominion..." (*Dan* 7:13-14). To be sure, Jesus used the title "son of man" and his kingdom is forever.

617 More prophecies of the Messiah

In your last column you wrote about some of the prophecies of the Messiah in the Old Testament, which I found very interesting. What are some of the other prophecies and did Jesus ever say he was the awaited Messiah?

Another important prophecy is that the Messiah would have to suffer. Psalm 22 is especially graphic in portraying the sufferings Jesus in fact underwent, and indeed he quoted the psalm from the Cross: "My God, my God, why have you forsaken me?" The psalm goes on to say: "They have pierced my hands and feet – I can count all my bones – they stare and gloat over me; they divide my garments among them, and for my clothing they cast lots" (*Ps* 22:1, 16-18).

Isaiah, in chapters 50-53, describes what has come to be called "the suffering servant", another graphic portrayal of the Messiah's suffering. Among the verses especially applicable to Jesus are: "I gave my back to those who struck me, and my cheeks to those who pulled out the beard; I hid not my face from shame and spitting" (*Is* 50:6). "Behold, my servant shall prosper, he shall be exalted and lifted up, and shall be very high. As many were astonished at him – his appearance was so marred, beyond human semblance..." (*Is* 52:13-14).

As regards Jesus' suffering for our sins Isaiah says: "But he was wounded for our transgressions, he was bruised for our iniquities; upon him was the chastisement that made us whole, and with his stripes we are healed" (*Is* 53:4-5) "...yet he bore the sin of many, and made intercession for the transgressors" (*Is* 53:12).

Jesus referred these passages to himself when he told the two disciples on their way to Emmaus: "'O foolish men, and slow of heart to believe all that the prophets have spoken! Was it not necessary that the Christ should suffer these things and enter into his glory?' And beginning with Moses and all the prophets, he interpreted to them in all the Scriptures the things concerning himself" (*Lk* 24: 25-27).

Then too, the Messiah would come riding on a donkey: "Behold, your king comes to you; triumphant and victorious is he, humble and riding on a donkey, on a colt the foal of a donkey... and he shall command peace to the nations; his dominion shall be from sea to sea, and from the River to the ends of the earth" (*Zech* 9:9-10). Jesus fulfilled this prophecy in his entry into Jerusalem on Palm Sunday. St John relates: "So they took branches of palm trees and went out to meet him, crying, 'Hosanna! Blessed is he who comes in the name of the Lord, even the King of Israel!' And Jesus found a young donkey and sat upon it; as it is written, 'Fear not, daughter of Zion; behold, your king is coming, sitting on a donkey's colt!'" (*Jn* 12:13-15). St Mark describes how the people themselves realised that Jesus was their Messiah when they cried out, "Blessed is the kingdom of our father David that is coming!" (*Mk* 11:10)

As we have seen, Jesus applied the verses of Isaiah about the suffering servant to himself as the Messiah. Also, when the Samaritan woman at the well said that she knew the Messiah was coming, Jesus said, "I who speak to you am he" (*Jn* 4:26). And when in his Passion Jesus was called before the Sanhedrin and the high priest asked him, "Are you the Christ, the Son of the Blessed?", Jesus answered, "I am; and you will see the Son of man sitting at the right hand of Power, and coming with the clouds of heaven" (*Mk* 14:61-62).

Jesus also applied to himself some verses of Isaiah referring to the God who was to come to save his people: "the blind receive their sight and the lame walk, lepers are cleansed and the deaf hear, and the dead are raised up, and the poor have good news preached to them" (cf. *Is* 35:4-6; *Mt* 11:5).

If Jesus so clearly fulfilled the prophecies of the Messiah, and said he was the Messiah, why didn't more of the Jews believe in him and become his disciples? There can be a variety of reasons, but one of the most compelling is that at the time of Jesus the idea of the Messiah had become politicised and the people were expecting a Messiah who would free them from the domination of the Romans. But Jesus obviously had not come for that, his kingdom was not of this world, and therefore many Jews did not believe in him.

618 Proof of the Resurrection of Christ

My nephew, who is very intelligent and a real sceptic, challenges much of our Catholic faith, including the Resurrection of Christ. What arguments can I use to convince him?

We can begin with what the New Testament tells us about the facts. First, we have Jesus' own prophecy on several occasions that he would rise from the dead. Among the most detailed is his prediction of the way he would die and of his Resurrection: "Behold we are going up to Jerusalem; and the Son of man will be delivered to the chief priests and scribes, and they will condemn him to death, and deliver him to the Gentiles to be mocked and scourged and crucified, and he will be raised on the third day" (*Mt* 20:18-19).

Second, it is certain that Christ actually died on the cross. St John, who was there, records that the soldiers came to break the legs of the two men who had been crucified with him but "when they came to Jesus and saw that he was already dead, they did not break his legs" but "pierced his side with a spear, and at once there came out blood and water" (*Jn* 19:32-34). Even the Roman historian Tacitus (ca 55-120 AD) says that "Christ was put to death by Pontius Pilate, the procurator of Judaea, in the reign of Tiberius" (*Annals,* xv, 44). No one would accept that Christ had risen from the dead if it were not certain that he had actually died.

Third, the tomb where Christ was laid was found empty on the third day, that is on the Sunday morning. All four gospels tell us this. The apostles began to preach the Resurrection of Christ in Jerusalem itself and, again, no one would believe in the Resurrection if it could be shown that his body was still lying in a tomb just outside the city.

Fourth, over the next forty days Jesus appeared numerous times to various people, including five hundred at once. On the day of the Resurrection itself he appeared to Mary Magdalene, to several women, to Peter, to two disciples on their way to Emmaus and to ten of the apostles plus others in the Upper Room. In this last appearance he said: "See my hands and my feet, that it is I myself; handle me, and see; for a spirit has not flesh and bones as you see that I have" and he went on to eat a piece of broiled fish before them (*Lk* 24:39, 43). So he had truly risen in the flesh. It was not just a vision of the spirit of a deceased person.

Fifth, the Resurrection of Christ and his appearances completely transformed the apostles. From frightened, discouraged men they were transformed into bold preachers of the gospel. All but John would die martyrs for the faith. There is no way to explain this sudden change except by attributing it to the reality of the Resurrection. No one would be prepared to spend his life preaching and then die for something he knew was not true.

Sixth, nowhere does anyone claim to have found the mortal remains of Jesus. We know where the remains of most of the apostles are, yet there is no claim anywhere to the remains of Christ.

Moreover, it was the custom in the first century to erect a shrine at the site of a holy person's remains and in Jesus' time there were numerous such sites around Israel. The fact that no such shrine was ever erected for someone as well-known and revered as Jesus suggests that he truly rose from the dead and returned to his Father in heaven.

Seventh, the very origin and survival of the early Church argue powerfully in favour of the Resurrection. We recall the advice to the Sanhedrin of Gamaliel, a Pharisee and teacher of the law, who reminded the members that a certain Theudas had about four hundred followers but he was slain and his followers dispersed. After him Judas a Galilean had a number of followers but he too died and his followers were scattered (cf. *Acts* 5:34-37). This would certainly have happened to the followers of Jesus too if he had not risen from the dead.

As it was, the preaching of the apostles brought thousands of converts from the day of Pentecost on. On that day St Peter told the Jews that they had crucified Jesus but that God had raised him up: "This Jesus God raised up and of that we all are witnesses" (*Acts* 2:32). Later we read that even "a great many of the priests" were converted (*Acts* 6:7). The very priests that had condemned Christ to death were now becoming his followers. This can only be explained by the fact of his Resurrection.

The Church

619 The Church is one

In the Creed we profess our belief that the Church is one. I am in my seventies but have never seen such division over questions like loyalty to the Pope, matters of doctrine, morals and discipline, etc. How can we still say that the Church is one?

No matter how many divisions or differences of opinion we may see, the Church will always be one. There have always been differences of opinion over certain issues. In the *Acts of the Apostles* we see the disagreement in Antioch over whether converts to the faith should be circumcised. We read there that "Paul and Barnabas had no small dissension and debate" with those who wanted to impose circumcision (*Acts* 15:2). When the apostles and elders met to discuss the matter in Jerusalem, again "there had been much debate" (*Acts* 15:7) but in the end they resolved the matter by common agreement.

The Church's unity is much deeper than the differences of opinion that may exist over particular matters. The *Catechism of the Catholic Church* lists six ways in which the Church is one.

First, the Church is one because of her *source*. The Second Vatican Council says that "the highest exemplar and source of this mystery is the unity, in the Trinity of Persons, of one God, the Father and the Son in the Holy Spirit" (*UR* 2). The ultimate source of the Church is the Blessed Trinity, one God in three persons, so the Church is one for this reason.

Second, the Church is one because of her *founder*. The Church has only one founder, Jesus Christ, and his will is embodied in everything the Church believes and practises. "The Word made flesh, the prince of peace, reconciled all men to God by the cross, ... restoring the unity of all in one people and one body" (*GS* 78 §3; *CCC* 813).

Third, the Church is one because of her *soul*. The soul of the Church is the Holy Spirit, "who brings about that wonderful communion of the faithful and joins them together so intimately in Christ that he is the principle of the Church's unity" (*UR* 2; *CCC* 813).

Fourth, the Church is one because she professes *one faith*, the faith received from the apostles. Unity in faith is a salient feature of the Catholic Church and distinguishes it from other Christian denominations which can often be very divided in what they believe. The faith of the Catholic Church was received from Christ through the apostles and has been developed and deepened ever since through ecumenical councils, the teaching of Popes and the study of theologians and saints later accepted by the Magisterium. It is one coherent body of teaching which today is found in readily accessible form in the *Catechism of the Catholic Church*.

Fifth, the Church is one because of her *common celebration of worship*. Everywhere in the world the Church worships God with the same seven sacraments, the sacrifice of the Mass, Adoration of the Blessed Sacrament, etc. People travelling overseas appreciate this unity when they attend Mass in a variety of countries with different languages and rites, but always with the same fundamental structure based on the Missal approved by the Holy See. Anywhere in the world a Catholic is "at home" in the Mass.

And sixth, the Church is one in her *government*. The Church is one single organisation, with one head on earth, the Pope, and one body of bishops in communion with him. The Pope has immediate jurisdiction over the whole Church and over each of the faithful.

The marvellous unity of the Church is described by St Irenaeus at the end of the second century: "Since the Church has accepted this preaching and this faith we have outlined, despite its spread throughout the world it keeps it carefully, as though it lived in one house only. The Church believes these truths, as if it had but one soul and one heart; it preaches them and hands them on as though it had but one mouth. For although there are many different languages in the world, even so the strength of tradition is one and the same. The

Church founded in Germany believes exactly the same and hands on the same as do the Spanish and Celtic Churches, and the ones in the East, those in Egypt and Libya and Jerusalem, the centre of the world" (*Adv. haeres.* 1, 10, 1-3).

620 The Church is holy

When we say in the Creed that the Church is holy I can become quite cynical, wondering how we can call the Church holy when there is such obvious and widespread sinfulness in so many of her members, including priests and bishops. How can we call the Church holy?

I think many people ask this question. The first thing to remember is that the Church is not just the sinful members – all 1.3 billion of us! – who make her up at any given time here on earth. The Church is the Mystical Body of Christ, with Christ as her head, the Holy Spirit as her soul, Mary as her mother, and the myriad of saints in heaven and suffering souls in Purgatory praying for us. A good way to describe the Church is the traditional expression *immaculata ex maculatis*: immaculate, unstained, though composed of stained members. No matter how many sins we members of the Church commit here on earth, the Church herself will always be holy because she is the Mystical Body of Christ. This is the first reason why we can call the Church holy, but there are others.

Second, the Church is holy because she was founded by Jesus Christ, the very Son of God, who is all holy. Other religions have been founded by men, some of them notorious sinners, but the Catholic Church was founded by God himself, through his Son Jesus Christ.

Third, the Church teaches that all are called to holiness of life. Quoting the Second Vatican Council, the Catechism says that "all the faithful, whatever their condition or state – though each in his own way – are called by the Lord to that perfection of sanctity by which the Father himself is perfect" (*LG* 11 §3; *CCC* 825). The Church does not teach a morality of mediocrity, where all can do whatever they please, but rather calls us to true holiness of life, modelled on the holiness of Christ himself, "perfect God and perfect man" (*Athanasian Creed*). In the words of the Second Vatican Council, "All the activities of the Church are directed, as toward their end, to the sanctification of men in Christ and the glorification of God" (*SC* 10).

Fourth, the Church offers us all the means we need to grow in holiness. It is in the Church that "the fullness of the means of salvation" is deposited, and in her "by the grace of God we acquire holiness" (*UR* 3; *LG* 48; *CCC* 824). The means of salvation are, of course, especially the seven sacraments, but also the Mass and other liturgical rites, the reading of Scripture etc. It is up to us to make use of these means, receiving regularly especially the sacraments of Penance and the Eucharist. Pope St Paul VI's *Credo of the People of God* (1968) states: "The Church is therefore holy, though having sinners in her midst, because she herself has no other life but the life of grace. If they live her life, her members are sanctified; if they move away from her life, they fall into sins and disorders that prevent the radiation of her sanctity" (*CPG* 19; *CCC* 827).

Fifth, the Church is holy because many of her members have lived lives of exceptional holiness and have been canonised by the Church, a recognition that they practised heroic virtue and lived in fidelity to God's grace. They are proposed as models and intercessors and, as such, they help us here on earth to aspire to holiness and to make this world a better place. Quoting Pope St John Paul II, the Catechism says: "The saints have always been the source and origin of renewal in the most difficult moments in the Church's history... Holiness is the hidden source and infallible measure of her apostolic activity and missionary zeal" (*CL* 16, 3, 17, 3; *CCC* 828).

Sixth, the Church is holy in the many ordinary people here on earth who lead lives of exemplary holiness. They are "the saints next door", as Pope Francis calls them in *Gaudete et Exsultate*, (*GE*, 6-9). In this sense he says: "Holiness is the most attractive face of the Church" (*GE* 9). We should all strive to be these saints.

Seventh, the Church is holy in her teaching. She not only calls us to holiness but teaches a demanding moral code, with respect for life at all stages, a demanding way of living marriage and sexual morality, concern for the poor, social justice, etc. Here the words of *Deuteronomy* come to mind: "And what great nation is there, that has statutes and ordinances so righteous as all this law which I set before you this day?" (*Dt* 4:8)

So yes, the Church is indeed holy in spite of our sins.

621 The Church is catholic

In the Nicene Creed we say that the Church is one, holy, catholic and apostolic. Why is the word catholic not capitalised?

When we write the word Catholic as the name of the Church we always capitalise it, as it is the proper name of our Church. But when we say in the Creed that the Church is catholic we are using that word as a generic adjective which comes from a Greek word meaning "universal." As the Catechism explains, the word universal is used here in the sense of "according to the totality" or "in keeping with the whole" (*CCC* 830). The Church is catholic in two ways.

In the words of the Catechism, "First, the Church is catholic because Christ is present in her. 'Where there is Jesus Christ, there is the Catholic Church'" (St Ignatius of Antioch, *Ad Smyrn.* 8, 2; *CCC* 830). St Ignatius died a martyr around the year 107, so the Church was already being called Catholic early in the second century.

The Catechism goes on to explain why the presence of Christ makes the Church catholic: "In her subsists the fullness of Christ's body united with its head; this implies that she receives from him 'the fullness of the means of salvation' which he has willed: correct and complete confession of faith, full sacramental life, and ordained ministry in apostolic succession. The Church was, in this fundamental sense, catholic on the day of Pentecost and will always be so until the day of the Parousia" (*UR* 3; *AG* 6; *CCC* 830).

That is, the Church is catholic because she has within herself the fullness, the totality of all she needs to carry out her mission. She is catholic, complete, all-embracing. She has received from God the fullness of the deposit of faith and she passes on to us all we need to know in order to grow in holiness and go to heaven: the truth about God one and triune, about Jesus Christ in his divinity and humanity, about the Church herself, life after death, morality, etc.

In addition, the Church has and offers us the fullness of the means of salvation in the seven sacraments, which accompany us from our birth through the various stages of life to our death. What is more, because the bishops and priests of the Church have apostolic succession – they can trace their ordination back in an unbroken line to the laying on of hands by the apostles themselves – the sacraments they confer are valid and confer all the grace we need.

So, in this first sense, the Church is catholic because she is complete, full. She has within herself all she needs to lead human beings to heaven.

"Secondly, the Church is catholic because she has been sent out by Christ on a mission to the whole of the human race. 'All men are called to belong to the new People of God. This People, therefore, while remaining one and only one, is to be spread throughout the whole world and to all ages in order that the design of God's will may be fulfilled: he made human nature one in the beginning and has decreed that all his children who were scattered should be finally gathered together as one'" (*LG* 13, 2; *CCC* 831).

Christ came that all might be saved, and he wants his teaching and the means of salvation to reach all. The Church in this second sense is truly catholic or universal: she is for people of all nationalities, all walks of life, rich and poor, married and single, young and old, educated and uneducated, saints and sinners. In this sense too, the Church was catholic on the day of Pentecost, even though at that time she consisted of only a handful of faithful. She was destined for all.

In the fourth century St Cyril of Jerusalem spoke of the catholicity of the Church in both these senses: "The Church, Catholic or universal, gets her name from the fact that she is scattered through the whole world from one end of the earth to the other, and also because she teaches universally and without omission all the doctrines which are to be made known to mankind, whether concerned with visible or invisible things, with heavenly or earthly things. Then again because she teaches one way of worship to all men, nobles or commoners, learned or simple; finally, because she universally cures and heals every sort of sin which is committed by soul and body. Moreover, there is in her every kind of virtue in words and deeds and spiritual gifts of every sort" (*Instr. to cat.* 18, 23-25).

622 The Church is apostolic

In the Nicene Creed we say that the Church is one, holy, catholic and apostolic. I have always understood "apostolic" to mean that the Church engages in the apostolate, in evangelisation, in spreading the faith to others, but a friend says this is not correct. What is correct?

While spreading the faith is part of what we mean when we say that the Church is apostolic, the original meaning is much deeper than that. It means primarily that the Church is founded on the apostles, and this in three ways.

First the Church was, and continues to be, built on the foundation of the apostles. Our Lord chose the apostles to be the foundation of the Church, the first bishops. He formed them and sent them out to all nations to spread the faith and form new communities, exercising the authority he had received from the Father and in turn passed on to them (cf. *Mt* 28:18-20; *Jn* 20:21). They did go out, with Thomas going as far as India, James to Spain, Peter to Rome, etc. The communities they founded, afterwards led by bishops and priests on whom they laid hands, were truly apostolic, in the sense that they were founded by the apostles themselves.

As the years passed, the number of new communities continued to grow and to spread to more and more parts of the world until today the Church is everywhere. But all the communities today can trace their origin back to the apostles and they are built on the foundation laid by the apostles.

Second, the Church is apostolic in that she hands on the teaching she received from the apostles. Christ spent long hours instructing the apostles (cf. *Mk* 9:30) and before he ascended into heaven he sent them out to pass on to others what he had taught them: "Go therefore and make disciples of all nations, ... teaching them to observe all that I have commanded you" (*Mt* 28:19-20). He also told them, "He who hears you hears me" (*Lk* 10:16) so that the teaching of the Church today, received from the apostles, is the teaching of Christ himself.

Today, the Church has a rich body of teaching that has expanded greatly over the years, as the Church goes ever deeper into the deposit of faith handed on by Christ and the apostles. The Catechism says that "with the help of the Spirit dwelling in her, the Church keeps and hands on the teaching, the 'good deposit,' the words she has heard from the apostles" (*CCC* 857).

Third, the Church is apostolic in that she is taught, sanctified and ruled by the bishops, who are the successors of the apostles. In the words of the Catechism, she "continues to be taught, sanctified and guided by the apostles until Christ's return, through their successors in pastoral office: the college of bishops, 'assisted by priests, in union with the successor of Peter, the Church's supreme pastor'" (*AG* 5; *CCC* 857).

This continuity of transmission of the bishops' authority, with the apostles laying hands on their successors and these in turn laying hands on others in an unbroken line down to the present, is what is known as apostolic succession. Through it, the power and authority Christ gave the apostles is transmitted faithfully to each successive generation. Apostolic succession guarantees that the bishops and priests today have indeed the power to change bread and wine into the Body and Blood of Christ, to forgive sins, etc.

Tertullian, at the end of the second century describes how the Church grew out of the one Church founded by Christ on the apostles, always remaining faithful to their teaching: "Again they [the apostles] set up Churches in every city, from which the other Churches afterwards received the shoot of the faith and the seeds of doctrine and continue to receive them every day, in order to become Churches. By this they are themselves reckoned apostolic as being the offspring of apostolic Churches... These Churches, then, numerous as they are, are identical with that one primitive apostolic Church from which they all come" (*Praescr.* 20).

So the Church is indeed apostolic, having grown out of the one Church founded by Christ on the apostles, and she continues to believe and live out everywhere what Christ taught the apostles.

623 Fathers of the Church

I have often heard of a saint being called a Father of the Church. What does this mean and who decides who is a Father? Also, could you give me the names of some Fathers?

We are accustomed to speaking about the Fathers of the Church, yet many people, like yourself, are not exactly sure what we mean by the expression. The term is used for early saints who had three characteristics in common: antiquity, holiness of life and orthodoxy of writing.

As regards antiquity, we mean that they lived in the early centuries of the Church. While there is no universally accepted cut off point, it is quite common to say the seventh century is the end of this period in the West, so that saints like St Gregory the Great and St Isidore of Seville would be included. In the East it is extended to the eighth century, so as to include St John Damascene.

Holiness of life is essential if someone is to be included among the Fathers. This is usually indicated by their inclusion in the list of the canonised saints.

Orthodoxy of writing is also essential. There are some early writers like Tertullian and Origen, most of whose writings are highly regarded and frequently quoted, but who are not generally regarded as Fathers because at one time or another they embraced heresy. They are often called simply ecclesiastical writers.

Who gives someone the title Father of the Church? The answer is no one in particular. Rather it was the living Tradition of the Church which recognised them as such. Among the characteristics that led to someone being included among the Fathers were: citation of his writings by an ecumenical council or by a pope; his inclusion in the Roman Martyrology, a list of saints, as "outstanding in holiness and doctrine"; public reading of his writings in churches and citation of his works with praise by other great Fathers. There is no official list of Fathers of the Church as there is, for example, of Doctors of the Church (cf. J. Flader, *Question Time 2*, q. 283). There are far more Fathers than Doctors.

It is to be understood that the Fathers were generally in agreement with each other on major points of doctrine, especially once those points had been defined in an ecumenical council. Nonetheless there could be individual Fathers who had their own teaching on certain points. When the Fathers were in complete agreement in the interpretation of certain passages of Scripture, both the Council of Trent in the sixteenth century and the First Vatican Council in the nineteenth declared that it was not licit to depart from their interpretation.

The Fathers can be divided into different groups. It is customary to call the earliest ones Apostolic Fathers. They lived at the end of the first century and beginning of the second, and were formed by the apostles or their disciples. Among them are St Clement of Rome, the fourth Pope, who wrote important letters to the Church in Corinth and who died around AD 97; St Ignatius of Antioch, a disciple of St John the apostle, who wrote seven letters to various Churches on his way to Rome to be martyred around 107; St Polycarp, bishop of Smyrna, a disciple of St John who died around 155; and Papias, bishop of

Hierapolis, another disciple of St John and a friend of St Polycarp, who wrote the *Exposition of the Sayings of the Lord* and who died in 163.

Next came the Apologists, who defended the faith in the face of non-believers. The most important of them is St Justin, a convert to Christianity who moved from the East to Rome, where he set up a school of philosophy. He wrote the *Dialogue with Trypho* and two *Apologies* to the Emperor Antoninus Pius, describing the life of the Christians and urging the emperor to stop persecuting the Church. He was beheaded in 163. Lesser Apologists were Aristides of Athens, who also wrote to Antoninus Pius; Athenagoras, who wrote to Marcus Aurelius, and Theophilus, Bishop of Antioch, who wrote three books of apology addressed to a certain Autolycus.

After these the Fathers are sometimes grouped together as pre-Nicene Fathers (those who lived prior to the Council of Nicaea in 325) and post-Nicene Fathers. Likewise, they can be divided into Eastern Fathers, who lived in the Eastern part of the Roman Empire, and Western Fathers.

624 Eastern Fathers of the Church

Can you tell me a little about some of the Eastern Fathers of the Church so that I can know who they are?

The Eastern Fathers lived in the Eastern part of the Empire and wrote predominantly in Greek. By the way, when the works of the Fathers are quoted the citation usually includes the letters PG or PL. The abbreviations stand for *Patrologia Graeca* and *Patrologia Latina*, Greek Patrology, or study of the Greek Fathers, and Latin Patrology. Together they form a collection of hundreds of volumes compiled by J.P. Migne in the nineteenth century. The writings of the Greek Fathers alone comprise 166 volumes.

In the East, as in the West, there are four Fathers who are customarily known as the Great Church Fathers, so let us begin with them. In the

East they are Saints Athanasius, Basil the Great, Gregory of Nazianzus and John Chrysostom.

St Athanasius (296-373), was a great theologian and archbishop of Alexandria. He is perhaps best remembered for his role in the first ecumenical council, held in Nicaea in 325, where he defended the divinity of Christ against the errors of Arius.

St Basil the Great (330-379), bishop of Caesarea, was the older brother of St Gregory of Nyssa (332-395), who was bishop of Nyssa and also a prominent Eastern Father. Together with their close friend St Gregory of Nazianzus, they are known as the Cappadocian Fathers.

St Basil, along with the other Cappadocians, showed that Christians could dialogue with learned Greek-speaking intellectuals. They argued that the Christian faith, while contrary to many ideas of the Greek philosophers, was at the same time a scientific belief system. They were significant contributors to the theology of the Trinity as defined in the First Council of Constantinople in 381, from which came the Nicene-Constantinopolitan Creed.

St Gregory of Nazianzus (329–389) was Patriarch of Constantinople and highly regarded as an orator and philosopher. He made a significant contribution to the theology of the Blessed Trinity and is sometimes remembered as the "Trinitarian Theologian."

The fourth great Eastern Father was St John Chrysostom (347-407). He was archbishop of Constantinople and is remembered for his eloquence in preaching and public speaking. The sheer volume of his sermons and writings make him the most prolific of the Eastern Fathers. A testimony to his eloquence is the name Chrysostom, meaning golden mouthed, which was given him after his death or, according to some sources, during his lifetime.

Another great Eastern Father was St Cyril of Alexandria (378-444), bishop of that city when it was at the height of its influence in the Roman Empire. He wrote extensively and was a leading protagonist in the controversy over the person of Christ in the fourth and fifth centuries. He played a leading role at the Council of Ephesus (431) which declared, against the errors of Nestorius, that Christ was one person, the divine person of the Word, and therefore Mary was truly the Mother of God. He is sometimes called the "Pillar of Faith" and "Seal of all the Fathers".

One cannot speak of great Eastern Fathers without mentioning Maximus the Confessor (580-662), also known as Maximus the Theologian and Maximus of Constantinople. In his early life he was a civil servant and an aide to the Byzantine Emperor Heraclius but he gave up this life to become a monk. He defended the two wills in Christ, the human and the divine, against the error known as monothelitism, but his strong teaching on the question resulted in his torture and exile and eventually his death. His *Life of the Virgin* is thought to be the earliest complete biography of Our Lady.

Finally, of the many more Eastern Fathers who could be mentioned, comes St John Damascene (676-749). He was a Syrian monk and priest who wrote books and composed hymns which are still in use in Eastern monasteries. He is well known for defending the use of icons during the iconoclast controversy in the eighth century. He wrote on the Assumption of Mary.

625 Western Fathers of the Church

Could you tell me a little about some of the Western Fathers so that I can know who they are?

As with the Eastern Fathers, there are four Western Fathers who are known as the Great Church Fathers. They are Saints Ambrose, Augustine, Jerome and Gregory the Great and it will be appropriate to deal with them first. In a later column I will write about other Western Fathers.

St Ambrose (340-397) was born into a Christian family and was raised in present-day Germany. His mother was a woman of considerable intellect and piety and his brother Satyrus and sister

Marcellina are also venerated as saints. Ambrose studied law in Rome and in 372 he was named Governor of Aemilia-Liguria in Italy. When in 374 there was an uproar between Arians and orthodox Catholics over the election of a new bishop of Milan, Ambrose went to restore calm but because he was so popular with the people, they began to chant "Ambrose, bishop". He energetically refused the position because he had not even been baptised nor trained in theology. Eventually he had to accept and a week later he was baptised and ordained a bishop. St Ambrose is known for his preaching, which led to the conversion of St Augustine, and for his many theological writings, especially on the virginity of Mary and her role as Mother of God.

St Augustine (354–430), a philosopher and theologian, is one of the most important figures in western Christianity. He was born in present-day Algeria to a very Christian mother, St Monica, but he resisted her efforts to have him become a Christian. He was educated in North Africa and began to live a dissolute life, taking a mistress with whom he lived for fifteen years and who bore him a son whom they named Adeodatus, meaning given by God. He studied rhetoric and philosophy and for a time followed the Manichean heresy. He later went to Rome, where he read widely in Greek and Roman philosophy and set up a school of rhetoric, and then to Milan, where he came under the influence of St Ambrose and was baptised in 387. He was ordained a priest in 391 and was later made bishop of Hippo, in present-day Algeria. His most important works are the *Confessions*, his autobiography; *The City of God*, a defence of Christianity against pagan critics which proposed the idea of the Church as the city of God as distinct from secular society, the city of man; his mammoth treatise on the Trinity *De Trinitate*; hundreds of preserved sermons, letters and works defending the faith against heresies, commentaries on Scripture, books on marriage…

St Jerome (347-420) was born in the Roman Province of Pannonia and went to Rome, where he studied the classical writers and learned Latin and Greek. Around 373 he went to Syria, where he began to study the Bible and took up the monastic life, learning Hebrew at the same time. After being ordained a bishop, he returned to Rome where he served as secretary to Pope Damasus I from 382 to 385. While in Rome he began a revision of the Latin Bible, basing his translation on the Greek manuscripts of the New Testament. This was the beginning of his most notable achievement, the Latin translation of the Bible known as the Vulgate, starting from the Hebrew and Greek manuscripts. In 385 he returned to the Middle East, where he spent the rest of his life, working for the last years in a cave near Bethlehem. Among his other writings are numerous commentaries on Scripture, lives of important Christians, many letters and several writings defending Catholic doctrine against heresies.

Pope St Gregory the Great (540-604) was the son of a Senator and himself prefect of Rome at the age of 30 before entering a monastery and later returning to public life. He was Pope from 590 to 604. It was he who sent St Augustine of Canterbury to convert the pagan Anglo-Saxons of England to Christianity. Also under his leadership the Franks, Lombards and Visigoths left their Arian beliefs to be united with the Catholic Church. He introduced substantial revisions in the liturgy of the Mass, and the plainchant known as Gregorian Chant is attributed to him. Among his most important writings are the *Moralia*, a commentary on the book of Job; the *Book of Pastoral Rule* on the role of bishops; the *Dialogues* on the miracles done by saints; and many sermons and letters. He was canonised by acclamation of the people shortly after his death.

626 More Western Fathers of the Church

Apart from the four Great Western Fathers of the Church about whom you wrote recently, who are some of the other important Western Fathers?

As with the Eastern Fathers, there are dozens of important Western Fathers, so I will have to make a selection of some of the more significant ones, basing this selection especially on the importance of their life and writings.

We can begin with St Irenaeus of Lyons (140-202), who is regarded as the most important theologian of the second century. He was a native of Asia Minor, probably from Smyrna, where he had been a disciple of St Polycarp. It is not certain when he went to France but he was there as a highly regarded member of the clergy of Lyons shortly before the death of the martyred bishop St Pothinus, whom he succeeded in the year 177 or 178. True to his name, which comes from the Greek word for peace, he tried to make peace around the year 190 between Pope Victor and St Polycrates of Ephesus, who was threatened with excommunication. His most important work is the well-known and often quoted *Adversus haereses*, a refutation of the gnostic heresy. It consists of five books written in Greek between 180 and 199.

Another great Western writer is Quintus Septimius Florens Tertullianus (ca 155/160-240/250), better known as Tertullian. He is normally called an ecclesiastical writer rather than a Father of the Church, since in his later life he lapsed into the rigorist heresy of Montanism. But his early writings are so abundant and widely quoted that it would not be right to omit him. He was born in Carthage of pagan parents and became a lawyer of much repute. After his conversion to the faith around 193 he turned his expertise to the defence of Christianity, being the first author to write in Latin. Among his many writings the *Apology*, a defence of the faith, is generally regarded as the most important. Among his other writings are those on prayer, patience, Baptism, chastity, marriage, the soul, the resurrection from the dead, idolatry, etc.

A unique Western Father is the anti-Pope St Hippolytus of Rome, who died in 235. He probably came from the East but his whole career took place in Rome. In a dispute with Pope St Callistus over the readmission of sinners to the Church, Hippolytus was elected Pope by a small group of followers between 217 and 222 and he remained an anti-Pope until 235, when he and the Pope of the day, St Pontianus, were exiled to Sardinia by the emperor. The two were reconciled there and died soon after as martyrs. St Hippolytus' writing was prodigious, although only a few of his works have survived intact. Among his most important works is *The Apostolic Tradition*, a comprehensive description of the liturgy and organisation of the Church around 215.

Another important Western Father is St Cyprian, bishop of Carthage in North Africa. He was born in Carthage between 200 and 210 of wealthy pagan parents and was converted to Christianity around 246, being ordained a priest shortly afterwards and bishop of Carthage in 248 or 249. He was involved in a long-running controversy over how to treat those who had lapsed from the faith during persecution and who later desired reconciliation. One of his important writings, *The Lapsed*, is about this issue. Other important writings are *The Unity of the Catholic Church*, a beautiful commentary on *The Lord's Prayer*, writings on almsgiving and patience and numerous letters.

Finally, a brief word about four more Western Fathers. St Hilary of Poitiers (315-367) was bishop of that city in France and a staunch defender of the faith against Arianism, most notably in his book *De Trinitate*. He is a Doctor of the Church.

St John Cassian (360-435), after visiting Eastern monasteries especially in Egypt, brought monasticism to the West and founded the monasteries known as the Abbey of St Victor near Marseilles.

St Gregory of Tours (538-593), bishop of Tours, is best known for his ten-volume *History of the Franks* and his *Eight Books of Miracles*.

Lastly, St Isidore of Seville (560-636) is generally regarded as the last of the Western Fathers. He was Archbishop of Seville and one of the most learned men of his time, known especially for his twenty-volume encyclopedia *Etymologies* and for presiding over important councils and synods. He too is a Doctor of the Church.

627 The Fathers of the Church and conversions

I remember hearing how a convert from Protestantism found reading the Fathers of the Church extremely helpful in his conversion. Can you tell me why this might have been?

Many converts from Protestantism have found the Fathers instrumental in their conversion. The reasons may vary but one important one is that the Fathers put us in touch with the early Church and how the Church interpreted the message of Christ though its life and teaching.

Protestantism, based on the teaching of Martin Luther, follows the principle of *Sola Scriptura*, Scripture alone as the source of our knowledge of the teachings of Jesus Christ. Based on Scripture alone Protestants draw many conclusions which are different from the faith as professed from the beginning by the Catholic Church. When someone goes back to the Fathers and finds that the early Church believed and lived out not what Protestants do but what the Catholic Church does today, they are often led into the Church.

After all, the Church didn't begin in the sixteenth century, when Protestantism fractured its unity. It began with its foundation by Jesus Christ in the first century and it has a long history. If someone is searching for the true Church founded by Jesus Christ they will find it in the one that lives out today what the early Church did. That Church is the Catholic Church. Let me give one example of the many that could be given: the Church's teaching on the Eucharist.

Protestants do not celebrate the Eucharist as a sacrifice offered to God through the ministry of a priest, nor do they believe in the Real Presence of Christ in the Eucharist. The early Church did all of this. Already at the end of the first century, a document known as the *Didache* describes the Eucharist as a sacrifice three times, among them: "Give thanks after having confessed your transgressions, that your sacrifice may be pure (Ch. 14)." At the end of the second century St Irenaeus writes succinctly: "The oblation of the Church is judged by God to be a pure and acceptable sacrifice. The Lord gave instructions that it should be offered throughout the world" (*Adv. Haer.* 4.18).

A detailed description of the Mass as it was celebrated around the year 155 is given by St Justin Martyr. The Mass at that time followed the same plan as ours today. It had the Liturgy of the Word, with readings from the Old Testament and the apostles, the homily, the Prayers of the Faithful, the collection of gifts for the poor, the Sign of Peace, the Offertory Procession, the Presentation of the Gifts of bread and wine mixed with water, the Eucharistic Prayer addressed to the Father, the Great Amen at the end of the prayer, and Communion distributed by deacons to the baptised who were living in keeping with their faith (*Apol.* 1, 66-67; cf. *CCC* 1345). Any Church which calls itself Christian and does not celebrate the Eucharist in a way similar to this is simply not the Church Jesus Christ founded.

As regards belief in the Real Presence, this is already clear in the Scriptures. In the synagogue of Capernaum Jesus spoke about eating his flesh and drinking his blood (cf. *Jn* 6:53-57) and in the Last Supper he instituted the Eucharist and gave it to the apostles, saying: "Take, eat; this is my body" (*Mt* 26:26). Protestants interpret these words as if the Eucharist were merely a symbol of Our Lord's body. Yet the Church from the beginning believed that the Eucharist is truly the body and blood of Christ.

Already around the year 107 St Ignatius of Antioch wrote: "They [the heretics] abstain from the Eucharist and from prayer, because they do not confess the Eucharist to be the flesh of our Saviour Jesus Christ..." (*Ad Smyrn.* 6, 2). A few years later St Justin wrote: "Likewise, we have been taught that the food blessed by the prayer of his word – and from which our own blood and flesh are nourished and changed – is the flesh and blood of Jesus who was made flesh" (*Apol. 1*, 66). The Fathers of the Church were unanimous in teaching the Real Presence.

And as regards the need for an ordained priest to celebrate Mass, St Ignatius of Antioch wrote: "Let that be deemed a proper Eucharist which is administered either by the bishop or by one to whom he has entrusted it" (*Ad Smyrn.* 7, 1).

From this one example it is easy to understand how when Protestants read the Fathers and discover these truths they are led more easily into the Catholic Church.

628 Dogmas and doctrines

I am involved in the RCIA in my parish and we are to ensure that converts have "an appropriate acquaintance with dogmas." Are dogmas the same as doctrines and, if not, what is the difference?

A simple answer to your question is that all the teachings of the Church are doctrines, but only some of them are dogmas.

What is a dogma? The *Catechism of the Catholic Church* answers: "The Church's Magisterium exercises the authority it holds from Christ to the fullest extent when it defines dogmas, that is, when it proposes, in a form obliging the Christian people to an irrevocable adherence of faith, truths contained in divine Revelation or also when it proposes, in a definitive way, truths having a necessary connection with these" (*CCC* 88).

Two elements enter into the concept of a dogma. First, the truth has been revealed by God and is therefore contained in the sources of Revelation, which are Scripture and Tradition. And second, the truth has been proposed for belief by the teaching authority of the Church. Once a truth has been so defined, the faithful are to give their "irrevocable adherence of faith" to it. That is, they are to believe it with divine and Catholic faith: divine by virtue of its revelation by God and Catholic by virtue of its proclamation by the Church.

The proposal for belief by the Church may be done either in an extraordinary manner, through a solemn proclamation of the dogma by the Pope or an Ecumenical Council, or through the ordinary and general magisterium of the Church. This latter is less common.

The last two dogmas proclaimed through a solemn proclamation by the Pope were those of the Immaculate Conception of the Blessed Virgin Mary by Pope Pius IX in 1854 and the bodily Assumption of Our Lady into heaven by Pope Pius XII in 1950.

As regards Councils, while the Second Vatican Council did not intend to define any new dogmas, various Ecumenical Councils including the Council of Trent in the sixteenth century and the First Vatican Council in the nineteenth certainly did. A customary form of definition of a dogma in a Council is a statement with wording like "If anyone should say... let him be anathema." Succinct statements like these are to be held definitively. Among the dogmas defined by a Council was the infallibility of the Pope by the First Vatican Council, held in 1869-70.

As we saw in the Catechism, the Church can also teach definitively a truth having a necessary connection with a truth contained in divine Revelation. An example is the declaration by Pope John Paul II in 1994 that the Church does not have the authority to ordain women to the priesthood. In his Apostolic Letter *Ordinatio sacerdotalis* he wrote: "Wherefore, in order that all doubt may be removed regarding a matter of great importance, a matter which pertains to the Church's divine constitution itself, in view of my ministry of confirming the brethren (cf. *Lk* 22:32) I declare that the Church has no authority whatsoever to confer priestly ordination on women and that this judgment is to be definitively held by all the Church's faithful" (n. 4).

These dogmas and other definitive statements are a great help in our journey of faith. They are beacons that light up our way to heaven, just as the stars guide sailors across the seas. The Catechism says of them: "Dogmas are lights along the path of faith; they illuminate it and make it secure" (*CCC* 89).

It is interesting to know that the denial of a dogma or of some other definitive teaching of the Church is heresy, which is defined in the Catechism as "the obstinate post-baptismal denial of some truth which must be believed with divine and catholic faith, or it is likewise an obstinate doubt concerning the same" (*CCC* 2089).

Apart from the relatively few dogmas and other truths which are to be held definitively the Church teaches many other doctrines. They include, for example, all the teachings in the *Catechism of the Catholic Church*, the general teachings of Ecumenical Councils and Popes, etc. Our response to them should be, in the words of the Second Vatican Council, "loyal submission of intellect and will" (*LG* 25).

629 The Leuven Project

I have my children in a Catholic school and have heard talk about the Leuven Project for assessing Catholic school identity. I don't know anything about it. Can you enlighten me?

The name Leuven is the Flemish name for the Catholic University of Leuven, in Belgium. The university is perhaps better known by its French name Louvain. Since 1968 the University has been divided into a Flemish-language campus in Leuven and a French-language campus in Louvain-la-Neuve.

The Leuven Project was an initiative of the Catholic Education Commission of Victoria, which in 2006 entered into an agreement with the University of Leuven to undertake research in Catholic schools in order to respond to increasing secularisation and religious diversity. Researchers in Leuven came up with this program, officially known as the Enhancing Catholic School Identity Project (ECSIP). It is presently being used in many dioceses in this country, although many parish priests have opted not to have it in their schools.

In order to understand the Project it is helpful to know something of the theory behind it. The principal researchers were Didier Pollefeyt, Professor of Theology and Religious Studies, and his research assistant Jan Bouwens. Underpinning their research, however, was the work of Lieven Boeve, a theologian who maintains that the Christian "meta-narrative" has little or no meaning for people who are immersed in pluralist Western societies, and that belief in Christ and the teachings of the Church has been replaced by what he calls "post-critical belief", a belief system which is symbolic rather than grounded in objective truths. For ECSIP "post-critical belief" is the ideal for Catholic schools and parishes.

ECSIP is based too on a process known as "recontextualisation", whereby the Catholic school enters into dialogue with the ideas and values of the pluralist secular society in which it operates, receiving much from that society without attempting to assert its own beliefs.

Needless to say, these presuppositions are at best questionable and at worst a frontal attack on everything the Catholic school system was established to achieve: the teaching of the truths of the Catholic faith, so as to lead students to know their faith well and love Jesus Christ personally. The knowledge of the truths of the faith is critical too for the Church's work of evangelisation, the spreading of the truth and love for God which Pope Francis has done so much to promote.

Significantly, the goals of Catholic education were set out beautifully by the bishops of New South Wales in their pastoral letter *Catholic Schools at a Crossroads* in 2007. Among other things, that document expressed the aim of "ensuring that our schools are truly Catholic in their identity and life, are centres of the new evangelisation, enable our students to achieve high levels of Catholic religious literacy and practice, are led and staffed by people who will contribute to these goals."

One can see the presuppositions and agenda of ECSIP in many of the questions on the "Post-Critical Belief Scale", where the person answers on a seven-point scale ranging from "strongly disagree" to "strongly agree". For example: "The Bible is a guide, full of signs in the search for God and not a historical account." "Even though this goes against modern rationality, I believe Mary was truly a virgin when she gave birth to Jesus." "Too many people have been oppressed in the name of God to still make believing possible." "Because Jesus is mainly a guiding principle for me, my faith in him would not be affected if it would appear that he never actually existed as a historical individual." "Ultimately, religion is a commitment without having absolute certainty." "God grows together with the history of humanity and therefore is changeable." "I am well aware, that my beliefs are only one possibility among so many others." "There is no absolute meaning in life, only direction-giving, which is different for each one of us."

I can understand that some people would find ECSIP a good way for Catholic schools to dialogue with a pluralist culture, but frankly I think it undermines everything the schools were set up to achieve. I can understand why many priests have refused to have it in their schools.

630 Plenary Councils

Now that Australia is preparing for a Plenary Council to be held in 2020, can you please tell me exactly what a Plenary Council is, and how it differs, say, from a national assembly or some other national gathering by a different name?

It is not surprising that you are unfamiliar with the term Plenary Council since the last such gathering in this country took place in 1937, before most of us were born. In simple terms a Plenary Council is a gathering of the bishops of a particular territory, along with a number of priests and others, to consider matters of importance for the Church in that territory and to pass legislation on them. Any such legislation must first be approved by the Holy See (cf. *CCL*, Can. 446).

The principal reason why Plenary Councils have not been held in this country since 1937, and why they are exceedingly rare in other countries as well, is that the Second Vatican Council gave rise to bishops conferences, in which the bishops of a given territory gather periodically to consider matters of importance and make decisions on them. In this country the Australian Catholic Bishops Conference ordinarily meets twice a year for periods of a week or more to consider such matters. The Second Vatican Council entrusted to bishops conferences a large number of matters to be decided for each territory, and the bishops of this country have met and ruled on them and other matters often over the years.

If the bishops conference can already discuss and legislate on these matters, why have a Plenary Council? The obvious answer is that in a meeting of the bishops conference only the bishops take part, whereas in a Plenary Council representatives of the clergy and laity can also participate. In fact, as the Australian bishops have indicated, there is to be a process of preparation for the 2020 Plenary Council in which all Catholics in the country are invited and encouraged to express their views on how they see the Church at the present time and what suggestions for change they would like to see implemented. All of these observations will be gathered and considered before the Council meets in 2020.

It is a very important opportunity for everyone to contribute to this Council and it shows how the bishops value the thoughts of every single Catholic. We all have ideas on these matters and now is the time to express them. This can be done through parish gatherings and also directly online at the website of the Council: plenarycouncil.catholic.org.au. There the bishops say: "We invite all Australians to engage in an open and inclusive process of listening, dialogue and discernment about the future of the Catholic Church in Australia. Your voice is needed – join in!"

As to who can actually take part in the Plenary Council itself the *Code of Canon Law* is very clear. In the first place all the bishops are to attend and it is only they who have what is called a deliberative vote, meaning that only their votes count in passing any legislation (cf. Can. 443, §1).

Other categories of persons who are to be called are vicars general and episcopal vicars. Major Superiors of religious institutes and Societies of Apostolic Life of both men and women are to be called in a number determined by the bishops conference. Rectors of ecclesiastical and Catholic universities along with their deans of theology and canon law are also to be called, as are some of the rectors of major seminaries (cf. Can. 443, §3). The vote of all these is consultative, meaning that it is taken into account by the bishops but does not count in passing legislation.

Finally, priests and other members of the faithful may also be called, but their total number is not to exceed half of all the others mentioned and their vote too is consultative (cf. Can. 443, §4).

In summary, the number of those attending is clearly established and limited, as is the nature of their vote. In this sense, a plenary council is very different from a national assembly, where as many people can attend as the bishops determine. But a national assembly has no power to pass legislation as does a Plenary Council.

Let us get involved by making our voice heard in the preparatory phase and let us pray for the fruits of the Council, which can be very important for the future of the Church in this country.

631 The Church is hierarchical

I have been following the Synodal Assembly in Germany in 2020, where lay people, priests and bishops are discussing such matters as changing the Church's teaching on basic moral issues and even its structures. Can you comment on this?

Some of those involved in the Synodal Assembly held recently in Germany seem delighted that the synod involved the laity in a decision-making process in a new way. Yet Cardinal Rainer Maria Woelki of Cologne expressed the fear that the synodal path had installed a form of Protestant church parliament. He told the German Catholic news agency KNA: "My impression is that ... one believes that one can shape the Church in a completely new and different way."

All of this has implications for the first session of the Australian Plenary Council 2020 to be held in Adelaide in October. Indeed, the "Final Report for the Plenary Council Phase I" in Chapter 7 on "Leadership and Church Governance" includes ideas expressed by some of the participants which are at variance with the Church's teaching on its hierarchical structure. For example, the report speaks of "dissociating the ordained minister (whether bishop, priest, or deacon) from institutional power or the ecclesiastical office", "women to participate more fully in Church leadership positions that included senior administration and decision-making", "an inverted pyramid model of Church with the laity at the top", "a strong need to discard the old hierarchical model and develop an entirely new one", "an autonomous Australian Catholic Church" which is "completely detached from Rome and all decisions are made locally", etc.

Anyone with a minimal understanding of the Church would realise that views such as these are unacceptable. After all, it was Christ himself who gave the Church its structure of governance. He chose twelve apostles, giving them the power of the keys (cf. *Mt* 18:18) and sending them out to all nations to baptise and teach (cf. *Mt* 28:19-20). These would be the first bishops and they would lay hands on other men to ordain them deacons, priests and bishops.

From among the apostles Christ chose Peter to be their head and the head of the whole Church, telling him he would be the rock of the Church and giving him the keys to the kingdom of heaven so that whatever he bound on earth would be bound in heaven (cf. *Mt* 16:18-19). After his Resurrection he made Peter, and Peter alone, the chief shepherd of the Church when he said: "Feed my lambs, feed my sheep" (*Jn* 21:15-17). Peter was to be, of course, the first Pope.

We see Peter exercising his leadership when he told the brethren that they should choose one of the men among them to succeed Judas "in this ministry and apostleship" and they chose Matthias (*Acts* 1:15-25). Later it was Peter again who addressed the apostles and elders in the so-called Council of Jerusalem to decide what to impose on Gentile converts to the faith after controversy arose over this issue in Antioch (cf. *Acts* 15:6-11). After making their decision, they wrote a letter to the Church in Antioch, Syria and Cilicia in which they manifested their authority over the whole Church, telling the faithful that some persons had troubled them, "although we gave them no instructions" (*Acts* 15:24). When the faithful in Antioch received the letter, "they rejoiced at the exhortation", thereby acknowledging the authority of the apostles (*Acts* 15:31).

This structure of governance of the Church, with the Pope and the college of bishops exercising supreme authority, has existed from the beginning and it cannot be changed. It comes from Christ himself. We call this structure hierarchical, from the Greek word for sacred, because those who exercise authority in the Church are in the sacred ministry of Holy Orders. The Catechism explains that "from the beginning of his ministry, the Lord Jesus instituted the Twelve as the seeds of the new Israel and the beginning of the sacred hierarchy" (*CCC* 877).

With this structure we can be confident that those with authority in the Church have all studied philosophy, theology, canon law, scripture, the history of the Church, etc., and so have a deep understanding of what they are passing on to us. They may not all be great preachers or canonisable saints, but they have been well trained to look after our pastoral care, which they do with generosity in a spirit of service. We can help them in carrying this burden by our prayer and our respect for their authority, passing on to them too our concerns.

632 Decision-making in the universal Church

A number of friends who have made submissions to the Plenary Council 2020 are proposing that lay people should have a role in decision-making in the Church, even at the highest level. Is this something that might be accepted by the Church?

In answering your question I will take the word "lay" to mean all those not in Holy Orders, hence including men and women religious as well.

The "Final Report for the Plenary Council Phase I", in Chapter 7 on "Leadership and Church Governance", includes many proposals along this line, among them: "numerous changes to be made to the leadership and decision-making processes within the Church," "women to participate more fully in Church leadership positions that included senior administration and decision-making", etc.

As I wrote recently, Christ established a Church which is hierarchical, where those in authority at every level are men in Holy Orders, as bishops and priests. The Church is not a democracy, where everyone has a say in how things are done. This makes sense, since the mission of the Church is the vital one of leading souls to heaven. To carry out their task bishops and priests receive extensive philosophical, theological and spiritual formation and they must answer to God for how they carry out their pastoral ministry. The Church is not just one more large organisation, with a big bureaucracy. It is the People of God.

At the level of the universal Church, decision-making is done by the Pope and the College of Bishops. The *Code of Canon Law* says of the Pope: "He is the head of the College of Bishops, the Vicar of Christ, and the Pastor of the universal Church here on earth. Consequently, by virtue of his office, he has supreme, full, immediate and universal ordinary power in the Church, and he can always freely exercise this power" (Can. 331). That is, the Pope, as chief shepherd, has supreme and immediate power over the whole Church and over each member of it. And he can always exercise this power freely; that is, without needing the agreement of anyone else.

The Pope governs the Church with the help of the Roman Curia, consisting of offices known as Congregations, Secretariats, Councils, etc. The *Code of Canon Law* says: "The Supreme Pontiff usually conducts the business of the universal Church through the Roman Curia, which acts in his name and with his authority for the good and for the service of the Churches" (Can. 360). These offices, or dicasteries as they are known, assist the Pope but ultimately they act with his authority and in his name. The Pope takes responsibility for their decisions.

The members of the dicasteries include many lay people, including women. In particular the Congregation for Institutes of Consecrated Life and for Societies of Apostolic Life has a number of women as full members, meaning they have voting rights equal to those of bishops and priests. In addition, in January 2020 Pope Francis appointed an Italian woman Under-Secretary of the Secretariat of State in the Section for Relations with States, where she is responsible for managing the Vatican's relationship with multilateral organisations such as the

United Nations. Two other women in senior roles are the head of the Vatican Museums and the deputy head of the Holy See's press office. While the Pope has to approve major decisions, there are lay people assisting him in these bodies with senior decision-making roles.

Apart from the Pope acting on his own, the government of the universal Church also rests in the College of Bishops, whose head is the Pope. The *Code of Canon Law* says: "This College of Bishops, in which the apostolic body abides in an unbroken manner, is, in union with its head and never without this head, also the subject of supreme and full power over the universal Church" (Can. 336).

The College of Bishops exercises its role in solemn form in an Ecumenical Council, whose decrees must be approved by the Pope (Can. 337 §1, Can. 341). It can also exercise this power when the bishops are dispersed throughout the world and the Pope accepts its decisions (cf. Can. 337 §2). In both of these cases only the Bishops have a vote and there is no place for lay people in decision-making. But, as we have seen, there are lay people in very senior positions in the Church.

633 Decision-making in the local Church

Can the Plenary Council 2020 legislate to allow lay people to be involved in decision-making at the level of the diocese or parish?

Numerous submissions along the lines of what you ask were made in the preparatory phase of the Council. Among the ones included in the "Final Report for the Plenary Council Phase I", in Chapter 7, were: "lay people to run or administer parishes", "Parishioners need to be able to appoint their own lay Parish Administrators and Parish Boards of Management", "Every parish should have an elected pastoral council, which functions as a decision-making body", "Independent Catholic churches – Parishioners 'own' their parish in this model and have all the authority for decision-making."

Most of these proposals unfortunately reflect a Protestant mindset, where lay people have a significant say in running the Church, especially at the parish level. As I wrote earlier, the Catholic Church founded by Jesus Christ is hierarchical, where leadership is vested at all levels in those in Holy Orders. Nonetheless, there are many possibilities for lay people to be involved in some capacities.

At the level of the diocese, the bishop is the head, and he has the final responsibility for pastoral leadership, for decision-making. He must answer to God for his decisions. In the words of the *Code of Canon Law*: "By divine institution, Bishops succeed the Apostles through the Holy Spirit who is given to them They are constituted Pastors in the Church, to be the teachers of doctrine, the priests of sacred worship and the ministers of governance" (Can. 375 §1).

Bishops, like the Pope himself, carry out their work with the help of the diocesan curia and other bodies, many of which include lay faithful. Most of these agencies, including the Catholic Education Office, Catholic Care and others are headed by lay people, often with large budgets and great decision-making authority, even if in the end they must answer to the bishop.

The *Code of Canon Law* also provides the possibility that lay people may be judges in diocesan tribunals (cf. Can. 1421 §2). The bishop himself is the judge in first instance, but he may exercise this role through others (cf. Can. 1419 §1).

Another body where lay people are to be involved is the diocesan pastoral council, composed of clerics, religious "and especially lay people", selected in such a way that they reflect the entire diocese, taking account of the different regions, social conditions and professions, etc. (Can. 512). The council, nonetheless, has only a consultative vote, meaning the bishop consults it but he has the final say on the matters discussed (cf. Can. 514 §1).

Where lay people have an important role in the diocese is on the finance committee, since the members are to be "expert in financial affairs and civil law" (Can. 492 §1). In addition, the financial administrator, or business manager, of the diocese is usually a lay person, who administers the goods of the diocese under the authority of the bishop (cf. Can. 494). In matters of extraordinary administration, as determined by the Bishops' Conference, the bishop actually needs the consent of the finance committee, so that lay people in this case have a very important decision-making role (cf. Can. 1277).

Turning to the parish, the parish priest or administrator has charge of the pastoral care of the faithful of the parish under the authority of the bishop, who appoints him (cf. Can. 519, Can. 523). The lay faithful can of course make their wishes known as regards the sort of priest they would like as their pastor, but the bishop has the final say on whom he appoints.

If the parish has a pastoral council, it is presided over by the parish priest and is usually composed mainly of lay people, whose role is to "give their help in fostering pastoral action". The pastoral council has only a consultative vote, meaning the priest consults it but retains the final say in what is to be done (Can. 536). Each parish is to have a finance committee to help the parish priest in the administration of goods, and this body will normally be composed of lay people (cf. Can. 537). The parish priest has the final say in financial matters since he is regarded in law as the administrator of all parish goods (cf. Can. 1279).

634 The *sensus fidei*

Can you please tell me the meaning of the phrase sensus fidei, *which is being used a lot in conjunction with the Plenary Council 2020?*

Sensus fidei, literally "sense of faith", also called *sensus fidelium,* "sense of the faithful", is described by the *Catechism of the Catholic Church* as "the supernatural appreciation of faith on the part of the whole people" (*CCC* 92). In the previous point the Catechism says: "All the faithful share in understanding and handing on revealed truth. They have received the anointing of the Holy Spirit, who instructs them and guides them into all truth" (*CCC* 91; cf. *Jn* 16:13). In simple terms, the expression refers to the fact that the faithful of the Church, guided by the Holy Spirit, have a sense of what is right and true in matters of faith and morals.

The Second Vatican Council goes so far as to say that the faithful, including their pastors, are infallible when they are in agreement on some matter of truth: "The whole body of the faithful ... cannot err in matters of belief. This characteristic is shown in the supernatural appreciation of faith (*sensus fidei*) on the part of the whole people, when, 'from the bishops to the last of the faithful,' they manifest a universal consent in matters of faith and morals" (*LG* 12; *CCC* 92).

It is clear that this does not mean that every individual is always right in whatever he or she may think, but rather that the whole body of the faithful, guided by their pastors, is led by the Holy Spirit into the truth. The Second Vatican Council's Dogmatic Constitution on the Church taught that the discernment of the faithful in matters of faith and morals "is exercised under the guidance of the sacred teaching authority, in faithful and respectful obedience to which the people of God accepts that which is not just the word of men but truly the word of God" (*LG* 12).

Pope Benedict XVI insisted on this point in a speech to the International Theological Commission on 7 December 2012. He said that, in its proper understanding, the *sensus fidei* "is certainly not a kind of public ecclesial opinion, and invoking it in order to contest the teachings of the Magisterium would be unthinkable, since the *sensus fidei* cannot be authentically developed in believers except to the extent in which they fully participate in the life of the Church, and this demands responsible adherence to the Magisterium, to the deposit of faith."

What is not a proper understanding of the *sensus fidei*, therefore, is the idea that if a group of sincere Catholics, even a large group, believes something, they are therefore guided by the Holy Spirit. Since some Catholics today believe there should be women priests and women deacons, that contraception, abortion and euthanasia should be allowed in certain circumstances, and that Communion should be given to non-Catholics, practising homosexuals and people in irregular marriage situations, it would follow that, since they are guided by the Holy Spirit, the Church should change its teaching on these matters.

The Congregation for the Doctrine of the Faith, in its Instruction *Donum veritatis* (1990), explicitly rejected the notion that the opinion of a large number of Catholics would be an expression of the *sensus fidei*: "Not all the ideas which circulate among the People of God are compatible with the faith. This is all the more so given that people can be swayed by a public opinion influenced by modern communications media. Not without reason did the Second Vatican Council emphasise the indissoluble bond between the *sensus fidei* and the guidance of God's People by the magisterium of the Pastors. These two realities cannot be separated" (n. 35).

Finally, Pope Francis, in an address to the International Theological Commission on 6 December 2013, said: "By the gift of the Holy Spirit, the members of the Church possess a 'sense of faith'. This is a kind of 'spiritual instinct' that makes us *sentire cum Ecclesia* [think with the Church] and to discern that which is in conformity with the apostolic faith and is in the spirit of the Gospel. Of course, the *sensus fidelium* [sense of the faithful] cannot be confused with the sociological reality of a majority opinion. It is something else. It is, therefore, important – and one of your tasks – to develop criteria that allow the authentic expressions of the *sensus fidelium* to be discerned."

With the Plenary Council commencing its deliberations in 2020, it is very important for everyone to have a clear understanding of what is, and what is not, the *sensus fidei*.

635 A Vatican document on the *sensus fidei*

I found your column on the sensus fidei *interesting and helpful. I mentioned it to a friend who said the Vatican had issued a document on that topic some years ago. Are you aware of it and, if so, can you fill me in on some of its ideas?*

The document, "*Sensus fidei* in the life of the Church", was issued in

2014 by the International Theological Commission (ITC), an advisory body to the Holy See. I will use it to write here about the historical development of the *sensus fidei*.

One of the many scriptural foundations for the *sensus fidei* is in St John's first letter: "You have been anointed by the Holy One, and all of you have knowledge… As for you, the anointing that you received from him [Christ] abides in you, and so you do not need anyone to teach you. But as his anointing teaches you about all things, and is true and is not a lie, and just as it has taught you, abide in him" (*1 Jn* 2:20, 27).

The ITC document comments: "As a result, the faithful have an instinct for the truth of the Gospel, which enables them to recognise and endorse authentic Christian doctrine and practice, and to reject what is false. That supernatural instinct, intrinsically linked to the gift of faith received in the communion of the Church, is called the *sensus fidei*, and it enables Christians to fulfil their prophetic calling" (n. 2).

Already in the first centuries, the Fathers of the Church and theologians considered the faith of the whole Church, that is the universal belief on some matter of faith, to be a sure point of reference for discerning the authentic content of the apostolic Tradition. The Fathers refuted the errors of heretics by appealing to the belief and practice of all the churches.

For Tertullian, the fact that all the churches had substantially the same faith testified to Christ's presence and the guidance of the Holy Spirit in them. St Augustine said *Securus judicat orbis terrarum:* the judgment of the whole world is sure (*Contra epistolam Parmeniani*, III, 24). And St Vincent of Lerins proposed as a sure norm of belief the faith that was held "everywhere, always and by everyone" (*Commonitorium* II, 5).

To resolve disputes the Church Fathers appealed not only to what was believed by all but also to what was practised by all. Thus St Jerome justified the veneration of relics by pointing to the common practice of the bishops and the faithful and St Epiphanius defended

Mary's perpetual virginity by asking whether anyone had ever dared to utter her name without adding "the Virgin".

The *sensus fidei* of the bishops together with the laity was decisive in determining which of the many books circulating among the churches were to be accepted as divinely inspired and hence part of the canon of Scripture, as it was for defining major doctrines such as the divinity of Christ, the perpetual virginity and divine motherhood of Mary, and the veneration of the saints.

In later centuries the universal belief of the faithful was used to defend the Real Presence of Christ in the Eucharist, the Beatific Vision enjoyed by souls immediately upon their arrival in heaven, the Immaculate Conception of Our Lady and the infallibility of the Church. The Scholastics, including St Thomas Aquinas, held that the Church cannot err in matters of faith because she is taught by God through the Holy Spirit, who would lead her into the truth.

In refuting the arguments of the Protestants in the sixteenth century, the Council of Trent appealed repeatedly to the belief of the whole Church in the previous centuries, that is to Tradition. At that same time, Melchior Cano defended the infallibility of the Church in believing, and of the pastors in teaching, because they were guided by the Holy Spirit.

The nineteenth century saw a renewed study of the *sensus fidei* by theologians such as Johann Adam Möhler, Giovanni Perrone and St John Henry Newman. Newman wrote *An Essay on the Development of Christian Doctrine* (1845) in which he used St Augustine's norm *Securus judicat orbis terrarum* to spell out the characteristics of faithful development in understanding doctrine, arguing that an infallible authority was also necessary to maintain the Church in the truth. Later he wrote *On Consulting the Faithful in Matters of Doctrine* (1859) to demonstrate that the faithful, as distinct from their pastors, have their own active role to play in preserving and transmitting the faith.

As is clear, the *sensus fidei* is the faith of the whole Church, not that of a handful of believers.

636 Practical consequences of the *sensus fidei*

Did the Second Vatican Council have anything to say about the sensus fidei *and what are some practical consequences of this sensus?*

The Second Vatican Council spoke of the *sensus fidei* in its Dogmatic Constitution on the Church *Lumen gentium*. As we know, it was the belief for centuries that the Holy Spirit would not allow the whole Church to be led into error. *Lumen gentium* goes further and teaches formally the infallibility of the Church as a consequence of the *sensus fidei*: "The whole body of the faithful who have an anointing that comes from the holy one (cf. *1 Jn* 2:20, 27), cannot err in matters of belief. This characteristic is shown in the supernatural appreciation of the faith (*sensus fidei*) when, from the bishops to the last of the faithful, they manifest a universal consent in matters of faith and morals. By this appreciation of the faith, aroused and sustained by the Spirit of Truth, the People of God, guided by the sacred teaching authority (*magisterium*), and obeying it, receives not the mere word of men, but truly the word of God" (*LG* 12). We see here how the People of God are infallible in their believing when they are united with their bishops and they obey the magisterium, the teaching authority of the Church.

The International Theological Commission's document *"Sensus fidei* in the life of the Church" makes the important point that over the centuries the lay faithful have had an important role to play in the development of the Church's teaching on such issues as the morality of receiving interest on a loan, matters of social doctrine and the question of human rights and religious freedom. In the end, however, it is up to the magisterium of the Church to judge which contributions of the lay faithful "actually correspond to the truth of the Tradition received from the Apostles" (n. 77).

It has sometimes been said that only upon the acceptance of Church teaching by the faithful, including bishops, priests and lay faithful, does a teaching have authority. This is false. The First Vatican Council taught that infallible definitions of the Pope are irreformable "of themselves and not from the consent of the Church" (*Pastor Aeternus*, Ch. 4). The ITC's document comments that "such teaching of the Pope, and by extension all teaching of the Pope and of the bishops, is authoritative in itself because of the gift of the Holy Spirit, the *charisma veritatis certum* [the certain charism of truth] that they possess" (n. 79).

What happens when a teaching of the Church is met with opposition from a body of the faithful, as has sometimes happened? The document says that in this case action is required on both sides: "The faithful must reflect on the teaching that has been given, making every effort to understand and accept it. Resistance, as a matter of principle, to the teaching of the magisterium is incompatible with the authentic *sensus fidei*. The magisterium must likewise reflect on the teaching that has been given and consider whether it needs clarification or reformulation in order to communicate more effectively the essential message" (n. 80).

How does public opinion, even a majority opinion, on Church matters relate to the *sensus fidei*? The document answers that "the *sensus fidei* cannot simply be identified with public or majority opinion in the Church. Faith, not opinion, is the necessary focus of attention. Opinion is often just an expression, frequently changeable and transient, of the mood or desires of a certain group or culture, whereas faith is the echo of the one Gospel which is valid for all places and times." Moreover, "In the history of the people of God, it has often been not the majority but rather a minority which has truly lived and witnessed to the faith" (n. 118).

The document concludes by acknowledging that all the faithful "have the right, indeed at times the duty, in keeping with their knowledge, competence and position, to manifest to the sacred Pastors their views on matters which concern the good of the Church", but in doing so "they must always respect the integrity of faith and morals" and "show due reverence to the Pastors" (*CCL*, Can. 212, §3; n. 120).

The Plenary Council 2020 provides a splendid opportunity for all the faithful to express their views, always respecting the integrity of faith and morals taught by the Church and showing due respect for their pastors. This is the true meaning of the *sensus fidei*.

637 Seventh-Day Adventists and the Church

One of my workmates is a Seventh-Day Adventist. He is a very fine person and I am curious to know more about his church and its beliefs.

The Seventh-day Adventist church is a Protestant Christian denomination which, as its name suggests, observes Saturday, the seventh day of the week in Christian and Jewish calendars, as its day of rest and worship. The name Adventist comes from the fact that the church grew out of the Adventist movement, which began in the 1840s in upstate New York and believed that the Second Coming (advent) of Jesus Christ was imminent. This was later changed to the belief that Christ would enter the heavenly sanctuary.

For about twenty years the Adventist movement consisted of a small, loosely knit group of people from many churches who were united through James White's periodical *The Advent Review and Sabbath Herald*. Among its most prominent figures were Joseph Bates, James White and Ellen White, who was regarded as having the gift of prophecy. The Seventh-day Adventist church was eventually established formally in Battle Creek, Michigan, in 1863.

The official teachings of the church are set out in its 28 Fundamental Beliefs, adopted by a General Conference in 1980. Among these teachings are belief in the Trinity, the infallibility of Scripture, the resurrection of the dead, justification by faith alone, Baptism by immersion, creation in six literal days and of course the observance of Saturday, not Sunday, as the day of rest and worship. The church has been widely accepted as a Protestant denomination.

Among the more particular Seventh-day Adventist beliefs are that the Second Coming of Christ to earth will take place after a time of trouble and that it will be followed by a millennial reign of the saints in heaven. Also, for those who are saved there will be no consciousness after death but only "soul sleep". Their doctrine of "conditional immortality" holds that the wicked will not suffer eternal damnation in hell but rather will be permanently annihilated.

Adventists abstain from secular work on Saturdays and many also refrain from purely secular forms of recreation, such as competitive sport and watching non-religious programs on television. Nature walks, family-oriented activities and charitable work are encouraged.

The major weekly worship service on Saturday often commences with Sabbath School, a structured time of small group bible study at church. The church service that follows uses a typical evangelical format, with a sermon as the central feature. Singing, Scripture readings, prayers and an offering, including tithing, are standard features. A Communion service is held four times a year, preceded by a foot washing ceremony based on Christ's washing of the disciples' feet in the Last Supper. Communion is then received, consisting of unleavened bread and unfermented grape juice.

Emphasis is placed on wholeness and health, including abstinence from alcohol and tobacco, the practice of vegetarianism and adherence to Jewish kosher laws, with abstinence from pork, shellfish and other animals regarded as unclean. John Harvey Kellogg was one of the early promoters of Adventist health work in the U.S., and his brother William founded Kellogg's, the well-known producer of breakfast cereals. In Australia and New Zealand the church's Sanitarium Health and Wellbeing Company produces health and vegetarian products. Studies have shown that Adventists in California live four to ten years longer than other Californians, probably because they do not smoke or drink alcohol, they have a day of rest every week and they live a low-fat vegetarian diet.

Adventists have generally conservative moral views. They regard marriage as a lifelong commitment of a man and a woman and they do not perform same-sex weddings. Their official position is against abortion for reasons of birth control, gender selection and mere convenience, but they do allow it in the case of danger to the woman's life or health, for severe congenital defects in the foetus and in the case of rape or incest. They are against sex and cohabitation before marriage, homosexual activity and euthanasia.

Adventists try to dress in a simple, modest way and many are opposed to body piercing and tattoos, and even the wearing of jewellery.

638 Faith in the Church

My faith in the Church has recently been shaken by more allegations of widespread sexual abuse by clergy and even a call from a high-ranking ecclesiastic for the Pope to resign. What am I to make of this?

It has indeed been a troubling time for the Church, with many people expressing their concerns to me over it. Some have even ventured to call it one of the darkest hours for the Church. How are we to react?

First, the Church has been here for some two thousand years and has survived, and even thrived, through much darker times than the present one. Consider the persecutions by the Roman Empire for some 250 years from Nero in the first century to Diocletian at the beginning of the fourth. Tens of thousands of Christians were put to death for their faith and in the third century the emperor Valerian ordered all bishops, priests and deacons to be arrested and put to death in an effort to destroy the Church once and for all. The Church continued to grow through all that time.

In the fourteenth century came the so-called Schism of the West during which there were up to three claimants to the papacy at the same time.

In the sixteenth century the moral life of the clergy in Rome was in a dreadful state, with Alexander VI having been elected Pope even though he had fathered four children as a priest, bishop and cardinal. That was one of the contributing factors to Martin Luther leaving the Church after being excommunicated and taking millions of Catholics with him into various forms of Protestantism. But at the same time, millions were being converted to the faith in Mexico following the apparitions of Our Lady at Guadalupe.

In the twentieth century countless Catholics were martyred in the Mexican revolution, the Spanish civil war and in the autocratic regimes of Stalin and Hitler. Those were dark times indeed.

Second, the Church is made up of frail human beings who have inherited the effects of original sin and so there will always be people, even in high positions, who do the wrong thing. Even among the twelve apostles chosen by the Son of God himself, one of them betrayed him for thirty pieces of silver, the prince of the apostles denied three times that he even knew him, and they all ran away in the garden when Judas went with the soldiers and priests to arrest him.

Pope Pius XII, in his encyclical *Mystici corporis* in 1943, put us on guard for times such as these: "If something is perceived in the Church which points to the infirmity of our human condition, this is not be attributed to her juridical constitution, but to the lamentable tendency of individuals toward evil, a tendency which her divine founder suffers to exist even in the higher members of his Mystical Body, for the testing of virtue of both flock and pastors, and for the greater merit of Christian faith in all... Christ did not will sinners to be excluded from the society he had founded; if therefore some members are spiritually infirm, this is no reason for lessening our love toward the Church, but rather for increasing our compassion toward her members."

Finally, the Church is more than the sinful individuals who make her up in any moment of history. She is the Mystical Body of Christ, with Christ as her head, the Holy Spirit as her soul, Mary as her Mother, and the saints in heaven and souls in purgatory interceding powerfully for her. So we can have absolute trust that the Church will remain firm no matter what crises she may go through.

For our reassurance, when the barbarians were invading the Roman Empire St Augustine wrote: "The Church will shake if her foundation shifts; but can Christ be moved? As long as Christ remains her immovable base, the Church will remain strong until the end of time" (*Enarr. in psalmos*, 103, 2, 5). And around the same time St John Chrysostom said: "Nothing is stronger than the Church. Your hope is the Church; your salvation is the Church; your refuge is the Church. It is higher than the heavens and broader than the earth; it never grows old, its vigour is eternal" (*Homily 2 on Eutropius*, 6).

So the conclusion is simple. First, we should never lose hope in the Church, which is the Mystical Body of Christ and will be here until the end of time. And second, we should pray very much for the Church: for the Pope, the bishops and priests, the religious and all the lay faithful.

639 Prayer for the Church

I was somewhat surprised to hear that in 2018 Pope Francis asked all Catholics to pray the rosary each day in October followed by the Prayer to St Michael the Archangel and the prayer "Sub tuum praesidium" to Our Lady. Can you tell me what is behind this?

I too was surprised but very happy to hear that the Pope has asked for these prayers. What is behind it is simply that, as we are well aware, the Church is going through troubled times, seen above all in the reports of widespread sexual abuse by priests and others in the Church. The Vatican press release in which the Holy Father asked for these prayers said that we are to ask Our Lady and St Michael "to protect the Church from the devil, who always seeks to separate us from God and from each other" and it referred to "moments of spiritual turbulence".

As we recall, the situation in the Church was such that it moved the Pope to write a Letter to the People of God on 20 August 2018 inviting the whole Church "to a penitential exercise of prayer and fasting" which "can awaken our conscience and arouse our solidarity and commitment to a culture of care that says 'never again' to every form of abuse."

Now the Holy Father has asked in particular that we pray the rosary every day in the month of October, followed by the two prayers you mentioned. October is the month of the rosary, as proclaimed by Pope Leo XIII in his Encyclical *Supremi Apostolatus* of 1 September 1883. In view of the many dangers afflicting the Church at that time, Pope Leo asked that the rosary and the Litany of Loreto be recited each day of October that year in every parish church throughout the world (cf. J. Flader, *Question Time 1*, q. 132). What Pope Francis has asked for now echoes that petition of 135 years ago, since once again the Church is experiencing special difficulties. The rosary is a very rich prayer and, independently of the circumstances in which we say it, it always benefits us enormously so let us take up this request of the Holy Father.

We should not forget that from October 3-28 the Synod of Bishops is meeting in Rome to discuss the important topic of young people, the faith and vocational discernment, so we can add that as an important intention for our prayers this month.

As for the prayer to St Michael the Archangel, again it was Pope Leo XIII who gave it to the Church. One day while attending a Mass of thanksgiving he saw evil spirits gathering over Rome and he had a vision of God granting Satan the choice of a century in which to do his worst work against the Church. The devil chose the twentieth century. Greatly disturbed, the Pope wrote the prayer to St Michael the Archangel and in 1886 he ordered it to be said all over the world after every Low Mass. The prayer was said until 1964, when the Church no longer required it. Nonetheless, on 24 April 1994 Pope St John Paul II recommended that the faithful continue to say it "to obtain help in the battle against the forces of darkness and against the spirit of this world" (cf. J. Flader, *Question Time 1*, q. 137).

Pope Francis has spoken about the devil repeatedly from the earliest days of his pontificate (cf. J. Flader, *Question Time 3*, q. 307) and on 5 July 2013 he consecrated the Vatican to St Michael and blessed a new statue of him in the Vatican gardens. The idea for the statue had come during the pontificate of Pope Benedict XVI, who was present for the blessing. On that occasion Pope Francis said: "In consecrating the Vatican City State to St Michael the Archangel, let us ask him to defend us from the Evil One and cast him out." So in these special times let us take up the Pope's plea and say the prayer to St Michael with fervour.

As for the prayer "Sub tuum praesidium", it is one of the most ancient prayers to Our Lady, having been found on an Egyptian papyrus dating to the third or fourth century. It is one of the Marian hymns that may be used after Night Prayer in the Liturgy of the Hours. It reads: "We fly to thy protection, O Holy Mother of God; despise not our petitions in our necessities, but deliver us always from all dangers, O Glorious and Blessed Virgin."

If we take up this petition of the Holy Father and say these prayers, we will grow in love for the Church and help her greatly and we will grow in holiness at the same time.

640 Prayer for the Pope

In the four years that Pope Francis been in office, I have heard all sorts of things about him: that he is a great pope, a liberal, a heretic or even that his election was not valid. What should I think about him and how should I react to all this?

I too have heard all these remarks and I can understand how many people are confused over this pope, who has been described as a "pope of surprises". How should we react?

First, we cannot question the validity of his election. Everything was handled according to the norms for papal elections, no one questioned the validity of the election at the time and we should not do so now. The Holy Spirit inspired the cardinals to give us the pope God wants for us.

Second, Pope Francis has done the world of good for the Church. From the beginning he endeared himself to the Church and the world by his smile, his outgoing manner, his simple lifestyle, his choosing to live in the Domus Sanctae Marthae in the Vatican rather than in the papal apartments so that he could be closer to the people, his obvious love for the poor and marginalised, his appeal to mercy rather than the strict enforcement of rules, and so much more.

He is truly popular, not only with Catholics but also with many non-Catholics. When he became the first pope to open an Instagram account in March 2016 he broke all records, gaining over one million followers in under twelve hours. He was *Time* magazine's "Man of the Year" in 2013 and many other publications have featured him on their front cover.

Pope Francis has given us some memorable teaching. His first encyclical, *Lumen Fidei* on the important virtue of faith, came out in June 2013 only a few months after his election. His Apostolic Exhortation *Evangelii gaudium* came in November 2013 and gave great impetus to the work of evangelisation, of spreading the Gospel more effectively in today's world, particularly through the joy of our life. Evangelisation, which is central to the mission of the Church – "the Church exists to evangelise", wrote Pope Paul VI – is vital for the Church at the present time and Pope Francis has made it a central theme of his pontificate.

His second encyclical *Laudato si'* on care for the environment, our common home, came in June 2015. It was widely acclaimed and pointed to our need to be responsible stewards of the planet God gave us. This issue too is important at the present time, but many critics seized on certain opinionable statements, on which we are free to disagree with the pope in any case, and overlooked the core perennial teaching.

One of the biggest targets for the pope's critics was his Apostolic Exhortation *Amoris laetita* on the family, which came in April 2016. The critics focussed on one particular footnote and a few other statements in Chapter 8, which seemed to open the door to giving Communion to the divorced and remarried civilly, and which have indeed given rise to great divisions among cardinals and bishops. But leaving those statements aside, *Amoris Laetitia* is a marvellous document on marriage, full of practical hints on how to help couples and families stay together and grow in love in these challenging times. Everyone should read it.

And what to say about the Jubilee Year of Mercy, which helped us experience God's mercy particularly through the sacrament of Penance and to show more mercy to others?

Is the pope a liberal? You cannot apply political terms like this to any pope. They simply don't apply. If to be a liberal is to be concerned for the poor, the sick, the elderly, the refugees, the marginalised and the environment, then yes, the pope is liberal. But what could be more conservative or traditional than Pope Francis' repeated references to the devil, to the need for confession, to devotion to St Joseph, Our Lady and the Eucharist, to upholding Catholic teaching on birth control, abortion and the impossibility of ordaining women to the priesthood?

And Pope Francis is certainly not a heretic. There is nothing to suggest that. He might be unclear at times but he is not a heretic.

What we should all do is heed his constant petition: "Pray for me". That is the best way to help him.

The Last Things

641 Predestination

I was recently reading St Paul's letter to the Romans where he talks about predestination. Does God really predestine some souls to heaven and others to hell? If so, to what extent are we still free to work out our own destiny? I am really confused.

The passage to which you refer reads: "We know that in everything God works for good with those who love him, who are called according to his purpose. For those whom he foreknew he also predestined to be conformed to the image of his Son, in order that he might be the first-born among many brethren. And those whom he predestined he also called; and those whom he called he also justified, and those whom he justified he also glorified" (*Rom* 8:29-30).

So St Paul does indeed speak of predestination. But to what extent does it affect a free person? Are there some people whom God has predestined to heaven and they will go there no matter how many sins they commit, even if they remain unrepentant when they die? And are there others whom God predestined to hell and there is nothing they can do to be saved? When expressed like this the thought of predestination is truly frightening. It makes a mockery of human freedom and personal merit for the good deeds we do or the punishment we deserve for our sins. And it makes a mockery too of God's mercy and justice.

Fortunately, that is not how we are to understand predestination. The Catholic Encyclopedia says: "Predestination, taken in its widest meaning, is every divine decree by which God, owing to his infallible prescience of the future, has appointed and ordained from eternity all events occurring in time, especially those which directly proceed from, or at least are influenced by, man's free will." In other words, God's plan of predestination takes into account the free acts of man, which he foresees from all eternity.

In understanding how predestination relates to human freedom we must situate it within four fundamental premises or presuppositions. The first is that God wants all to be saved, both Christians and non-Christians. St Paul, in his first letter to Timothy, speaks of "God our Saviour, who desires all men to be saved and to come to the knowledge of the truth" (*1 Tim* 2:4). St Peter writes in a similar vein, saying that God "is forbearing toward you, not wishing that any should perish, but that all should reach repentance" (*2 Pet* 3:9). So God does not predestine anyone to suffer forever in hell. The *Catechism of the Catholic Church* says as much: "God predestines no one to go to hell; for this a wilful turning away from God (a mortal sin) is necessary, and persistence in it until the end" (*CCC* 1037).

The second premise is that God grants everyone sufficient grace to be saved. This follows from the first premise, and it leads St Augustine to say: "One must not despair of even the greatest sinner as long as he lives here on earth" (*Retract.* I, 19, 7). The Second Vatican Council says with respect to the salvation of those who do not know God: "Nor shall divine providence deny the assistance necessary for salvation to those who, without any fault of theirs, have not yet arrived at an explicit knowledge of God, and who, not without grace, strive to lead a good life" (*LG* 16).

The third premise is that our good deeds and the merit deriving from them are already the fruit of the grace God has predestined to grant us beforehand. The Catechism says: "The merit of man before God in the Christian life arises from the fact that God has freely chosen to associate man with the work of his grace. The fatherly action of God is first on his own initiative, and then follows man's free acting through his collaboration, so that the merit of good works is to be attributed in the first place to the grace of God, and then to the faithful" (*CCC* 2008).

At the same time, and this is the fourth premise, God grants us this grace foreseeing that we will correspond to it. The Catechism says that when God "establishes his eternal plan of 'predestination' he includes in it each person's free response to his grace" (*CCC* 600). That is,

God grants us his grace, knowing that we will use it to do good deeds deserving of eternal life.

The question of predestination, even taking into account these four premises, still remains in some sense a mystery. But in the end, God is free to bestow his grace and love on whomever he chooses, and he does give everyone sufficient grace to be saved.

642 Pope Francis and hell

I understand Pope Francis has been quoted as saying that hell doesn't exist and that the souls of those who reject God at the end simply disappear. Did the Pope really say that?

Pope Francis most certainly did not say that. Like all faithful Catholics he believes in hell and he has spoken of it on several occasions in his five years as Pope. The source of the misleading statement was Eugenio Scalfari, a 93-year-old retired journalist, former editor of *La Repubblica* and avowed atheist who has become a good friend of the Pope. After a recent meeting with the Holy Father Scalfari wrote on March 28 that the Pope told him, "Hell does not exist" and that the souls of those who reject God at the end of their life simply cease to exist.

According to Vatican spokesman Greg Burke, Pope Francis invited Scalfari to have a "private meeting for the occasion of Easter" and the meeting was not a formal interview. In his earlier interviews with the Pope in 2013 and 2015, Scalfari took no notes and did not record the conversation, limiting himself to reconstructing the conversation later on the basis of his own memory, and that was obviously the case this time as well.

The reality is that Pope Francis has spoken several times about the existence of hell. In a warning to the Mafia in 2014 he said: "Convert! There is still time, so that you don't end up in hell. That is what awaits you if you continue on this path. You had a father and a mother: think of them. Cry a little and convert."

Then in his 2016 Message for Lent he wrote: "The danger always remains that by a constant refusal to open the doors of their hearts to Christ who knocks on them in the poor, the proud, rich and powerful will end up condemning themselves and plunging into the eternal abyss of solitude which is hell."

The teaching of the Church on hell is clear. In the *Catechism of the Catholic Church* we read: "To die in mortal sin without repenting and accepting God's merciful love means remaining separated from him for ever by our own free choice. This state of definitive self-exclusion from communion with God and the blessed is called 'hell'" (*CCC* 1033). The Catechism goes on to say: "The teaching of the Church affirms the existence of hell and its eternity" (*CCC* 1035).

So hell exists. And it is not God who sends people there but rather human beings who refuse to accept God's merciful love and thereby reject God and remain separated from him forever by their own free choice. Pope Benedict XVI comments: "God never, in any case, forces anyone to be saved. God accepts man's freedom. He is no magician, who will in the end wipe out everything that has happened and wheel out his happy ending. He is a true father; a creator who assents to freedom, even when it is used to reject him. That is why God's all-embracing desire to save people does not involve the actual salvation of all men. He allows us the power to refuse. God loves us; we need only to summon up the humility to allow ourselves to be loved" (*God is Near Us,* Ignatius 2003, pp. 36-37).

Fr John Wauck, who lectures at the Pontifical University of the Holy Cross in Rome, commented on the Scalfari statement in a radio interview on "The *Crux* of the matter": "My first reaction, especially because this wasn't the first time, was, 'There goes crazy Scalfari again.' He's getting a headline out of something outrageous that seems to be in complete contradiction to the Christian faith and other things Francis has said."

Rather than being scandalised, Wauck sees it as an opportunity to explain what the Church teaches on hell. He said: "Hell is actually God's way of taking us seriously. If we're able to determine our eternity in a good sense, meaning eternal life, God, happiness, delight, all of which will last forever on the basis of what we've done, it makes sense there's a flip side. Sometimes we think hell seems kind of disproportionate, but heaven's also disproportionate. God has skin in the game ... he's given us everything, and hell is a reminder of what we can turn our back on, which is something infinite."

So yes, let us take advantage of this "fake news" to talk with others about hell. The more the better. We rarely get as good an opportunity as we have now.

II. LITURGY AND THE SACRAMENTS

Liturgy in general

643 A new Sign of the Cross

A friend recently told me that in the Catholic school his son attends some teachers are now making the Sign of the Cross "In the name of the Father and of the Mother and of the Son and of the Holy Spirit." I was astounded. Is this acceptable?

When I read your question, I too was astounded. In total disbelief. Is this acceptable? Of course not. We should remember where we got the Sign of the Cross in the first place. The answer, of course, is from Jesus Christ himself, when he sent the apostles out to baptise "in the name of the Father and of the Son and of the Holy Spirit" (*Mt* 28:19).

From the very beginning, the Church took up this formula and used it in the sacraments, in the Mass and in personal prayer. It forms part of the living Tradition of the Church. For example, Tertullian, who died around the year 225, wrote: "In all our travels and movements, in coming in and going out, in putting on our shoes, at the bath, at the table, in lighting our candles, in lying down, in sitting down, whatever employment occupies us, we mark our foreheads with the sign of the cross. These practices are not commanded by a formal law of scripture, but Tradition teaches them, custom confirms them, and faith observes them" (*De cor. Mil.,* 3).

In the Blessed Trinity, whom we name and honour with the Sign of the Cross, there are three divine persons, not four. There is no mother who would be a divine person. Undoubtedly, those who have invented the new formula want to point out that the Father has motherly characteristics. Indeed he does.

The *Catechism* says: "God's parental tenderness can also be expressed by the image of motherhood, which emphasises God's immanence, the intimacy between Creator and creature" (*CCC* 239). This is revealed in numerous passages of Scripture. In the prophecy of Isaiah God speaks to his people: "As one whom his mother comforts, so I will comfort you" (*Is* 66:13). And again: "Can a woman forget her sucking child, that she should have no compassion on the son of her womb? Even these may forget, yet I will not forget you" (*Is* 49:15). In the book of Psalms, the psalmist speaks of being comforted by God like a child by its mother: "But I have calmed and quieted my soul, like a child quieted at its mother's breast; like a child that is quieted is my soul" (*Ps* 131:2). So we can say without hesitation that God, whom we call Father, has both paternal and maternal characteristics.

But these characteristics are in the one divine person whom we call Father. There is not another divine person who would be called Mother. We believe in the Blessed Trinity, not the Blessed Quaternity.

A good way to understand this is through the traditional triangle of the Blessed Trinity, with the names of the Father, Son and Holy Spirit at each angle. Along the sides of the triangle are the words "is not", so that the Father is not the Son, the Son is not the Holy Spirit and the Holy Spirit is not the Father. In the middle of the triangle is the word "God", connected to each of the angles with the word "is". So the Father is God, the Son is God and the Holy Spirit is God. There is no place in this diagram for a person called Mother, of whom it could be said that "The Father is not the Mother", "The Mother is not the Son", etc., and "The Mother is God". There is no God the Mother.

While the Father has motherly characteristics, these characteristics do not constitute a person distinct from the Father, a person who would be God. On the other hand, the Holy Spirit, who is the love between the Father and the Son, does constitute a separate person, distinct from the Father and the Son and yet God.

The *Catechism of the Catholic Church* sums it up: "Christians are baptised 'in the name of the Father and of the Son and of the Holy Spirit'. Before receiving the sacrament, they respond to a three-part question when asked to confess the Father, the Son and the Spirit: 'I do. 'The faith of all Christians rests on the Trinity'" (St Caesarius of Arles, *Sermo* 9, *Exp. symb.*; *CCC* 232).

In conclusion, we cannot change the words of the Sign of the Cross, which was revealed by the Son of God himself and which the Church has used from the earliest days. We would be tampering with the fundamentals of our Faith and using a formula which is, quite frankly, nothing short of blasphemous.

644 What can be blessed

I recently asked a priest to bless some holy cards and he seemed hesitant. Is there anything wrong with blessing holy cards? Also, if I have a rosary or holy cards with me during Benediction, are they blessed by the Blessed Sacrament? How about blessing a computer?

To answer your second question first, there can be no certainty that the blessing with the Blessed Sacrament during Benediction actually blesses objects in the church. It is most likely that it does not. So it is better to approach the priest personally to have these objects blessed.

One circumstance in which multiple objects are blessed with one blessing is the Pope's *urbi et orbi* blessing, given to "the city [Rome] and the world" on big feasts like Christmas and Easter. It is considered that all religious objects like rosary beads, crucifixes and medals that those present have with them are blessed by the Holy Father himself on that occasion.

Returning to your first question, there is no problem with blessing holy cards, by which we understand small cards, usually with a prayer and an image of a saint or other holy image on them. These are used for the devotion of the faithful, as are rosary beads, medals, crucifixes, statues and other holy images.

The *Book of Blessings* issued by the Holy See contains among its numerous blessings the blessing of articles meant to foster the devotion of the Christian people. While it doesn't specifically mention holy cards, these would clearly be included. The *Shorter Book of Blessings*, approved by the Holy See for use in the United States, says in the introduction to blessings of religious articles: "Since certain articles are used in connection with liturgical prayer or popular devotions, for example, rosaries and the like, celebration of a blessing of such articles is a helpful means of recommending them to the faithful. Further, the faithful have developed the commendable practice of using religious articles as they pray, of having objects of piety on their person, of placing religious statues or pictures in their homes, or of keeping there certain other blessed objects, even food or drink" (*SBB*, nn. 859-860). The reference to "using religious articles as they pray" would certainly include holy cards.

When the priest is asked to bless individual holy cards, a rosary, a religious medal, etc., he will usually do this by simply making the sign of the cross over it while saying quietly, "May this rosary [holy card, medal, etc.] and the one who uses it be blessed, in the name of the Father, and of the Son, and of the Holy Spirit" (*SBB*, 906).

How about blessing a computer, which is clearly not intended to foster the devotion of the faithful? Or a boat, an office, some tools, a football field? These too can be blessed. The *Book of Blessings* contains an extremely wide range of blessings which can be divided roughly into two main categories: on one hand things intended to be used for Christian worship and devotion, and on the other persons, places and things of a more secular sort.

The first category usually involves a blessing which makes the object a sacred object and is called a *constitutive* blessing. These objects are thereafter to be treated with the respect due to a sacred object. Apart from the blessing of churches and chapels, which are treated elsewhere, and articles for personal devotion like rosaries, medals, etc., this category includes the blessing of such articles for the church as the baptismal font, tabernacle, lectern, confessional, crucifix, vestments, sacred vessels, linens, holy water, Way of the Cross, etc.

The other category of blessings, called *invocative*, is extremely varied and extends to the most secular imaginable. The first type is blessings of people: the family, spouses, children, the woman before or after giving birth, the sick, those sent out to announce the Gospel, pilgrims, etc. Then there are blessings of buildings like a new home, seminary, religious house, school or university, hospital, office, shop, factory or gymnasium. And even the blessing of an athletics field, means of transportation, boats and fishing gear, tools and other equipment for work, animals, fields and flocks, etc.

In short, the Church as a good mother is there to bless practically all aspects of human life, including your computer.

645 Incense in the liturgy

I have always liked ceremonies in which incense is used but have wondered what exactly the meaning is of this aspect of the liturgy.

The use of incense goes back to the Old Testament. For example, we read in the book of Exodus when Moses was erecting the Tent of Meeting: "You shall make an altar to burn incense upon; of acacia wood shall you make it... And Aaron shall burn fragrant incense on it; every morning when he dresses the lamps he shall burn it, and when Aaron sets up the lamps in the evening, he shall burn it, a perpetual incense before the LORD throughout your generations" (*Ex* 30:1, 7-8).

The incense was to be very fragrant: "Take sweet spices, stacte, and onycha, and galbanum, sweet spices with pure frankincense (of each shall there be an equal part), and make an incense blended as by the perfumer, seasoned with salt, pure and holy; and you shall beat some of it very small, and put part of it before the covenant in the tent of meeting where I shall meet with you; it shall be for you most holy. And the incense which you shall make according to its composition, you shall not make for yourselves; it shall be for you holy to the LORD" (*Ex* 30:34-37). Already here we see that the incense was for God, for his worship, not for man.

The burning of incense twice a day at the time of the sacrifice was to symbolise the people's prayer rising to God. King David says: "Let my prayer be counted as incense before you, and the lifting up of my hands as an evening sacrifice" (*Ps* 141:2).

We find the use of incense and the same symbolism in the book of Revelation in the worship of the Lamb: "And another angel came and stood at the altar with a golden censer; and he was given much incense to mingle with the prayers of all the saints upon the golden altar before the throne; and the smoke of the incense rose with the prayers of the saints from the hand of the angel before God" (*Rev* 8:3-4).

In New Testament times the Jews were still using incense in their worship as attested to by St Luke, who describes how Zechariah, the husband of Elizabeth, served as a priest in the temple in Jerusalem and "it fell to him by lot to enter the temple of the Lord and burn incense" (*Lk* 1:9).

Given the use of incense in Old Testament worship it is only natural that the practice would be taken up by the early Church. One of the earliest recorded uses in this regard was in funeral rites, for which there is a sizeable body of evidence. The practice was later extended to the relics and tombs of martyrs and the dedication of churches.

The earliest recorded use of incense in a church in Rome dates from the fourth century, and the purpose seems to have been above all to produce a pleasant aroma, as was the practice in Roman homes. The liturgies of Saints James and Mark, dating from around the fifth century, speak of the use of incense in the worship of God, and a Roman Ordo of the seventh century mentions its use in the procession of the bishop to the altar on Good Friday.

In the seventh and eighth centuries there are records of incense being used in the liturgy in Rome to honour the Pope and the book of the Gospels. This may have been inspired by the Roman civil practice of using incense to honour magistrates and the book of statutes.

The incensing of the altar, the clergy and the gifts of bread and wine was introduced in the ninth century, probably influenced by the liturgical practice of France and Germany at the time. By about the year 1350 the rubrics regarding how the incensing was to be done were fairly well established. Although incense honours a sacred person or an object, it is above all an act of the worship of God, where the ascending fragrant smoke represents the prayers of the Church.

At present, incense is used in many ceremonies, among them more solemn Masses, where it is used to incense the altar, the crucifix, the priest and people, the book of the Gospels, the gifts on the altar and the consecrated species at the elevation. It is also used in funerals to incense the coffin, in Exposition and Benediction of the Blessed Sacrament, in the dedication of a church or altar, in solemn celebrations of the Divine Office, etc.

It adds a note of solemnity and sacredness to the celebration and raises our hearts to God.

Baptism

646 Baptism in the early Church

My son-in-law was recently baptised and the priest explained that the ceremonies of Baptism are very ancient. Is this true and, if so, can you please elaborate on it?

The ceremonies are indeed ancient, going back to the first centuries. Fortunately, we have numerous documents that describe how Baptism was performed in the early Church. A helpful resource is Mario Righetti's four-volume history of the liturgy *Storia Liturgica* (1959). Here I will describe some of the ceremonies and later I will continue the study.

We can begin with Scripture itself, where we know that Our Lord sent the apostles out to all nations to baptise in the name of the Father and of the Son and of the Holy Spirit (cf. *Mt* 28:19). This trinitarian formula has always been used as what is called the "form" of Baptism.

On the day of Pentecost, after St Peter had addressed the multitude gathered in Jerusalem, many were converted and St Luke tells us that "those who received his word were baptised, and there were added that day about three thousand souls" (*Acts* 2:41). We see here how entry into the Church was brought about through Baptism.

Another account of an early Baptism comes when the deacon Philip explained the faith to the Ethiopian eunuch on the way to Gaza: "And as they went along the road they came to some water, and the eunuch said, 'See, here is water! What is to prevent my being baptised?' And he commanded the chariot to stop, and they both went down into the water, Philip and the eunuch, and he baptised him" (*Acts* 8:36-38). Here we see the common practice in the early Church of the person to be baptised going down into the water along with the baptiser.

As regards the symbolism of Baptism we have the words of St Paul:

"Do you not know that all of us who have been baptised into Christ Jesus were baptised into his death? We were buried therefore with him by baptism into death so that as Christ was raised from the dead by the glory of the Father, we too might walk in newness of life" (*Rom* 6:3-4). Just as immersion in water symbolises death to sin and entry into the tomb with Christ, so coming up from the water represents resurrection to the new life of grace brought about by the sacrament.

Apart from the Scriptures, one of the earliest Christian documents that speaks of Baptism is the *Didache*, which dates to the end of the first century. It says: "And concerning baptism, baptise this way: having first said all these things, baptise into the name of the Father, and of the Son, and of the Holy Spirit, in living water. But if you have not living water, baptise into other water; and if you cannot in cold, in warm. But if you have not either, pour out water thrice upon the head into the name of Father and Son and Holy Spirit. But before the baptism let the baptiser fast, and the baptised, and whatever others can; but you shall order the baptised to fast one or two days before".

By living water is meant flowing water, as in a stream. Thus Baptism could be done either by immersion or by pouring water three times on the head, and its importance was such that fasting was to precede it.

Before the actual Baptism, the water was blessed. In the early Church this blessing had a twofold meaning. It was both an exorcism, ordering the devil to leave in keeping with the widespread belief that wells or fountains were the habitat of evil spirits, and also an epiclesis, a calling down of the Holy Spirit upon the water. The latter rite is preserved in the blessing today when the priest touches the water with his right hand, calling the Holy Spirit down upon it.

Another ancient ceremony in Baptism was the *Ephphetha*, in which the minister touched the ears and nostrils of the person, saying "Be opened", as Our Lord did to cure the man who was deaf and dumb (cf. *Mk* 7:32-35). In the early centuries the minister used his saliva in touching the senses, as Jesus did, and he pronounced words of exorcism, ordering the devil to flee. As to why he touched the nostrils and not the mouth, as Jesus did, St Ambrose explained that it was not fitting for the minister to touch the mouth of a woman. Today the *Ephphetha* comes after the actual Baptism and the minister touches the ears and the mouth.

647 More ceremonies of Baptism in the early Church

After the Ephphetha *what other ceremonies were there in Baptism in the early Church?*

After the *Ephphetha*, which was done prior to the Baptism itself since it involved a prayer of exorcism, came the anointing with the oil of catechumens. A fifth-century work *De Sacramentis*, sometimes attributed to St Ambrose, says that the person to be baptised was anointed as an athlete of Christ, like a fighter going into battle. Some early writings accompany the anointing with a prayer of exorcism to ward off the devil. The person was anointed on the chest and back, although in the East the whole body was anointed, with deaconesses assisting in the anointing of women.

Before the Baptism the person renounced Satan and made a profession of faith, as is done today. For the renunciation of Satan and all his works the person faced West, the direction of darkness and evil, and afterwards he faced East, the direction of the rising sun, the light of Christ. The profession of faith was done, as it is today, in the form of three questions from the Apostles' Creed, one on each of the three divine persons. For example, the person was asked, "Do you believe in God the Father almighty…?" and the person answered "I believe". In the first centuries the Baptism was done during this profession of faith by having the person immersed in water or having water poured over the head once after each question.

A common practice was for the person to stand in shallow water perhaps up to the knees with the priest or deacon, also in the water, pouring water over the head three times. Many early baptistries were in fact very shallow so that this was clearly the practice. Nonetheless, some documents speak of the person immersing at least the head in the water, assisted by the minister.

Baptism by immersion was the preferred practice until the fourteenth or fifteenth century, when infusion, pouring water over the head, became more common. In the East immersion has always been the common practice.

A number of early documents speak of the persons being baptised taking off their clothes for the Baptism and women were to take off any jewellery or other adornments they were wearing. This suggests the possibility that men and women might have been baptised separately, and that women may have been assisted by a widow or deaconess. One early document speaks of the woman standing behind a veil and a deaconess helping her to be under the water when the priest or deacon poured it. The symbolism was clear: the person was putting off the old garment of sin in order to be clothed with the new life of grace.

The ordinary minister for solemn Baptism in the early Church was the bishop, although he could delegate a priest or deacon to perform the ceremony if he was unable to do it.

And from the beginning the person baptised had a sponsor or godparent, who presented the candidate to the bishop, assisted in the ceremony and helped to dry and clothe the person after the Baptism. From the eighth century on two or even more godparents were allowed.

After the Baptism the person was anointed again, this time with the oil of chrism. There are references to this anointing already in the second century. The anointing was done on the head and it signified the infusion of sanctifying grace through the action of the Holy Spirit. Through it the person came to share in the priestly, prophetic and kingly mission of Christ and in some places it was the custom to put a crown on the person's head after the anointing.

The person was then vested in a white garment as a sign of the interior cleansing from sin and the new life of grace. St Paul's words were often invoked: "For as many of you as were baptised into Christ have put on Christ" (*Gal* 3:27). The custom of the white garment seems to have been introduced in the fourth century, first in the East and then in the West. The neophytes baptised in the Easter Vigil wore their white garments all week, at least in Mass which they attended every day.

Finally, the newly baptised person was given a lighted candle with words that recalled the lamps of the wise virgins. The most ancient formula speaks of the person being able to go out to meet the Lord when he comes to the nuptial banquet of heaven.

The Eucharist

648 Candles in the Mass

I remember that years ago candles for Mass were made primarily of beeswax, but now we see them made from much cheaper substances like paraffin. Is this permitted? Also, how many candles are to be lit for Mass?

In the Old Testament everything related to the worship of God was to be made of the finest materials. Thus, for example, the ark of the covenant was made of acacia wood overlayed with gold inside and out, and the mercy seat and the two cherubim on top of it were of pure gold (cf. *Ex* 25:10-22). The seven-branched lampstand, or *menorah*, was made of pure beaten gold (cf. *Ex* 25:31-40) and the oil for a lamp to burn day and night inside the tent of meeting, the *ner tamid*, was pure beaten olive oil (cf. *Ex* 27:20).

This is the spirit that should permeate the worship of God, or liturgy. Materials should be of the finest quality and the ceremonies well performed. Since the liturgy is directed to God himself, man should not offer him anything defective. Just as we give our loved ones on earth expensive gifts within our means, we do the same for God.

As you say, years ago candles were usually made of beeswax, often either sixty-five per cent or thirty-five percent. Since the candle symbolises Christ, the light of the world, it should be as pure as possible, as he was. The Vatican's Congregation for Rites prescribed in 1904 that the paschal candle and the two candles used in Mass were to be made from candles with a majority of beeswax, while other candles were to have at least a notable quantity of beeswax. Candles made wholly of other materials such as tallow or paraffin were actually forbidden.

In 1850 the Congregation of Rites made an exception for missionaries in Oceania who, on account of the impossibility of obtaining wax candles, were allowed to use candles made from sperm whales.

With the passing of time the composition of candles in the liturgy has changed considerably. One of the problems with candles with a majority of beeswax is that in hot weather they can soften and bend over, making them unsightly and thus unsuitable for giving true glory to God. In any case all wax candles tend to drip wax down the sides and thus look unsightly unless they are cleaned regularly, which can be time consuming.

This has led over the years to the increased use of candlesticks with a metal tube which looks somewhat like wax, into which a narrower candle made from paraffin or some other substance is inserted. Alternatively, the inner candle may be of oil in a glass tube. These are quite acceptable and much more practical, even though beeswax candles would be preferable.

The sanctuary lamp which burns constantly before the Blessed Sacrament in the tabernacle undoubtedly owes its origin to the *ner tamid* in the Old Testament tent of meeting. It continues to be used in Jewish synagogues today. The name means "eternal light" and in the Jewish understanding it symbolises God's eternal and imminent presence among his people. How much more in a Catholic church does it not only symbolise but actually accompany the Real Presence of God! For Catholics it also symbolises the faithful's prayer rising to God day and night.

The sanctuary lamp, usually inside a red or clear glass tube, can be made either of wax or of oil. In some churches it is electric and made to look like a flickering candle. In this regard Bishop Peter Elliott, in his book *Ceremonies of the Modern Roman Rite* (Ignatius Press 1995) comments: "Electric votive candles virtually eliminate the symbolism of the personal offering of a living natural flame" (p. 84). One could add that they look cheap and if there is a power outage the lamp goes out, which destroys its significance.

As regards the number of candles, the *General Instruction of the Roman Missal* (2012) indicates that there are to be "at least two in any celebration, or even four or six, especially for a Sunday Mass or a Holyday of Obligation" (n. 117). When the diocesan bishop celebrates, there is a seventh candle in the middle of the altar.

649 Has the Pope changed the Our Father?

Recently several friends have told me that the Pope has changed the wording of the Our Father. Is this true and, if so, what is the new wording?

It is not true that the Pope has changed the Our Father, although he has said something about it. The facts as they unfolded are the following.

First, the French bishops adopted a new translation of the Lord's Prayer in the Roman Missal which went into effect on the first Sunday of Advent 2018. The translation changed "lead us not into temptation" to the French equivalent of "do not let us fall into temptation."

Sometime later Italian television aired an hour-long interview with Pope Francis in which he was asked about the new translation. He commented: "It's I who fall. It's not He who pushes me into temptation, as if I fell. A father doesn't do that. A father helps you to get up right away. The one who leads into temptation is Satan."

What the Pope says is true. God does not lead us into temptation; the devil does. But "lead us not into temptation" are the words Our Lord himself gave the apostles when he taught them the Our Father (cf. *Mt* 6:13) and they are the words we have used in English ever since. Both the Greek and the Latin can be translated as "lead us not into temptation."

St Jerome's Latin Vulgate Bible translation, taken from the Greek, is *ne nos inducas in tentationem*, which is literally "lead us not into temptation."

As regards the Greek, the *Catechism of the Catholic Church* teaches: "This petition goes to the root of the preceding one, for our sins result from our consenting to temptation; we therefore ask our Father not to 'lead' us into temptation. It is difficult to translate the Greek verb used by a single English word: the Greek means both 'do not allow us to enter into temptation' and 'do not let us yield to temptation'" (*CCC* 2846).

Thus the words "lead us not into temptation" are to be understood in the sense of asking God not to let us fall into temptation. In the words of the Catechism: "We ask him [God] not to allow us to take the way that leads to sin. We are engaged in the battle 'between flesh and spirit'; this petition implores the Spirit of discernment and strength" (*CCC* 2846).

More recently, at the beginning of June 2019, Pope Francis approved the translation of the third edition of the Roman Missal prepared by the Italian bishops' conference. This translation, like the French, has changed the wording of the Our Father, in this case to "do not abandon us to temptation".

So to date Pope Francis has approved new translations of the Lord's Prayer in the missals of two countries. He has not changed the translation for the whole world. It is for the bishops of each language group to propose the change, which must be approved by the Holy See.

As regards the English, the translation of the third edition of the Roman Missal was issued back in 2011 and it is the one we use at present. It has the traditional rendering of the Our Father, with expressions like "hallowed be thy name" and "thy kingdom come." The thinking of the English-language bishops was obviously that the words of the Our Father are so traditional and familiar that they should not be changed.

But is the English translation too about to change? A spokesperson for the bishops of England and Wales has said that the International Commission on English in the Liturgy (ICEL) "is not currently considering the Lord's Prayer," and that "there are no plans at present for [the Our Father] to change in English."

A spokesperson for the Scottish bishops said there were no plans to adopt the changes, while the Irish bishop in charge of liturgy said that, "In consultation with bishops from other English-speaking countries, the Irish Catholic Bishops' Conference will give close attention to the reported change to the Lord's Prayer. The bishops will look at the implications for both the Irish and English translations of this much loved and universal prayer."

In the meantime we will continue to say the Our Father both in Mass and in our personal prayers in its traditional form.

650 Receiving Communion kneeling

I have been receiving Communion standing but now am considering receiving it kneeling and on the tongue as a sign of greater respect. Very few people in our parish receive it this way and I don't want to stand out. Is this a good thing to do?

You have every right to receive Communion kneeling and on the tongue. To be sure, this was the way everyone received it for a thousand years until after the Second Vatican Council (cf. J. Flader *Question Time 1*, q. 71). And it is still received this way when Mass is celebrated in the Extraordinary Form, or Tridentine Rite, and also in some parishes, especially where they have retained altar rails.

Even though in the early Church Communion was given to the faithful in the hand, already at the time of the Fathers of the Church this practice became more and more restricted in favour of distributing Communion on the tongue. The reason was twofold: first to avoid, as much as possible, fragments of the host falling on the ground; and second to increase among the faithful devotion to the Real Presence of Christ in the Eucharist by not taking it in the hand as one would with ordinary bread.

By the eleventh century the practice of receiving Communion

on the tongue was practically universal. In the thirteenth century St Thomas Aquinas wrote: "... out of reverence towards this Sacrament, nothing touches it but what is consecrated; hence the corporal and the chalice are consecrated, and likewise the priest's hands, for touching this Sacrament. Hence, it is not lawful for anyone else to touch it except from necessity, for instance, if it were to fall upon the ground, or else in some other case of urgency" (*STh*, III, 82, 3).

As regards receiving Communion kneeling, the words of St Augustine in the fifth century are very relevant: "No one eats that flesh without first adoring it; we should sin were we not to adore it" (*Enarrationes in Psalmos* 98, 9).

The need for reverence in receiving Communion was emphasised most recently by Cardinal Robert Sarah, Prefect of the Vatican's Congregation for Divine Worship, in the foreword to a book on the distribution of Communion: "The most insidious diabolical attack consists in trying to extinguish faith in the Eucharist, sowing errors and favouring an unsuitable manner of receiving it. Truly the war between Michael and his Angels on one side, and Lucifer on the other, continues in the heart of the faithful: Satan's target is the Sacrifice of the Mass and the Real Presence of Jesus in the consecrated host.

"Why do we insist on communicating standing in the hand? Why this attitude of lack of submission to the signs of God? [Receiving kneeling and on the tongue] is much more suited to the sacrament itself. I hope there can be a rediscovery and promotion of the beauty and pastoral value of this manner. In my opinion and judgment, this is an important question on which the Church today must reflect. This is a further act of adoration and love that each of us can offer to Jesus Christ."

In his foreword Cardinal Sarah also criticises such "outrages" against the Blessed Sacrament as satanic "Black Masses", the sacrilege of receiving Communion while in a state of mortal sin, and "intercommunion" – the reception of Communion by non-Catholics.

He adds that we should not receive Communion like any other food but should retain a sense of the sacred: "Why are we so proud and insensitive to the signs that God himself offers us for our spiritual growth and our intimate relationship with Him? Why do we not kneel down to receive Holy Communion on the example of the saints? Is it really too humiliating to bow down and kneel before the Lord Jesus Christ?"

While the faithful may receive Communion either standing or kneeling, on the hand or on the tongue, it is clear from all this that receiving it kneeling and on the tongue is the way that by itself shows the greatest respect for Our Lord's Real Presence. In conclusion, anyone should feel free to kneel down and receive Communion on the tongue, even though they may be in the minority.

651 Communion for Protestants

I read recently that the Vatican has turned down a proposal of some German bishops to allow Mass-going Lutheran spouses of Catholics to receive Holy Communion. Wouldn't this be a good way to promote eventual union with Protestants?

The facts are as you say. A group of German bishops – not all the bishops, by the way – drafted a document granting permission to give Communion to Mass-attending Lutheran spouses of Catholics, and the Vatican rejected it. More specifically, a letter published on June 4 on the Italian blog *Settimo Cielo* and signed by Cardinal-designate Luis Ladaria, SJ, Prefect of the Congregation for the Doctrine of the Faith, said of the German document: "The Holy Father has reached the conclusion that the document has not matured enough to be published."

The Prefect had hosted a meeting on May 3 with a group of German bishops, including both supporters and opponents of the document, along with officials from the Pontifical Council for Promoting Christian Unity and the Pontifical Council for Legislative texts.

In his letter Fr Ladaria said he had spoken with Pope Francis about the proposed guidelines on two occasions and he said that the proposal raises "a series of problems of notable importance." He listed three main issues. First, "The question of the admission to Communion of Lutheran Christians in interconfessional marriages is a theme that touches on the faith of the Church and has relevance for the universal Church." Second, "Such a question has effects on ecumenical relations with other churches and other ecclesial communities that cannot be undervalued." And third, the matter also involves Church law, particularly the interpretation of canon 844 of the *Code of Canon Law*, which states: "If the danger of death is present or if, in the judgment of the diocesan bishop or conference of bishops, some other grave necessity urges it, Catholic ministers administer these same sacraments licitly also to other Christians not having full communion with the Catholic Church, who cannot approach a minister of their own community and who seek such on their own accord, provided that they manifest Catholic faith in respect to these sacraments and are properly disposed."

The letter said that because of varying interpretations of the canon, "the competent dicasteries of the Holy See already have been charged with producing a timely clarification of such questions on the level of the universal Church. In particular, it appears opportune to leave to the diocesan bishop the judgment about the existence of a 'grave necessity' that would permit Christians of other denominations to receive the Eucharist at a Catholic Mass."

Returning to your question, why is the Church so opposed to giving Communion to well-meaning Protestants who wish to receive it? The answer is that reception of Holy Communion implies full communion with the Church and all its teachings. It is to receive Jesus Christ himself and all he stands for. It is the "source and summit" of Christian life, as the Second Vatican Council said (cf. *LG* 11). It is the high point of one's relationship with Christ and the culmination of the journey into the Church, not a step along the way of that journey.

This is seen clearly in the early Church, where the catechumens who were to enter into full communion with the Church in the Easter Vigil could attend the first part of the Mass, the Liturgy of the Word or

"Mass of the Catechumens," but were ushered out of the Church before the Presentation of the Gifts, when the Liturgy of the Eucharist, the "Mass of the Faithful", began. The catechumens were being instructed in the teachings of the Church and they accepted all of them, but they were only admitted to Holy Communion after their Baptism in the Easter Vigil.

This criterion is found also in the *Didache,* which dates to the end of the first century. There we read: "Let no one eat or drink of your Eucharist unless they have been baptised... If anyone is holy let him come, if anyone is not so, let him repent." Here it is clear that to receive Our Lord in Communion one must not only be baptised but must also be living in keeping with the faith. That is, if a person was not holy, not in the state of grace, he or she must first repent and be absolved in the sacrament of Penance. This is the practice today, as we see in the *Catechism of the Catholic Church (cf. CCC* 1415).

652 Communion in a nursing home

I am an extraordinary minister of Communion and regularly take Communion to an aged care home. What should I do when a new patient arrives so as to ensure that they are properly disposed to receive Communion?

This is an important question since, as we all know, "Anyone conscious of a grave sin must receive the sacrament of Reconciliation before coming to Communion" (*CCC* 1385). Given that fewer and fewer Catholics are attending Mass regularly these days, it is likely that many people entering a nursing home are not regular Mass goers and have not been to confession for a long time.

What the extraordinary minister should not do is simply take Communion to a new person on the list without finding out the state of their soul. Among other reasons, the patient may very well know that he or she needs to go to confession before receiving Our Lord and, if this is not made available, may be led to receive Our Lord anyway even though they know they are not in the state of grace.

What then should you do? You should approach the matter with great tact and kindness and this ordinarily requires a little time and a relaxed atmosphere. If you go to the home only once a week you might visit the new patient after distributing Communion to the others, so that you can introduce yourself and sit down for a chat.

In the conversation you can say that you were given the patient's name as being a Catholic and would be very happy to take him Communion in the future. You might then ask general questions to put the person at ease such as where he is from, what his family situation is, how long he has been a Catholic, where he went to school and church, whether he has been going to Mass and receiving Communion regularly, etc.

If it is clear that he has not been practising the faith regularly, you can explain that in order to receive Communion again it will be important to go to confession first and that you can arrange for a priest to come and visit him. Most people will understand that to receive Communion after a long time some form of reconciliation with God is necessary. And of course if the patient has been attending Mass regularly, you can still ask if he would like to see a priest and go to confession and you can arrange for the priest to visit him. At the end of the conversation it is good to say a few prayers with the patient and tell him you look forward to seeing him on your next visit.

Another situation the extraordinary minister may face is going to an aged care home for the first time and being given a list of patients who have received Communion there in the past. Can you assume that all the patients are properly disposed, in the state of grace, or should you first find out? Here, as in a parish Mass, you can give them the benefit of the doubt and assume that those who regularly receive Communion are properly disposed and so you can take Communion to them. You do not need to speak privately with each one beforehand.

But since there may be some who are not in the state of grace, it would be good to visit each one personally at some stage, simply to introduce yourself, get to know them and have a pleasant chat with them. They will generally be very appreciative of this conversation as it shows that you are not simply carrying out a duty of taking them Communion but rather you care about them as persons and want to get to know them. In the course of this conversation you can easily find out the state of their soul.

As always, you can offer to have the priest go to visit them, whether or not they are in the state of grace. After all, people in the state of grace may also want to chat with a priest and go to confession from time to time. Since for the fact of being in an aged care home they are in their advanced years, they will tend to think more often of their eventual meeting with God and they will want to prepare well for it.

It is good to remember too that even faithful of the Orthodox Churches can be given Communion in these circumstances if they ask for it (cf. Can. 844, §3). But, as I wrote some years ago, the wishes of their respective priest should be taken into account (cf. *Question Time 1,* q. 62).

653 The Eucharistic miracle of Santarem

A friend recently returned from Fatima and told me about a Eucharistic miracle that had taken place near there many centuries ago. Can you tell me something about it?

Until I received your question I hadn't heard about the miracle, but it is very impressive. It took place in the thirteenth century in the Portuguese town of Santarem, not far from Fatima.

According to a document commissioned by King Alfonso IV in 1346, a young woman in Santarem was unhappy with her marriage, convinced that her husband did not love her and was unfaithful to her. Her efforts to win back his love were unsuccessful. As a last resort, in 1266 she consulted a sorceress, who told her that her husband would love her again if she went to the church and brought back a consecrated Eucharistic Host.

The woman was understandably frightened at this suggestion since she knew that to do this was a sacrilege, but she finally gave in. She went to Mass in the church of St Stephen and received Communion, but instead of consuming the Host she left the church immediately, took the Host out of her mouth and placed it in her veil. She then went to the house of the sorceress.

Along the way the Host began to bleed inside the veil. The woman was not aware of it until passers-by brought it to her attention, thinking it was she that was bleeding. Filled with panic, the woman then rushed home instead of going to the sorceress. She put the veil containing the Host in a trunk, not knowing what else to do. When her husband arrived home she said nothing.

Later that night they were awakened by bright rays of light coming from the trunk and lighting up the whole room. The wife then confessed her sin to her husband and they knelt in adoration for the remaining hours until dawn, when they called for the parish priest.

The Host was then taken in procession, accompanied by priests and lay faithful, to the church of St Stephen, where it was encased in wax to contain the blood and Host and placed in the tabernacle. Years later, apparently in 1340, when the tabernacle was opened another miraculous event was discovered. The wax that had encased the Host had broken into pieces and the Host was found enclosed in a crystal pyx, along with the Precious Blood. In 1782 this was placed in a gold and silver pear-shaped monstrance with a "sunburst" of thirty-three rays. It can still be seen in that vessel today.

After an investigation and approval by the Church authorities, the church of St Stephen was renamed "The Church of the Holy Miracle". In 1684 the house where the miracle occurred was converted into a chapel.

Throughout the centuries on various occasions the Host has given off new emissions of Blood, and in some cases images of Our Lord were seen on the Host. Among the visitors to the miracle was St Francis Xavier, who visited the Shrine before being sent to the missions in India by the King of Portugal in the sixteenth century.

Another famous visitor was Queen St Elizabeth of Portugal, who in 1295 and 1322 went to pray before the miraculous Host. On her second visit she prayed especially for reconciliation between her husband, King Dionisio, and her son, the future Alfonso VI. She asked that the Sacred Host be taken in procession through the streets and, wearing simple clothes without any royal regalia, she accompanied the procession, walking barefoot and covered with ashes with a rope around her neck. Her prayer was granted.

From the time of the miracle until now, every year on the second Sunday of April the events of the miracle are re-enacted by local actors. The monstrance containing the miraculous Host is taken in procession from the house where the miracle took place to the church of St Stephen.

Miraculously, after 750 years the Precious Blood still remains in liquid form, defying the natural laws of nature. The Host is irregularly shaped, resembling real flesh with delicate veins running from top to bottom. Some of the Blood is collected in the crystal.

Over the years various Popes have granted plenary indulgences to pilgrims who visited the church of the miracle and to the brothers of the Royal Brotherhood of the Sacred Miracle who look after the church. The Popes include Pius IV, St Pius V, Pius VI, and Gregory XIV.

654 The Eucharistic miracle of Amsterdam

A friend who is very interested in Eucharistic miracles recently told me about a miracle that took place many centuries ago in Amsterdam. Can you tell me something about it?

The miracle took place, as you say, in Amsterdam, the Netherlands, in 1345. On 12 March of that year, a few days before Easter, a devout man named Ysbrand Dommer, thinking he was near the end of his life, sent for the parish priest of the Oude Kerk, or Old Church, to receive the Last Rites. Shortly after receiving Holy Communion, he vomited everything into a small basin. The priest, foreseeing this possibility, had told the family that if the man threw up, which he was known to do after taking food, they were to empty the contents into the fire in the fireplace, which they did. By the next day Dommer had recovered his health completely.

Early the next morning one of the maids attending him went to rake the fire and, to her amazement, saw the Sacred Host still intact surrounded by a light. She put her hand into the fire to take out the Host, doing so without suffering any burns. She was surprised to discover that the Host was not hot but cold.

At this point there are two diverging accounts. One says that the maid called in a neighbour lady and asked her to take the Host to her home. The neighbour took a clean cloth, placed the Host on it and locked it in a box. She took it to the maid's home, where her husband asked to see it. When he tried to pick it up he was unable to do so, as if Our Lord were saying he did not want to be touched by his hands. They then called for a priest, who placed the Host in a pyx, a small vessel for taking Communion to the sick. When he went to wash the cloth on which the Host had rested and return it to the original box, he noticed that the pyx had been moved and the Host was gone. The next morning the neighbour returned for her box and the cloth. When she opened the locked box she once again found the Sacred Host in it!

The other account, which is more probable in view of the respect for the Blessed Sacrament that the people would have had, is that Ysbrand himself wrapped the Host in a linen cloth, placed it in a case and took it to the parish priest. But when the priest opened the case the Host was not there. It miraculously reappeared in Ysbrand's house and the priest went there to recover it. But again, and even a third time, it disappeared and reappeared in Ysbrand's house. It was then decided to make a chapel for it in Ysbrand's house.

On Easter Sunday everyone who had witnessed the miracle, along with the mayor, compiled a report of what had happened. The report was delivered to Bishop Jan van Arkel of Utrecht, who authorised devotion to the Sacred Host. As early as 1360 public processions were held with many pilgrims taking part. In 1452 a fire destroyed a great part of Amsterdam, including the chapel of the Sacred Host, but strangely the monstrance containing the Host was left intact. In 1456 a new chapel was built, surrounded by a beautiful church.

In 1665 the city council authorised Father Jan van der Mey to convert one of the houses of a former convent of the Beguines into a chapel for the Host. The Beguines were a community of women who lived quasi-religious lives without taking vows, and devoted themselves to prayer and good works, especially looking after the poor. They were numerous in Northern Europe from the twelfth century on and were very popular in the Netherlands. Each woman lived in a separate house in a cluster of houses in the same place.

The monstrance with the Sacred Host was transferred to the Beguine chapel but shortly afterwards it was stolen by thieves and was never seen again. The only objects that remain from the Eucharistic miracle are the case that contained the Host, the documents that describe the miracle and some paintings housed in the Historical Museum of Amsterdam.

Every year in March a *stille omgang,* or silent walk, is held in Amsterdam to commemorate the miracle. In the 1950s up to 90,000 people from all over the Netherlands would take part in the procession. In recent years there have still been several thousand participating each year. The Silent Walk is done on the night of Saturday to Sunday following the start of the Miracle Feast, which is on the first Wednesday after March 12.

655 A Eucharistic miracle in Mexico

I know you have written about recent Eucharistic miracles in Argentina and Poland, and now I hear there has been another one in Mexico. Is this true?

There was indeed a Eucharistic miracle in Mexico in 2006. It took place on October 21 that year during a retreat in the parish of St Martin of Tours in Tixtla, in the diocese of Chilpancingo-Chilapa. The parish priest, Fr Leopoldo Roque, was distributing Communion during Mass assisted by Fr Raymundo Reyna Esteban, who was leading the retreat, and a religious sister. The sister approached Fr Raymundo with tears in her eyes and showed him a host which had begun to give off a reddish substance. They put the host aside and informed the bishop.

The bishop, Most Reverend Alejo Zavala Castro, then convened a theological commission to investigate the matter to determine if this was a hoax or a genuine miracle. In October 2009, he invited Bolivian-born Dr Ricardo Castañón along with a team of other scientists to conduct research on the host.

He chose Dr Castañón Gómez because the scientist had investigated a Eucharistic miracle that took place in Buenos Aires in 1996, invited by Archbishop Jorge Bergoglio, later to become Pope Francis. Crucial to that investigation was the intervention of Australians Michael Willesee and Ron Tesoriero, who in 2004 had a sample of the Argentinian host analysed by forensic pathologist Frederick Zugibe in New York. Zugibe found that the host had turned into human heart tissue from the left ventricle and that the person from whom the sample was taken had suffered trauma about the chest (cf. J. Flader, *Question Time 3*, q. 367).

Dr Castañón's team concluded their investigation of the Mexican host in October 2012 and presented their conclusions on 25 May 2013 during an international symposium organised by the diocese of Chilpancingo. They reported the following:

1. The reddish substance analysed corresponds to blood in which there are haemoglobin and DNA of human origin.

2. Two studies conducted by eminent forensic experts with different methodologies have shown that the substance originates from the inside, excluding the hypothesis that someone could have placed it from the outside.

3. The blood type is AB, similar to the one found in the host of Lanciano and in the Holy Shroud of Turin.

4. A microscopic analysis of magnification and penetration reveals that the upper part of the blood has been coagulated since October 2006. Moreover, the underlying internal layers reveal, in February 2010, the presence of fresh blood.
5. There are intact white blood cells, red blood cells, and active macrophages that engulf lipids. The tissue in question appears lacerated and with recovery mechanisms, exactly as occurs in a living tissue.
6. A further histopathological analysis determines the presence of protein structures in a state of deterioration, suggesting mesenchymal cells, very specialised cells, characterised by an elevated biophysiological dynamism.
7. The immune-histochemical studies reveal that the tissue corresponds to the muscle of the heart (Myocardium).

In view of the scientific results and the conclusions reached by the theological commission, on 12 October 2013 Bishop Zavala Castro issued a Pastoral Letter with the following statement: "This manifestation brings us a marvellous sign of the love of God that confirms the Real Presence of Jesus in the Eucharist... In my role as Bishop of the Diocese I recognise the supernatural character of the series of events relating to the Bleeding Host of Tixtla.... I declare the case a 'Divine Sign.' The event does not have a natural explanation. It does not have paranormal origin. It is not traceable to manipulation of the enemy."

Surprisingly, in all the bleeding hosts and other Eucharistic miracles where human DNA was found, scientists have not been able to sequence the DNA to obtain a genetic profile.

Penance

656 The seal of confession

Now that the Royal Commission has recommended that priests be required to inform the authorities of sins of sexual abuse that they hear in confession, I am wondering if the Church can allow priests to do this. Is the teaching on the confidentiality of confession a new or an old one?

This has been a matter of much discussion of late and it is good to have clear ideas about what the Church can and cannot allow. We are speaking of course about what is known as the seal of confession. By it, a priest is forbidden to disclose to anyone the sins he hears in confession. This is an old and constant teaching, not a new one.

Already in the twelfth century Gratian, a Camaldolese monk and teacher of theology at the monastery of Saints Nabor and Felix in Bologna, Italy, wrote of the Church's prohibition of disclosing what is heard in confession. Around the year 1151 in his work *Concordia discordantium canonum*, more often referred to as the Decree of Gratian, he collected in one volume the numerous legal texts that existed in different documents at the time. It includes this norm: "Let the priest who dares to make known the sins of his penitent be deposed" (*Secunda pars*, dist. VI, c. II). He goes on to say that anyone who violates this law should be made a lifelong, ignominious wanderer. It should be understood that Gratian was not the initiator of this norm but was merely stating what had already been in existence for some time.

In the following century the Fourth Lateran Council (1215) decreed: "Let the priest absolutely beware that he does not by word or sign or by any manner whatever in any way betray the sinner: but if he should happen to need wiser counsel let him cautiously seek the same without any mention of person. For whoever shall dare to reveal a sin disclosed to him in the tribunal of penance we decree that he shall be not only deposed from the priestly office but that he shall also be sent into the confinement of a monastery to do perpetual penance" (Canon 21).

St Thomas Aquinas (1225-1274) in his *Summa Theologiae* quotes this Canon and explains the reason for the seal: "Now God hides the sins of those who submit to him by Penance; wherefore this also should be signified in the sacrament of Penance, and consequently the sacrament demands that the confession should remain hidden, and he who divulges a confession sins by violating the sacrament. Besides this there are other advantages in this secrecy, because thereby men are more attracted to confession, and confess their sins with greater simplicity" (*STh* Suppl. q. 11, art. 1).

In that same century the Council of Durham (1220) in England declared: "A priest shall not reveal a confession – let none dare from anger or hatred or fear of the Church or of death, in any way reveal confessions, by sign or word, general or special, as for instance, by saying 'I know what manner of men ye are' under peril of his Order and Benefice and if he shall be convicted thereof he shall be degraded without mercy".

The Catholic Encyclopedia records that in thirteenth century Spain an unnamed Spanish writer stated that under King James I of Aragon a priest convicted of a breach of the seal of confession was to have his tongue cut out. The seal was taken seriously indeed!

In sixteenth century England King Henry VIII, in his *Defence of the Seven Sacraments*, acknowledged the importance of the seal of confession and attributed its universal observance to the grace of God: "For the people could never, by any human authority, be induced to discover their secret sins, which they abhor in their consciences, and which they are so much concerned to conceal, with such shame, and confusion, and so undoubtedly to a man that might, when he pleased, betray them. Neither could it happen, that among such great numbers of priests, some good, and some bad, indifferently hearing confessions, they should all retain them; and that also, when some of them can keep nothing else secret, if God himself, the author of the sacrament, did not, by his especial grace, defend this so wholesome a thing."

So the seal of confession is a longstanding norm in the Church. It cannot be changed.

657 Would priests violate the seal of confession?

If priests were required by law to inform the authorities of sins of sexual abuse that they hear in confession, would the Church accept such a law and allow priests to obey it?

As we have seen, from at least the thirteenth century the Church has insisted on the importance of priests keeping strict confidence about what they hear in confession. The norm at present is the same, as we read in the *Catechism of the Catholic Church*: "Given the delicacy and greatness of this ministry and the respect due to persons, the Church declares that every priest who hears confessions is bound under very severe penalties to keep absolute secrecy regarding the sins that his penitents have confessed to him. He can make no use of knowledge that confession gives him about penitents' lives. This secret, which admits of no exceptions, is called the 'sacramental seal', because what the penitent has made known to the priest remains 'sealed' by the sacrament" (*CCC* 1467).

The "severe penalties" are contained in the *Code of Canon Law*: "A confessor who directly violates the sacramental seal, incurs a *latae sententiae* excommunication reserved to the Apostolic See; he who does so only indirectly is to be punished according to the gravity of the offence" (Can. 1388 §1). That is, if a priest were to violate the seal, he would be automatically and immediately excommunicated by the law itself. Moreover, the lifting of the excommunication is reserved to the Holy See. The violation of the seal is indeed a grave offence.

It is interesting to note that at one time the civil law too in Australia and New Zealand forbade priests to reveal what they heard in confession. The state of Victoria's Evidence Act 1890 declared: "No clergyman of any church or religious denomination shall, without consent of the person making the confession, divulge in any suit, action or proceeding whether civil or criminal any confession made to him in his professional character according to the usage of the church or religious denomination to which he belongs" (S. 55). And New Zealand's Evidence Act 1908 stated: "A minister shall not divulge in any proceeding any confession made to him, in his professional character, except with the consent of the person who made such confession" (S. 8, 1).

It would thus be a major change if the civil law were now to compel a priest to divulge what he heard in confession. What would a priest do in these circumstances? He would simply refuse to comply with the law. If this involved contempt of court and he was put in jail, he would happily go to jail rather than violate the sacrosanct seal of confession.

Why is this so serious? Because if the Church did not protect the confidentiality of what is said in confession, people would not trust their priests and they would not confess anything that might incriminate them. Just as they trust their doctor, psychologist, lawyer or counsellor to respect their confidentiality, so all the more do they trust their priest.

Paedophiles and other people with serious problems would simply not go to confession out of fear that the confessor would take the matter to the police. They would thereby deprive themselves of the forgiveness of their sins, the grace of the sacrament and a very valuable aid in overcoming their sinful habit. This could lead, ironically, to an increase in child sexual abuse.

But if a paedophile confesses this most serious sin, shouldn't the priest be able to take some action? Yes, he should and he will. He will strongly urge the person to address his problem: to seek professional help, to resign his position, to inform the relevant people and possibly even to give himself up to the police. And of, course, if the priest sees that the paedophile is not sorry for what he has done and is not prepared to take necessary action, the confessor can refuse to absolve him.

What the confessor should not do is ask the penitent to see him outside of confession and to repeat what was said, giving the priest permission to reveal to others the content of this conversation. The contents of this conversation too would be covered by the seal of confession and therefore what was said in it could not be made known to others.

Even if the law is changed so as to require priests to divulge what they have heard in confession, the Church will not and cannot change its teaching on the seal of confession and priests will not violate this important norm.

658 The consequences of state legislation on the seal of confession

Now that some Australian states have legislated to require priests to inform the authorities of sins of child sexual abuse they hear in confession, what will happen? Will priests obey the law?

As you say, some states, including South Australia and Tasmania, along with the Australian Capital Territory, have passed legalisation requiring priests to report to the police any cases of child sexual abuse they hear in confession. The law thus removes the exemption from mandatory reporting for priests hearing confession and puts them on an equal footing with such professionals as social workers, teachers and medical professionals, who are required to report child abuse to the police.

It is a shame, a big shame, that these states have done this. The Church has had the requirement of the sacramental seal for many centuries and the governments of the world have largely respected it. Now, with advancing secularisation and decreasing respect for the Church and all it has done to advance the dignity of human beings, to provide health care, education and aid for the poor all over the world, governments think they can ride roughshod over the Church.

This new development is more a theoretical issue than a practical one. The theoretical issue is the fact that for the first time, at least in this country, governments have taken away the exemption from mandatory reporting by priests of what they hear in confession. This is a serious and most unfortunate development. It signals the increasing willingness of the state to dictate to the Church, not respecting her longstanding and wide-reaching contribution to society. And it tramples on the religious freedom of penitents to confess sins without fear of being reported to the police.

As a practical issue, the new legislation will have little effect and this for two reasons. First, people who commit sexual offences against children hardly ever go to confession. I am not aware of a single priest who has heard this sin confessed and in my own more than fifty years of priesthood I have not heard it either. I have certainly heard victims mention that they were sexually abused as children, but this almost always took place within the broader family circle.

What is more, if a perpetrator of abuse went to confession, he would be most unlikely to mention his name, so that the priest could not report it anyway. And with the new legislation, the fear of being reported will deter abusers all the more from confessing their sin, thus depriving them of the help they could have received from the priest and the sacrament.

Second, priests are simply not going to obey the legislation. They would prefer to pay a fine or go to jail rather than violate the seal of confession and with it the confidentiality of the penitent. The Church will never change the requirement of the seal of confession and priests will observe it.

Holy Orders

659 Voluntary priestly celibacy

One of the recommendations of the Royal Commission into Institutional Responses to Child Sexual Abuse was that priestly celibacy should be voluntary. Is this something the Church might consider implementing?

I would like to say three things in answer to your question. First, in a real sense priestly celibacy has always been voluntary. This statement may raise eyebrows. Celibacy has been voluntary in the sense that entry into the priesthood, which requires a celibate life, is itself voluntary. No one needs to be a priest. If a man chooses to follow the call of God to become a priest, he knows he is entering a life of celibacy and he freely embraces that state, just as a person entering marriage embraces fidelity and a girl entering religious life embraces celibacy.

As I wrote in an earlier column (cf. *Question Time 3,* q. 377) from the earliest centuries, when priests were allowed to be married, they were to abstain from marital relations with their wife. Later, at least since the Council of Trent in the sixteenth century, they could not be married, yet the call to the priesthood has been answered constantly by many men.

At present, there are over one hundred thousand seminarians preparing for the priesthood in the Latin rite all over the world, and they have freely chosen to embrace celibacy. That is one seminarian for every four priests in the world, a very healthy proportion, which augurs well for the future.

Second, priestly celibacy is a disciplinary matter, not a doctrinal one, and the Church could very well change it, although it is very unlikely to do so, at least in the near future. As we know, the Eastern rites of the Church allow married priests and there are also a good number of married priests of the Latin rite who were married priests in the various Orthodox Churches or in the Church of England who have converted to the Catholic faith and are now priests.

But it is clear that the mind of the Church at the present time is unequivocally in favour of maintaining the centuries-old practice of celibacy. The 1990 General Assembly of the Synod of Bishops on the formation of priests stated: "The Synod does not wish to leave any doubts in the mind of anyone regarding the Church's firm will to maintain the law that demands perpetual and freely chosen celibacy for present and future candidates for priestly ordination in the Latin Rite" (Proposition 11; in Pope John Paul II, Apost. Exhort. *Pastores dabo vobis*, n. 29). Note that the bishops speak here of "freely chosen celibacy".

The bishops went on to say that they would like to see celibacy presented "as a precious gift given by God to his Church and as a sign of the Kingdom which is not of this world, a sign of God's love for this world and of the undivided love of the priest for God and for God's People, with the result that celibacy is seen as a positive enrichment of the priesthood" (*ibid*).

We should bear in mind too that Australia is a tiny part of the universal Church, with some 5.5 million Catholics out of a total of some 1.3 billion faithful worldwide. The Church is not about to change a tradition which has existed from the beginning just because a Royal Commission in this country has recommended it.

Third, it is in my opinion disingenuous in the extreme to think that allowing Catholic priests to be married is the answer to child sexual abuse by the clergy. It is common knowledge that the immense majority of child sexual abuse in this country is perpetrated by family members or friends of the victim, whether fathers, step-fathers, uncles or other family members or friends, most of whom are married.

This is borne out by a Personal Safety Survey published in 2005 by the Australian Bureau of Statistics. The survey showed that for participants who had experienced sexual abuse before the age of 15,

13.5% identified that the abuse came from their father or stepfather, 30.2% from another male relative, 16.9% from a family friend, 15.6% from an acquaintance or neighbour, and 15.3% from another known person. That is a total of 91.5%.

The real solution to the problem, and it is already being implemented in all our seminaries, is a more thorough screening of candidates for the priesthood before they enter the seminary, to weed out men whose sexual orientation and tendencies would make them likely to commit sexual abuse. Let us pray that these measures will be fruitful. Married priests are not the answer.

660 The effects of laicisation

When a priest has been laicised and can no longer function as a priest does this mean that the sacraments he administered throughout his years as a priest are no longer valid? My children were baptised by such a priest and I am worried. Do they need to be baptised again?

Over the years this question has been asked not only about priests who have been laicised but also about those who have left the Church altogether and those who have been found guilty of grave sins and have even gone to jail for serious crimes. The thinking is that if these priests already had false ideas or were committing grave sins at a time when they were administering the sacraments, the validity of these sacraments must be called into question.

The simple answer is that all the sacraments these priests administered before they were laicised or ceased to function as Catholic priests were indeed valid and need not be repeated. But let me explain.

The question was addressed by the Church as far back as the fourth century. It arose during the persecution of the Church in North Africa, when many priests and lay faithful, to escape imprisonment or death, handed over the Scriptures to the Roman authorities as a sign that they had repudiated the faith. One who hands something over, in Latin, is a *traditor*, from the verb *tradere*. hence the English word traitor.

A heretical sect in Carthage known as the Donatists, named after their leader the bishop Donatus Magnus, taught that the Church was meant to be an assembly of saints, not sinners. Therefore, any sacraments celebrated by priests who were traitors or apostates, that is who denied the faith, were invalid. The Donatists went so far as to say that even if the priest later repented and returned to the Church the sacraments he celebrated after that would be invalid.

The Donatist heresy was condemned in the year 313 by a commission appointed by Pope Miltiades. Later St Augustine (354-430), bishop of Hippo in North Africa, taught that the sacraments derive their efficacy not from the holiness of the priest who administers them but from the power of the sacrament itself, in Latin *ex opere operato*, from the work carried out. Even more, the efficacy derives from Christ himself, who works through the sacraments, so that the sacraments are actions of Christ and have their efficacy *ex opere operato Christi*, from the work done by Christ.

St Augustine expressed it graphically: "Peter may baptise, but it is Christ who baptises; Paul may baptise, yet it is Christ who baptises; Judas may baptise, still it is Christ who baptises" (*On St John*, tract 6, no. 7)

Naturally, the disposition of the recipient of the sacrament plays a role in determining the fruitfulness of the sacrament. A person who receives the sacrament with faith, love, sorrow for sin, etc., will receive more grace than someone who receives it without faith or devotion. And someone who receives it in the state of mortal sin, will receive no grace. But as regards the sacrament itself, it always has the power to give grace by virtue of the action of Christ in the sacrament.

In view of this, even if a priest were in the state of mortal sin when he said Mass or administered Baptism or absolved sins in the sacrament of Penance, etc., the sacrament would still be valid. If the priest had an opportunity to go to confession before administering the sacrament but did not avail himself of it, he would be administering the sacrament unlawfully but the sacrament would still be valid. So if a priest has been laicised the sacraments he administered before that will be valid.

How about the sacraments he administers after laicisation? According to the *Code of Canon Law*, a priest who has lost the clerical state, i.e., who has been laicised, is prohibited from exercising the power of holy orders (cf. Can. 292). That is, he is not to celebrate Mass or administer any of the sacraments. Were he to disregard this provision of the law, any Mass he celebrated would be unlawful but, by virtue of the power of order which he received in his priestly ordination and which can never be lost, the Mass would be valid and he would bring about the Real Presence of Our Lord in Holy Communion.

But having lost his priestly faculties, or permission from a bishop to celebrate the sacraments, a laicised priest could not validly absolve sins or celebrate a marriage. The only exception is that any priest, including one who has been laicised, can validly and lawfully absolve any penitents who are in danger of death (cf. Canons 292 and 976).

661 The ordination of women and the Plenary Council

I have been following the correspondence in The Catholic Weekly regarding the ordination of women to the priesthood, including the suggestion that the issue should be discussed in the forthcoming Plenary Council. Is this something the Council might consider?

It is most unlikely that the Plenary Council will consider the possible ordination of women to the priesthood. This is an issue which was resolved once and for all in May 1994 by Pope John Paul II in the Apostolic Letter *Ordinatio sacerdotalis*.

At the beginning of that document Pope John Paul quoted Pope Paul VI's 1975 letter to the Archbishop of Canterbury, summarising the reasons for the Catholic position: "These reasons include: the example recorded in the Sacred Scriptures of Christ choosing his

Apostles only from among men; the constant practice of the Church, which has imitated Christ in choosing only men; and her living teaching authority which has consistently held that the exclusion of women from the priesthood is in accordance with God's plan for his Church."

Because the question had become the subject of debate among theologians, Pope Paul VI directed the Congregation for the Doctrine of the Faith to set forth the teaching of the Catholic Church on the matter. This was done in the Declaration *Inter insigniores*, on 15 October 1976, which the Pope approved and ordered to be published. That Declaration concluded that the Church "does not consider herself authorised to admit women to priestly ordination."

Prior to the publication of *Inter insigniores*, in April of 1976 the Pontifical Biblical Commission released a study of the question from the biblical perspective. It stated, among other things: "The masculine character of the hierarchical order which has structured the Church since its beginning ... seems attested to by scripture in an undeniable way... As a matter of fact, we see in the Acts of the Apostles and the epistles that the first [Christian] communities were always directed by men exercising the apostolic power." Nonetheless, "It does not seem that the New Testament by itself alone will permit us to settle in a clear way and once and for all the problem of the possible accession of women to the presbyterate."

Since in 1994 the matter was still considered by some to be open to discussion, Pope John Paul II wrote *Ordinatio sacerdotalis* to resolve the doubt. He acknowledged that "the presence and the role of women in the life and mission of the Church, although not linked to the ministerial priesthood, remain absolutely necessary and irreplaceable." Nonetheless, "in order that all doubt may be removed regarding a matter of great importance, a matter which pertains to the Church's divine constitution itself, in view of my ministry of confirming the brethren (cf. *Lk* 22:32) I declare that the Church has no authority whatsoever to confer priestly ordination on women and that this judgment is to be definitively held by all the Church's faithful" (n. 4).

The phrase "definitively held" implies that the teaching cannot be changed and it is to be held always and by all. A year later, on 28 October 1995, the Congregation for the Doctrine of the Faith clarified the binding nature of this teaching: "This teaching requires definitive assent, since, founded on the written Word of God, and from the beginning constantly preserved and applied in the Tradition of the Church, it has been set forth infallibly by the ordinary and universal Magisterium (cf. Second Vatican Council, Dogmatic Constitution on the Church *Lumen gentium* 25, 2). Thus, in the present circumstances, the Roman Pontiff, exercising his proper office of confirming the brethren (cf. *Lk* 22:32), has handed on this same teaching by a formal declaration, explicitly stating what is to be held always, everywhere, and by all, as belonging to the deposit of the faith." It is clear from this that the matter is no longer open to discussion.

There are other more important matters that the Plenary Council might discuss. Among some I have heard mentioned are: how to improve the quality of preaching so that it is more relevant to people's daily lives, how to make our parishes more welcoming so that people will be drawn back to them, how to improve the quality of religious education in our schools, how to carry out the mission of evangelisation effectively, etc. I encourage everyone to think about what they consider to be issues affecting the Church in Australia and to submit them to the Council.

Marriage

662 Weddings not celebrated in a church

I recently read the account of Pope Francis marrying a couple on a plane. It made me wonder in what circumstances it would be permissible to conduct a wedding in a place other than a church.

To remind our readers, Pope Francis did indeed celebrate the impromptu wedding of two flight attendants on the papal plane during a flight over Chile from Santiago to Iqique. The couple were seated next to the Pope for a group photo and the Pope asked if they were married. They answered that they were married civilly but their church wedding was cancelled when the 2010 earthquake in Chile destroyed the church where the wedding was to take place. The Pope offered to marry them and they readily agreed. He then conducted the ceremony and blessed their rings. The CEO of the airline acted as the witness and one of the cardinals used some airline paper to draw up a wedding certificate which they all signed.

The Holy Father commented afterwards: "This is the sacrament that is missing in the world, the sacrament of marriage. I hope this motivates couples around the world to marry." It was indeed a unique wedding, not the sort that would be contemplated in canon law, but then the Holy Father is the supreme legislator in the Church, and the one who makes the rules can also dispense from them. Normally before proceeding to marry a couple the celebrant would spend some time with them, making sure they understood and agreed to live by the commitments of Christian marriage, he would check their birth and baptismal certificates, etc.

Does canon law provide for marriages to be celebrated in a place other than a church? It does, in canon 1118 of the *Code of Canon Law*.

The first paragraph of the canon stipulates that a marriage between two Catholics or between a Catholic and a baptised non-Catholic is to be celebrated in the parish church, but by permission of the local Ordinary or the parish priest it may be celebrated in another church or oratory. The second paragraph says: "The local Ordinary can allow a marriage to be celebrated in another suitable place." The third says that a marriage between a Catholic and an unbaptised person "may be celebrated in a church or in another suitable place."

The distinction is thus made between a sacramental marriage between two baptised persons, where the permission of the bishop is required to celebrate it outside a church, and a non-sacramental marriage, when one of the parties is not baptised, where the priest or deacon officiating at the wedding can authorise the celebration outside a church.

The mind of the Church is clearly that a sacramental marriage ought to be celebrated in a sacred place, like a church or oratory, and indeed most Catholic weddings celebrated by a priest or deacon are conducted in such a place. In this way the very setting of the wedding is sacred, reminding the couple and those attending that the couple are committing themselves before God to be faithful to each other, and they are asking God's blessing on their marriage.

In what circumstances might a wedding be celebrated in another place? An obvious answer is the case of a marriage between a Catholic and a baptised non-Catholic, where permission can be given to celebrate the wedding in the church or place of worship of the non-Catholic. It should be remembered that the bishop can also grant a dispensation to allow a mixed marriage to be celebrated by a non-Catholic minister (cf. Can. 1127, §2). This could happen, for example, when the non-Catholic's father was a minister and he wanted to officiate at the wedding.

Other circumstances might be the sickness of one of the parties, which could warrant the wedding taking place in a hospital or a home; the danger of death of one of the parties, where the wedding could be celebrated in any suitable place; the celebration in a home in the country if there was no church in the vicinity or if a family member was housebound, etc.

What would not be acceptable is a wedding celebrated, for example, while sky-diving or under water or at a beach, simply because the couple liked these activities. It would make a mockery of the sacred nature of Christian marriage.

663 Convalidation of a marriage

I understand that when Pope Francis recently celebrated a wedding on the papal plane he was in fact not marrying the couple but convalidating their civil marriage. Could you please explain exactly what this means and in what circumstances it can be done?

The reason Pope Francis conducted the wedding ceremony for the couple, who had been married by a civil celebrant some years before, was that the Church only accepts as valid the marriage of a Catholic when the exchange of consent has been given according to what is called the canonical form; i.e. before a priest or deacon and two witnesses, or when the Catholic bishop has granted permission for the wedding to be celebrated in some other public form (cf. *Code of Canon Law*, Can. 1108, 1127, §1). Nonetheless, if a Catholic marries a non-Catholic of oriental rite before a minister of that rite without permission, the marriage is considered valid in the eyes of the Church (cf. Can. 1127, §2).

There are many Catholics in the situation of the Chilean couple you mention, couples who have been married by a civil celebrant or by a minister of another religion without permission of the Catholic bishop and whose marriage is not recognised as valid by the Church. What can be done to validate their marriage?

There are two possibilities. The first is what the Chilean couple did before Pope Francis: to exchange consent again before a priest or deacon and two witnesses. Strictly speaking, this is not a convalidation but a new celebration of the marriage. It has the effect of making their marriage valid in the eyes of the Church from that moment on and thus, in the broad sense, of convalidating it.

The other possibility is what is called a "retroactive validation". Here the couple do not need to exchange consent again. Presuming that their initial consent remains and that they intend to continue in the marriage, the bishop grants the validation of the marriage with retroactive effects, back to the time of the original marriage. With this, they are considered to have been married validly at the time of the original marriage.

This solution can be used whenever it is requested. One situation in which it is especially useful is when one, or both, parties regard their original marriage as valid and do not wish to go through another wedding ceremony. It can be granted even without the knowledge of one or both parties, but this is not to be done without a grave reason (cf. Can. 1164).

Is there then such a thing as a convalidation which is not a retroactive validation or a new celebration of the marriage? Yes, there is. It is called a simple convalidation and it is used when there was an impediment when the marriage was first celebrated or there was a lack of consent on the part of one or both parties.

For example, if at the time of the marriage one of the parties did not give true consent, when that party later consents as an internal act of the will, the marriage is convalidated from that moment on (cf. Can. 1159, §§1-2). Naturally, the other spouse and those who attended the wedding may not know that this has happened and in the public forum the marriage will be considered valid from the day of the original ceremony.

Another example is the existence of an impediment which was not dispensed by the authority at the time of the original wedding. For example, if by an oversight one party was under age (16 for men and 14 for women), when that party reaches the required age and their consent persists, the convalidation of the marriage takes place automatically.

If the impediment is public (like prohibited degrees of consanguinity, marriage to a non-baptised person, public vows of chastity or holy orders) the dispensation must be granted and the couple must exchange consent in a new celebration of the marriage (cf. Can. 1158, §1). Here again, it is not a matter of a convalidation but rather of a new celebration of the marriage.

Those who are aware of couples in these situations should do all they can to help them validate their marriage and so be able to receive the sacraments.

664 The internal forum solution

I remember reading some time ago that if a couple who have been divorced and remarried outside the Church sincerely believe that their first marriage was invalid, even though it was not declared null by a Church tribunal, they may receive Communion. Is this true?

Your question makes reference to what has come to be called the internal forum solution. To clarify concepts, the external forum is the forum of public acts observable by others. In this forum, for example, a couple are married in the Church before a priest or deacon and two witnesses and they are deemed to be validly married until such time as one of the spouses dies or the marriage is declared null by a Church tribunal.

The internal forum is the forum of a person's conscience before God and the Church. For example, it is the forum of the sacrament of penance. The acts here are not publicly known by others. In this forum a person may be convinced in conscience that their previous marriage was null for some reason, even though it was not declared null by a Church tribunal, either because the case was never taken to a tribunal or because the tribunal found that the marriage was valid.

Can people in this situation who are now in a new relationship with another person, either "married" civilly or in a de facto relationship, receive Communion?

There are a number of considerations to be borne in mind. The first and most important one is that since their irregular marriage situation is publicly known by at least some people in the parish, it would give scandal if they were to receive Communion. That is, since they are married only civilly, not in the Church, or they are in a de facto relationship, they are in the same situation as anyone else who is married civilly or in a de facto relationship and everyone knows they are considered to be "living in sin" and should not receive Communion.

The fact that they consider in conscience that their first marriage was null is not sufficient reason to receive Communion. Their first marriage was celebrated in the public forum and its nullity or validity should also be declared in that forum. Only in this way can pastors and other parishioners have security about their situation.

But can't they make a personal judgment about the nullity of their first marriage? Since time immemorial it is a premise of the judicial system of both Church and state that no one is a good judge in their own case. Cases are always referred to third persons to be judged since these persons are considered to be impartial. For this reason we have tribunals.

But couldn't the couple come to a judgment about the validity of their first marriage with the help of their pastor? Their pastor is usually not an expert in the canon law of marriage and he has not heard the evidence of the other party to the marriage and so cannot make a valid judgment. What is more, he too may be biased in favour of the couple. If he is an expert in canon law he will be the first one to say that the case needs to be judged by a Church tribunal.

To facilitate this judgment, in 2015 Pope Francis streamlined the judicial system for marriage cases to make it more accessible and to speed up the process. No longer is there required a second judgment by an appeals tribunal to confirm the judgment of the first tribunal, so that the whole process should ordinarily take no longer than a year. In addition, there is now a shorter process, to be judged by the bishop himself, when there are obvious grounds for nullity. This process may take as little as a few months.

So if a person is convinced in conscience that their first marriage was null they should take the case to a tribunal and have it judged by the Church. If they have already done so and the tribunal found the marriage to be valid, they have no choice but to accept that judgment.

So no, we cannot allow a couple to make a personal judgment about the nullity of their marriage. Marriage is a public state and we need security in the external forum about who is married and who is not. For this reason we have tribunals. If the tribunal finds that a person's first marriage was valid, the couple can sometimes be helped to live "as brother and sister", i.e., to abstain from sexual relations. In this case they could be admitted to Communion, preferably in a church where their marital status is not known, so as to avoid scandal. Or, if they have no children in their care, they could simply separate and thus be able to receive Communion.

665 Is divorce on the decline?

I read recently that divorce is on the decline in Australia. Could this possibly be true? And what can we do to help marriages stay together?

I too read an article which said that divorce is on the decline in Australia, quoting the Australian Bureau of Statistics. But we have to understand exactly what the article was saying. The figure quoted was what is known as the crude divorce rate, or the number of people out of every 1000 in the population who became divorced in a given year. On that basis, the rate declined from 2.0 divorces per 1000 estimated population in 2015 to 1.9 per 1000 in 2016.

But we have to take into account that a big factor leading to a decrease in the crude divorce rate is simply the fact that fewer people are marrying now than used to be the case. If they are not marrying but rather living together in a de facto relationship or simply remaining single, they cannot be divorced. That is, the crude marriage rate has also declined greatly over the years. In 1996 it was 5.8 per thousand and in 2016 4.9, a fall of some 16 per cent in only ten years. In that same period the crude divorce rate declined from 2.9 to 1.9, a fall of 34 per cent.

Another way to judge the divorce rate is to compare the number of divorces granted in any one year with the number of marriages celebrated in that year. In 1996 there were 49 divorces for every 100 marriages and in 2016 the number was down to 39, so on that basis the divorce rate does indeed appear to be declining.

Another positive factor is that the median length of marriage from the wedding to the time of the divorce has increased slightly over the last ten years, from 11.0 years to 12.0 years.

At the same time, God is getting increasingly pushed out of marriage, measured by the percentage of marriages celebrated by a minister of religion. In 1996 53.2 per cent of marriages were celebrated by a minister of religion and in 2016 the figure was down to only 23.6 per cent and falling.

Over the same period the percentage of couples living together before marriage has increased, from 76.1 per cent in 1996 to 80.8 per cent in 2016.

So even though the moral and spiritual life of Australian couples is declining markedly, the divorce rate is still falling and that is something for which to give thanks to God. But any divorce brings with it all the havoc and harmful effects on the children as well as on the spouses with which we are all too familiar.

What can be done to help spouses stay together?

Suitable marriage preparation is the first means to help couples, so that they understand what marriage and love are all about and they are prepared to give themselves truly to one another in a lifelong commitment. They should understand that true love involves not only the emotions and romance, but also sacrifice for each other. A happy and long-lasting marriage cannot be founded on feelings alone. The couple should seek out a good marriage preparation course and they should get advice on marriage from couples whose marriages have been successful.

The most influential preparation for marriage, as we all know, begins when a child is born and grows up witnessing the marriage of his or her parents, for better or for worse. The couple cannot change what they saw in their parents' marriage but they can at least prepare well to make their own marriage successful so that their children are better prepared to enter into marriage many years later.

Another important factor is to make sure God has an important role in their lives. The more a couple pray together, attend Mass and receive the sacraments, the stronger their marriage will be. It will be founded on rock and the spouses will receive the grace of God on a continuing basis to nourish their spiritual lives and their relationship with each other.

And couples should always remember that the most important relationship in the family is that between the husband and the wife. After all, they came first, before the children, and they should nourish their own relationship by showing love for each other even when they don't feel like it, spending time talking together, and going out together on a regular basis.

666 A right to same-sex marriage?

In discussing the forthcoming plebiscite on same-sex marriage I have a friend who argues that people with same-sex attraction should have the same right to marry as the rest of us. How do I answer her?

The "marriage equality" slogan of those in favour of same-sex marriage expresses the gist of your question. We agree that people with same-sex attraction should be equal before the law in all matters in which sexual orientation is irrelevant to the law in question. Thus they should have equal access to food, accommodation, health care, education, employment, etc.

But marriage is not something in which two people of the same sex are equal to the rest of the population. Marriage, by nature and as defined in the Australian Marriage Act 1961, is "the union of a man and a woman to the exclusion of all others, voluntarily entered into for life." By nature, as intended by God when he created us male and female and gave us the power to cooperate with him in bringing new human beings into existence through a sexual act, marriage is only for a man and a woman since it has a natural orientation to the children who will come into being through their love. This is the way marriage has always been understood and lived all over the world.

The union of two men or two women is radically different. It cannot by itself bring forth children. It is naturally sterile. And if a same-sex couple have a child by adoption, artificial insemination or in-vitro fertilisation, the child will grow up without the complementary nurturing roles of both a father and a mother, which by nature provide the best outcome for the child.

The truth of marriage as the union of a man and a woman is enshrined in such important documents as the International Covenant on Civil and Political Rights (ICCPR), which states in Article 23: "(1) The family is the natural and fundamental group unit of society and is entitled to protection by society and the State. (2) The right of men and women of marriageable age to marry and to found a family shall be recognised." As is clear, the right to marry is related to founding a family and is therefore a right only of men and women, not of two people of the same sex.

This was confirmed by the UN Human Rights Committee when it was asked to offer an opinion as to whether in light of the ICCPR same-sex couples too had a right to marry. It answered: "Article 23, paragraph 2, of the Covenant is the only substantive provision in the Covenant which defines a right by using the term 'men and women', rather than 'every human being', 'everyone' and 'all persons'. Use of the term 'men and women', rather than the general terms used elsewhere in Part III of the Covenant, has been consistently and uniformly understood as indicating that the treaty obligation of States parties stemming from article 23, paragraph 2, of the Covenant is to recognise as marriage only the union between a man and a woman wishing to marry each other" (Joslin v New Zealand, 17 July 2002).

If the upcoming plebiscite results in a majority in favour of same-sex marriage and Australia goes down the road of legalising same-sex marriage it will give legal recognition – and therefore moral acceptability in the eyes of many – to a way of life that is not in keeping with nature and does significant harm to the proper upbringing of children.

Professor Augusto Zimmerman, in an article in *Quadrant* magazine (18 August 2017), reports on numerous published studies which show, among other things, that the average same-sex relationship lasts only two to three years; that the level of verbal, physical and sexual abuse in lesbian relationships is significantly higher than in heterosexual relationships; that the children of same-sex couples are much more likely to develop homosexual behaviour themselves; and that children of same-sex couples are far more likely to be sexually abused by their "parents" than children of heterosexual couples. Do we really want to go down this road?

In view of this, the American College of Pediatricians in July 2017 declared: "Given the current body of research, the American College of Pediatricians believes it is inappropriate, potentially hazardous to children, and dangerously irresponsible to change the age-old prohibition on homosexual parenting, whether by adoption, foster care, or by reproductive manipulation."

667 Same-sex marriage: why not?

Now that the plebiscite on same-sex marriage is upon us, can you summarise the principal arguments in favour of traditional marriage, so I have them clear in my mind?

This plebiscite is to give the people of Australia their say on one of the most important issues any society can face: the very nature of marriage and with it the family. Marriage and the family are the backbone of any society. As the family goes, so goes the nation. If marriage is strong and the parents are united, the children grow up learning how to love and to be loved, they learn social virtues like kindness, generosity, forgiveness, and honesty, and they bring these into the broader community. Society is all the healthier when the family is healthy. But if marriage and the family are undermined, the whole of society suffers. So the plebiscite is vitally important.

What are the key issues? Let us consider six.

First, and very important, we are not against people with same-sex attraction. They are human beings like everyone else, they were redeemed by Jesus Christ and they have a place awaiting them in heaven if, like everyone else, they live and die well. We must always love and respect them. They are often our own children, brothers and sisters, friends, work colleagues...

Second, marriage is by nature the union of a man and a woman to bring children into the world. We cannot change that. That is just the way it is and it is why all countries have laws protecting marriage. The union of two people of the same sex cannot of itself bring forth children. It is simply not marriage. There can be no "marriage equality" between the union of a man and a woman and that of two men or two women. One is marriage; the other is not.

Third, a No vote is not discrimination against people with same-sex attraction. Parents can't marry their children, brothers can't marry their sisters, and two people of the same sex can't marry each other. They might love each other but this relationship is not marriage. This is not discrimination but rather the acceptance of the reality of human nature.

Fourth, the well-being of children is at stake. Numerous studies have shown that, overall, children raised in same-sex households fare worse on practically all scales compared with children raised by a father and a mother. To set out deliberately to deprive a child of the complementary nurturing role of a father and a mother is harmful to the child, no matter how much the child may be loved. It is true that many children of heterosexual couples end up being raised by only one of their parents when the other parent dies or leaves, but we know how much these children suffer as a result and we shouldn't set out to make this the norm. Moreover, the average length of same-sex relationships is two or three years. How can this be good for the children?

Fifth, other values will inevitably be sacrificed if same-sex marriage is legalised. We saw this recently when a television commercial for Father's Day featuring a father singing a lullaby to his child was dropped because it was considered too political. Where are we going? How soon will we not celebrate Father's Day or Mother's Day at all? And when a baby is born it will no longer have a father and a mother named on the birth certificate but rather Parent 1 and Parent 2 as in some countries overseas. These events are the "collateral damage" that naturally follow the legitimation of same-sex marriage. Not to mention the mandating of the Safe Schools program to show children that same-sex relationships are perfectly healthy and normal.

Sixth, as has been seen in numerous cases overseas and even in this country, religious freedom, freedom of speech to defend traditional marriage and the right of people to refuse on conscientious grounds to cooperate in a same-sex wedding have been called into question and even penalised. A brave new world of discrimination against those who uphold traditional values is just around the corner.

So the plebiscite is important for the future of this country – very important. What is at stake is the very well-being of society. We shouldn't change the law for the sake of a tiny minority of people. In Canada, after ten years of legalised same-sex marriage, only 0.24 per cent of all registered couples were same-sex married couples. The consequences for marriage, the family, children and society are too great. To vote No is to vote Yes for marriage and society.

668 Children in same-sex relationships

I was talking recently with a friend about the welfare of children in same-sex relationships and she said she would prefer to see a child raised by a loving same-sex couple than by a heterosexual couple in which there was domestic violence. How do I answer her?

If those are the only alternatives perhaps it would be better to be raised by a loving couple than by one where there was domestic violence. But when a country passes laws on the matter it is legislating not for individual cases but for a whole population. And in a whole population many surveys have shown that children fare much better when raised by a heterosexual couple than by a same-sex one. Professor Augusto Zimmerman wrote an article on the question in the August 2017 issue of *Quadrant* I will take most of what follows from that article, looking at five aspects.

First, same-sex relationships are far more likely to involve sexual infidelity than heterosexual ones. An important U.S. study of 156 long-term same-sex couples found that the majority were unable to be faithful for more than a year, and not a single couple was capable of being faithful for more than five years. We all know how children's sense of security suffers when one or both parents are unfaithful.

Second, same-sex relationships are notoriously short lived. A study published in 2010 showed that the average same-sex relationship lasted only two to three years. How can it be good for children when their "parents" are constantly breaking up?

Third, and perhaps surprisingly, domestic violence is more frequent among same-sex couples than among heterosexual ones. A 1991 study of 1099 American lesbians showed that they were more physically abused by their female partners than women in heterosexual relationships. Another survey of 350 lesbians who had previously been in relationships with men showed that the rates of verbal, physical and sexual abuse were significantly higher in their same-sex relationship: 57 per cent had been sexually victimised by a female, 45 per cent had experienced physical aggression, and 65 per cent had experienced physical/emotional aggression.

A comprehensive literature review published in 2014 revealed that domestic violence affected some 75 per cent of all lesbian, gay and bisexual couples, and another review published in 2015 showed that domestic violence was far more likely to occur among same-sex couples than among heterosexual ones. Again, the effect on the children can only be disastrous.

Fourth, children of same-sex couples are more likely to be sexually abused by their "parents". To cite just one example published in 1996, although heterosexual men outnumber homosexuals by thirty-six to one, heterosexual child molestation cases outnumber homosexual cases by only eleven to one, meaning that paedophilia is more than three times more common among homosexuals.

What is worse, a 1990 issue of the *Journal of Homosexuality* had an article portraying sexual relationships between men and small boys as "loving relationships", thus considering paedophilia something normal and good. Yet we all know the lifelong damage that paedophilia can cause to the child.

Fifth, children of same-sex couples are far more likely to be same-sex attracted themselves. One study showed that whereas only about three per cent of people in the U.S. are same-sex attracted, 75 per cent of adult men and 57 per cent of adult women raised by homosexual couples developed bisexual or homosexual behaviour. This in turn has other negative consequences. A 2001 study of some six thousand people in the Netherlands, a country known for its tolerance of homosexuality, found that homosexual youths were four times more likely to suffer major depression, three times as likely to suffer anxiety disorder, four times as likely to commit suicide, five times as likely to have nicotine dependence, six times as likely to suffer multiple disorders, and six times as likely to have at least once attempted suicide.

No wonder the American College of Pediatricians issued a policy statement in July 2017 declaring that "it is inappropriate, potentially hazardous to children, and dangerously irresponsible to change the age-old prohibition on homosexual parenting, whether by adoption, foster care, or by reproductive manipulation."

669 Blessings for gay couples

I read that a German Cardinal has raised the possibility of blessing gay couples. Is this something priests are likely to be doing in the future?

First, we should look at what the Cardinal in question, Cardinal Reinhard Marx of Munich and Freising and President of the German Bishops Conference, actually said. Since his remarks were misrepresented in the media, the German Bishops Conference issued a statement clarifying that when the Cardinal was asked in a radio interview on 3 February 2018 if he "can imagine that there might be a way to bless homosexual couples in the Catholic Church?" he responded: "There are no general solutions and I think that would not be right, because we are talking about pastoral care for individual cases, and that applies to other areas as well, which we cannot regulate, where we have no sets of rules."

In other words, he was not endorsing the idea of such blessings, saying rather that general solutions or rules would not be right since each couple is different and pastoral care has to be tailored to individual cases. He went on to say that in ministering to people who are homosexual, "We must be pastorally close to those who are in need of pastoral care and also want it. And one must also encourage priests and pastoral workers to give people encouragement in concrete situations. I do not really see any problems there. An entirely different question is how this is to be done publicly and liturgically. These are things you have to be careful about, and reflect on them in a good way."

It seems clear from this that the Cardinal was not endorsing the idea of liturgical blessing ceremonies for homosexual couples. German Catholic media interpreted the Cardinal's remarks as moving a step back from a suggestion made by Bishop Franz-Josef Bode of Osnabrück in January that the Catholic Church should debate the possibility of a blessing ceremony for Catholic gay couples involved in the Church.

In any case, the publicity given to Cardinal Marx's comments led other bishops to say that priests cannot conduct ceremonies for the blessing of gay couples. Archbishop Charles Chaput of Philadelphia, for example, wrote a letter to his priests and deacons on February 7 saying: "I want to remind us all that under no circumstances may a priest or deacon of the archdiocese take part in, witness or officiate at any civil union of same-sex persons, or any religious ceremony that seeks to bless such an event. This in no way is a rejection of the persons seeking such a union, but rather a refusal to ignore what we know to be true about the nature of marriage, the family, and the dignity of human sexuality."

In a February 6 column in his archdiocesan newspaper he offered two principles to guide the Church's response to this issue. "First, we need to treat all people with the respect and pastoral concern they deserve as children of God with inherent dignity." He added that this "emphatically includes persons with same-sex attraction."

"Second, there is no truth, no real mercy, and no authentic compassion in blessing a course of action that leads persons away from God." On his blog he wrote that "any such 'blessing rite' would cooperate in a morally forbidden act, no matter how sincere the persons seeking the blessing. Such a rite would undermine the Catholic witness on the nature of marriage and the family. It would confuse and mislead the faithful. And it would wound the unity of our Church, because it could not be ignored or met with silence."

In summary, while we can always bless an individual, no matter what their religious belief or way of life, in effect asking God to help them live in keeping with his law and to reach eternal happiness with him in heaven, we cannot give a liturgical blessing to a homosexual couple as such, since that would imply blessing a lifestyle that is inherently sinful. In the words of the *Catechism of the Catholic Church*: "Basing itself on Sacred Scripture, which presents homosexual acts as acts of grave depravity, tradition has always declared that 'homosexual acts are intrinsically disordered'" (*CCC* 2357; CDF, *Persona humana* 8).

So no, the Church will not have a liturgical blessing ceremony for gay couples.

III. MORAL LIFE IN CHRIST

General Moral Issues

670 Can freedom be diminished?

My son stopped practising the faith several years ago and now lives in sin with his girlfriend. He says he can't pray anymore and doesn't want to attend Mass. Sometimes I think he has practically lost his freedom to relate to God. Is this possible?

To answer your question we should first clarify what we mean by freedom. The *Catechism of the Catholic Church* defines it as "the power, rooted in reason and will, to act or not to act, to do this or that, and so to perform deliberate actions on one's own responsibility" (*CCC* 1731). Human beings have reason, or intellect, and free will, and so we can choose among different courses of action. Animals cannot do this. They do not have a rational intellect nor are they therefore free, and so they cannot make free choices. They can only follow their instincts.

In human beings we can distinguish between the ontological or fundamental freedom which all human beings have for the fact of being human, and the existential or actual freedom which each human being has in a given set of circumstances. As regards the first, for having an intellect and free will and being able to choose freely what to do, all human beings are fundamentally free. They cannot lose this freedom. But depending on how they use their freedom they can progressively increase or decrease their actual degree of freedom. In this sense it is correct to say that some people are more free than others.

To understand this, we must clarify the purpose of freedom. Why did God make us free? To do whatever we want, whether it be good for us or not? No, he gave us a share in his own freedom so that we could freely choose to serve him, to do what is right and good, and so to develop our humanity more fully and finally be with God forever in heaven.

The Second Vatican Council expresses it like this: "God willed that man should be left in the hand of own counsel, so that he might of his own accord seek his Creator and freely attain his full and blessed perfection by cleaving to him" (*GS* 17; *CCC* 1730). So we are free for a purpose: to seek God and thereby attain our human perfection and happiness, both here and hereafter. In this sense we speak of "freedom for" seeking God and fulfilling this noble purpose. It is not "freedom from" God and his law.

But depending on which choices we make we can gradually increase our freedom to seek God and fulfil his will, or decrease it. By praying, receiving the sacraments regularly, striving to follow our conscience, doing what we know to be right and avoiding what we know to be wrong, we grow in the virtues and thereby find it easier to serve God. We become progressively more free to do so.

Alternatively, we can stop praying and receiving the sacraments, ignore what our conscience is telling us, do whatever we feel like, and gradually drift away from God into a life of sin. This seems to be the case of your son. Then instead of growing in the virtues we grow in the vices and we find it harder to do what is right. We diminish our freedom. Naturally, God continues to give us the grace to pray and receive the sacraments, but we find it harder to respond to this grace.

St Gregory of Nyssa expresses it graphically: "We are ourselves in a certain sense fathers of ourselves when by our good intention and our own free choice we conceive and give birth to ourselves and bring ourselves to the light. This we do as a result of receiving God into ourselves, when we have been made children of God, children of the Power, children of the Most High. On the other hand we also turn ourselves into an abortion and make ourselves imperfect and sickly when there has not been produced in us, in the Apostle's words, 'the form of Christ'. For the man of God must be whole and perfect" (*Hom. on Ecclesiastes,* Hom. 6).

The Catechism sums it up: "The more one does what is good, the freer one becomes. There is no true freedom except in the service of what is good and just. The choice to disobey and do evil is an abuse of freedom and leads to the 'slavery of sin'" (*CCC* 1733; cf. *Rom* 6:17).

St Peter says something similar. Speaking of people who are steeped in sin and who invite others to follow them, he writes: "For, uttering loud boasts of folly, they entice with licentious passions of the flesh men who have barely escaped from those who live in error. They promise them freedom, but they themselves are slaves of corruption; for whatever overcomes a man, to that he is enslaved" (*2 Pet* 2:18-19).

How important it is to use our freedom wisely!

671 Freedom and responsibility

Often when I read something about freedom, there is mention at the same time about responsibility. What does responsibility have to do with freedom?

As you say, freedom and responsibility are often written or spoken about together. The reason is simple. With every free act there are consequences and the person doing the act is held responsible for them.

Among God's creatures only humans and angels are free. We have an intellect or mind and a free will and we can weigh up the consequences of our possible choices and then decide what to do. Animals cannot do this. They cannot think or make free choices. They simply follow their instincts and so they are not held responsible for their actions. If a kangaroo jumps out in front of a car and is hit, damaging the car, it cannot be blamed. That is what kangaroos do. And if a puppy poos on the carpet it cannot be blamed either. That is what puppies do.

But humans are different. Once we acquire the use of reason, which we are deemed to have at the age of seven, we have a sense of right and wrong, of what is appropriate behaviour and what is not, and we are therefore responsible for what we do. By responsible we mean answerable; we must answer, respond to others for our choices. We are responsible to them.

Responsible to whom? First, to God, our maker and father. We know that when we do what is right and good, God will reward us. He told us so in many places of the Scriptures, among them in the description of the Last Judgment, when those who gave food, drink, clothing and shelter to others were welcomed into eternal life (cf. *Mt* 25:34-46). Similarly, if we do what is wrong, God will punish us. In the same passage, those who failed to do these good deeds went to eternal punishment (cf. *Mt* 25:46).

But we must also answer to others for our actions, depending on who is affected by them. Children must answer to their parents and teachers, spouses must answer to each other, employees must answer to their employers, and we must all answer to society. When people do meritorious deeds they are often rewarded by those affected by them, and when they do what is wrong they are often punished. This bears witness to the fact that we acknowledge human freedom and we hold people accountable, responsible, for their actions. All countries have a set of laws and a court system and they punish those found guilty of violating those laws.

There are circumstances though in which people's responsibility can be diminished. An obvious case is those who suffer from an intellectual disability such that they have never reached the use of reason. They cannot make proper choices and so they are not held responsible for their actions. Similarly a person suffering from a mental condition like depression, paranoia or schizophrenia will have their freedom diminished to varying degrees and hence have diminished responsibility. One could add here the diminished responsibility of a person who is exceedingly tired or under great stress. And of course we are not responsible for what we do while asleep.

In the same way, someone under the influence of alcohol or drugs will have diminished responsibility for their actions in that state, although they are usually responsible for putting themselves in that situation in the first place.

Another circumstance which can diminish one's responsibility is the influence of the various passions or emotions. It is obvious that a person moved by fear of some threat or by anger caused by a hurt will have diminished responsibility for whatever they do as a result.

Ignorance of the moral law or of a fact is another circumstance that diminishes responsibility. If a person did not know that something was sinful, God will not hold him responsible for doing it. Or if he knew that taking a strong recreational drug was wrong but did not know that the particular substance someone gave him was that drug, he would be ignorant of that fact and hence not responsible for what happened when he took it.

Finally, an entrenched habit like using offensive language, alcohol abuse, gambling or seeking sexual pleasure reduces one's responsibility when he is trying to overcome the habit.

We thank God for making us free, but we must also struggle to use our freedom wisely.

672 The emotions and responsibility

My husband is prone to frequent strong bouts of anger towards me and our children. This hurts all of us greatly. In trying to understand this, I am wondering if his anger actually makes him less responsible before God rather than more responsible.

This is a good question and it fits into the broader one of how the emotions affect the morality of our acts. The emotions or passions, of which anger is one as are fear and love, are the response of our nature to certain events, people or things. The *Catechism of the Catholic Church* defines the passions as "emotions or movements of the sensitive appetite that incline us to act or not to act in regard to something felt or imagined to be good or evil" (*CCC* 1763). They are our response to some external stimulus and are, in this sense, something that happens to us rather than something we do. For example, in response to a danger we experience fear and in response to a present good we experience joy. We cannot help having these feelings; they are simply the way we respond in these circumstances.

When the Catechism speaks of the sensitive appetite it is referring to the level of the senses and their impact on the person. The sensitive appetite is distinguished from the intellect and the will, the higher powers of the human person. We have the sensitive appetite in common with higher animals, which also experience fear, anger, desire, contentment, etc.

The Catechism summarises nine basic passions: "The most fundamental passion is *love*, aroused by the attraction of the good. Love causes a *desire* for the absent good and the *hope* of obtaining it; this movement finds completion in the pleasure and *joy* of the good possessed. The apprehension of evil causes *hatred, aversion,* and *fear* of the impending evil; this movement ends in *sadness* at some present evil, or in the *anger* that resists it" (*CCC* 1765).

How do the passions influence our acts? Given that they are simply feelings, not acts of the will, they are neither sinful nor meritorious in themselves. Just as it is not sinful to feel hungry or cold, it is not sinful to feel angry or sad. Only when we freely choose to do something or not to do it can the passions influence the morality of our acts.

In the case of your husband, he feels angry when something upsets him and then he expresses his anger by words, looks or gestures. It should be understood that there is a justified expression of anger which parents or teachers sometimes need to show, but it should be moderate and in keeping with the circumstances (cf. J. Flader, *Question Time 2*, q. 224). This expression of anger is not sinful. But when the display of anger goes beyond the bounds of what is appropriate in the circumstances, it is sinful. This seems to be the case with your husband.

The anger influences our will by inclining us to react in a stronger manner than would be the case without the anger, thereby restricting our use of reason and freedom. There can be a situation in which the feeling of anger is so strong that it practically takes away the use of reason altogether. Then we act impulsively and abusively and we are not really in control. It is clear that when this happens our freedom to act appropriately has been severely hindered and so the guilt of the sin before God is greatly reduced.

This is not to excuse the anger. If a person has a persistent problem with immoderate or unduly frequent displays of anger he should get help with anger management. Even though any one outburst can have reduced culpability due to the emotion of anger, the person is still responsible before God and the family for getting the necessary psychological help. Likewise, if a person realises he is becoming angry and could easily react in an intemperate way, he should leave the scene and calm down, praying for patience and peace.

There is a situation too in which strong emotions like anger can actually increase the wilfulness and merit of our actions. This is the case when a person inwardly feels angry towards another but represses the feeling and acts with patience and kindness. Here the very fact of the anger makes the kindness more meritorious. It is obvious that to show kindness when one is feeling angry has more merit than showing kindness when one feels kindly toward the other.

In summary, your husband's anger makes him less, not more, responsible before God.

673 The principle of double effect

I recently heard someone speak of the principle of double effect as a way of resolving moral dilemmas and I had never heard of it before. Can you explain what it is?

As you say, the principle of double effect is a way of resolving moral dilemmas and it can be very useful. The reason it is called double effect is that it refers to a situation in which a proposed course of action has both a good effect and a bad one, leaving the person in a dilemma as to whether to do the act. Most moral dilemmas involve good effects along with bad ones and so the principle is very helpful in resolving them.

A classical example often given in the textbooks is that of a woman who is pregnant and then is diagnosed with cancer of the uterus. She is told that the cancer is aggressive and her uterus must be removed soon or she will die. She cannot wait for the operation until the baby is viable. The good effect is that the operation will save her life and the bad effect is that the baby will die. Can she go ahead with the operation?

According to the principle of double effect three conditions must all be met if the proposed course of action is morally justified:

1. *The act to be done must be morally good or at least indifferent.* That is, it must not be intrinsically evil, like murder, adultery, stealing, etc. Here the act is the removal of a diseased organ, a cancerous womb, which is morally good. If the woman were not pregnant there would be no question about proceeding with the operation.

2. *The intention must be good.* Here the intention is to save the woman's life by removing her cancerous uterus, a good intention. It would be different if she was happy about the operation because it will end the life of her child and also render her unable to have more children, something she was contemplating doing but now the cancer has made it easy for her. This would be a bad intention. But if she laments the fact that her baby will die and she will not be able to have any more children, she clearly has a good intention.

3. *There must be a proportionate reason to proceed with the act.* That is, there must be an adequate proportion between the good effect and the bad effect. Here the good effect is saving the life of the mother, which is proportionate to the death of her child, and so she can go ahead with the operation. If she did not have the operation both she and the child would die. Note that this is not a direct abortion. It is the removal of a cancerous womb, which indirectly brings about the death of the inviable foetus. It is what is known as an indirect abortion.

Another case is one I heard many years ago. A woman was four and a half months pregnant and had been suffering from severe vomiting, known as *hyperemesis gravidarum*, so that she was unable to hold down any food and was dying. It was clear that her body could not cope with the pregnancy and the only way to save her life was to remove the inviable foetus.

If we apply the three conditions of the principle of double effect, it is clear that although the second and third conditions are met, the first is not. Here the act to be done is a direct abortion, which is intrinsically evil. The woman in question was a Catholic nurse and she understood well the implications of having or not having the abortion. She chose not to have it and in fact she died along with her baby. As she expressed it, she did not want to kill her baby to save her own life.

Another possible solution to this case, had it happened today, would be to wait for a few more weeks, when the foetus would have some slight chance of survival and then induce delivery. If the baby did not survive it would at least have been given a chance. These are very difficult moral choices and one does not envy the people who have to make them. What is always clear, however, is that one can never do evil that good may come from it.

In short, the principle of double effect can be very useful in solving moral dilemmas in which one is faced with a choice that involves a good effect and a bad one. It is good to remember the three conditions and to seek advice if one is still in doubt.

674 Mortal sin and salvation

Our priest recently said that everyone is saved, even those who commit mortal sin. When I asked him later he said mortal sin is very rare because it needs three conditions for gravity. Yet Our Lady of Fatima showed the children a vision of hell and told them sinners do go there. Can you please clarify this matter?

As your priest said, in order for someone to commit a mortal sin they must fulfil three conditions, of which the Catechism says: "For a sin to be mortal, three conditions must together be met: 'Mortal sin is sin whose object is grave matter and which is also committed with full knowledge and deliberate consent'" (*CCC* 1857; *RP* 17 §2).

As regards what constitutes grave matter, we find it whenever the Catechism speaks of grave, serious or mortal sin. To mention just a few examples, sins such as sacrilege against the Eucharist (cf. *CCC* 2120), perjury (*CCC* 2152), deliberate failure to attend Mass on a Sunday (*CCC* 2181), abortion (*CCC* 2271), euthanasia (*CCC* 2277), masturbation (*CCC* 2352), fornication, i.e. sexual acts between two unmarried persons (*CCC* 2353), prostitution (*CCC* 2355) and adultery (*CCC* 2380) are sins whose matter is grave.

As for the condition of full knowledge, the Catechism says that mortal sin "presupposes knowledge of the sinful character of the act, of its opposition to God's law" (*CCC* 1859). It is generally taught that for a person to be guilty of a mortal sin he or she must know not only that the act is sinful but that it is mortally sinful.

The third condition is deliberate consent, of which the Catechism says that it "implies a consent sufficiently deliberate to be a personal choice" (*CCC* 1859). Normally a person has sufficient consent when committing a sin, although circumstances such as fear, anger, etc. can diminish this consent somewhat, at times even to the point where the act may not be a mortal sin.

Given the partial list of mortal sins mentioned above and an explanation of the three conditions necessary for a given act to be in fact a mortal sin, I would consider it naïve in the extreme to think that mortal sin is very rare. It probably abounds more at the present time than at any other period in recent history.

But the fact that someone has committed a mortal sin does not necessarily mean that he or she will go to hell. Here the Catechism is very clear and compassionate: "To die in mortal sin without repenting and accepting God's merciful love means remaining separated from him for ever by our own free choice. This state of definitive self-exclusion from communion with God and the blessed is called 'hell'" (*CCC* 1033).

In other words, as long as the person truly repents and is determined to try to avoid committing the sin in the future, including avoiding the occasions of that sin, he or she will not go to hell. God's merciful love will always be extended to the sinner, even at the last moment of their life. After all, Our Lord "desires all men to be saved and to come to the knowledge of the truth" (*1 Tim* 2:4).

If God is so merciful, does this mean that there is no one in hell? Again, it would be very naïve to think that. As the Catechism says of mortal sin, "If it is not redeemed by repentance and God's forgiveness, it causes exclusion from Christ's kingdom and the eternal death of hell, for our freedom has the power to make choices for ever, with no turning back" (*CCC* 1861). Many people live in defiance of God, saying he doesn't exist, and are full of pride and steeped in serious sin, so that it is very likely that some of them will not repent of their sins and they will go to hell.

What is more, as you say in your letter, Our Lady at Fatima showed the three children a vision of hell in which they saw many souls suffering there, and she invited them to say the prayer we now say after each mystery of the Rosary, which includes the words "save us from the fires of hell". Our loving Mother would not have invited us to say that prayer if she knew no one was going to hell.

And many other people, including Sr Josefa Menendez (cf. J. Flader, *Question Time 4,* qq. 487-488) and in more recent times Gloria Polo (cf. *Question Time 4,* q. 483) have seen hell.

675 The indirect voluntary

I recently read about a man high on alcohol who drove his car into a man working beside the road and seriously injured him. I was discussing it with my friends and some argued the courts should be lenient with him because he was under the influence of alcohol and others said they should be especially tough. Does the Church have a view on this?

The case you give is an example of what is known in moral theology as the indirect voluntary or voluntary in cause. We know, as the *Catechism of the Catholic Church* teaches, that "Freedom makes man *responsible* for his acts to the extent that they are voluntary" (*CCC* 1734). By voluntary we mean that the act was freely chosen. Therefore, going on with the Catechism, "Every act directly willed is imputable to its author" (*CCC* 1736). By imputable we mean that the person is held responsible for the act, whether it is a good act which merits a reward or a sinful act which deserves punishment. As long as the act is freely chosen, the person is responsible for it.

But what happens when, as in the case you give, someone freely chooses to do something which ends up having a very harmful consequence which he didn't set out to bring about, even though he might have foreseen that it could arise from his action? This is what is known as an effect which is indirectly voluntary or voluntary in cause. That is, the man freely chose to drive his car under the influence of alcohol, knowing that he might have an accident or even injure or kill someone. He did not directly will the accident and the injury but he could at least have foreseen the possibility.

The injury to the worker was not directly willed or directly voluntary but it was indirectly voluntary, since it resulted from something that was directly voluntary: driving his car under the influence of alcohol. Or, using the other term, it was voluntary in cause, inasmuch as the driver willed the cause of the injury, driving under the influence. In the words of the Catechism, "An action can be indirectly voluntary when it results from negligence regarding something one should have known or done: for example, an accident arising from ignorance of traffic laws" (*CCC* 1736).

The Catechism sums up the responsibility of the driver in this case, saying: "For a bad effect to be imputable it must be foreseeable and the agent must have the possibility of avoiding it, as in the case of manslaughter caused by a drunken driver" (*CCC* 1737). Thus, two conditions must be met for the bad effect to be imputable to the agent: it must be foreseeable and there must be the possibility of avoiding it. Both of these conditions are met in this case. Any person who has consumed too much alcohol knows he or she shouldn't drive because an accident could result, and that person has the possibility of not driving, choosing instead to take public transport or asking a friend to do the driving.

While it is true that a person who has drunk too much alcohol can have diminished use of reason and therefore diminished responsibility for his acts and the consequences which follow from them, the responsibility for getting into the car to drive and the eventual accident can be traced back to the decision to have another drink when the person was still reasonably in control and aware he should stop drinking.

The civil courts are in agreement with the Church on this point. They don't let the driver off or diminish the punishment because he was under the influence of alcohol, but rather find him guilty and perhaps even increase the punishment because of this aggravating circumstance. The courts generally mention that the driver could and should have foreseen the possibility of an accident and could have avoided it by not driving.

Another example of the indirect voluntary or voluntary in cause is the case of a person who watches a film with scenes which are unchaste and ends up committing acts of impurity with himself or with another. Or someone who watches a film with scenes of violence or blasphemy and ends up committing violent acts or using blasphemous language.

All of this can help us avoid doing something that can indirectly lead to harmful consequences.

676 Good and bad fruit

The gospel in Mass recently was about good trees bearing good fruit and bad trees bearing bad fruit. How are we to interpret this? Can we divide mankind into good people and bad people?

That is a good question. The text to which you refer reads: "Beware of false prophets, who come to you in sheep's clothing but inwardly are ravenous wolves. You will know them by their fruits. Are grapes gathered from thorns, or figs from thistles? So, every sound tree bears good fruit, but the bad tree bears evil fruit. A sound tree cannot bear evil fruit, nor can a bad tree bear good fruit. Every tree that does not bear good fruit is cut down and thrown into the fire. Thus you will know them by their fruits" (*Mt* 7:15-20).

What Our Lord means by this is clear. There may be people who appear good on the outside, like the false prophets, but who are quite malicious on the inside, like ravenous wolves. We can know people's character by their fruits, by their deeds. When we see bad or malicious deeds we can judge that at least on this occasion, at this time in their life, the person is moved in some way by evil intent, by Satan. Similarly, when we see habitual acts of kindness, of generosity, of cheerfulness, we can judge there is a lot of goodness in that person.

But naturally the person who does malicious deeds even most of the time also does good deeds some of the time. And the one who is normally kind and generous will have their bad days on which they can be impatient, sullen or angry.

So, to answer your question about whether there are some people who are simply bad, who do bad deeds all the time, and others who are good, who do good deeds all the time, the answer is no. There is no such thing as an intrinsically bad person and no such thing as an intrinsically good person, except in the sense that we are all good, having come from God.

But what about Hitler, or Stalin, who killed so many people? They did many extremely evil deeds but undoubtedly they also did some good deeds too. And a St Mother Teresa of Calcutta or St John Paul II, who were so good, would also have committed sins.

Alexander Solzhenitsyn, the Russian novelist, sums it up in his book *The Gulag Archipelago* about the Soviet prison camps: "The line separating good and evil passes not through states, nor between classes, not between political parties either – but right through every human heart – and through all human hearts. This line shifts. Inside us, it oscillates with the years. And even within hearts overwhelmed by evil, one small bridgehead of good is retained. And even in the best of all hearts, there remains… an un-uprooted small corner of evil."

In this sense I remember a little saying we learned in catechism class as children: "There is so much good in the worst of us and so much bad in the best of us that it ill-behoves none of us to talk about the rest of us."

Our Lord says on another occasion that he wants us to bear good fruit: "You did not choose me, but I chose you and appointed you that you should go and bear fruit and that your fruit should abide" (*Jn* 15:16). What is this fruit that abides? We can take it to mean the good deeds we do that store up treasure in heaven (cf. *Mt* 6:19-20) or, in a word, personal holiness, love of God.

What can we do to bear this fruit? Jesus answers in that same Chapter 15 of St John's gospel: "I am the vine, you are the branches. He who abides in me, and I in him, he it is that bears much fruit, for apart from me you can do nothing" (*Jn* 15:5).

We are united to the vine, to Christ, through such means as daily prayer, reading of the Scriptures and spiritual books, and of course through frequent reception of the sacraments, especially the Eucharist, where we live in Christ and he lives in us (cf. *Jn* 6:56), and Penance, where we are purified of our sins and strengthened in grace to be more Christlike.

If we live like this we will bring not only good deeds, good fruit, into the world, but through them Christ himself. We can ask Our Lady, of whom we pray "Blessed is the fruit of thy womb, Jesus" to help us be a sound tree that bears much good fruit.

Specific moral issues

677 The Sunday Mass obligation

In the 1950s I learned in Catholic school that it was a mortal sin if you missed Mass on Sunday through your own fault, but I haven't heard this in recent times. Is it still taught by the Church?

It is indeed still taught by the Church. The *Catechism of the Catholic Church* says: "The Sunday Eucharist is the foundation and confirmation of all Christian practice. For this reason the faithful are obliged to participate in the Eucharist on days of obligation, unless excused for a serious reason (for example, illness, the care of infants) or dispensed by their own pastor. Those who deliberately fail in this obligation commit a grave sin" (*CCC* 2181).

When the *Catechism* uses the term "grave sin", it means mortal sin, just as it does when it speaks of "serious sin". And of course Sunday itself is the foremost day of obligation, along with the other two holy days of obligation celebrated in Australia: Christmas and the Assumption of Our Lady (August 15).

But why is attending Mass on Sundays so important that failure to do so constitutes a grave sin? It is a matter of understanding what the Mass is and how good God is to us.

In the Old Testament, God gave his people the commandments, which included the commandment of keeping holy the Sabbath: "You shall keep the Sabbath, because it is holy for you; everyone who profanes it shall be put to death; whoever does any work on it shall be cut off from among the people" (*Ex* 31:12-14). God went on to say that the Sabbath obligation would remain forever: "Therefore the Israelites shall keep the Sabbath, observing the Sabbath throughout their generations, as a perpetual covenant" (*Ex* 31:16).

The observance of the Sabbath by the Jews was to be transformed into the observance of Sundays by Christians through attendance at Mass. On the night before he died on the Cross, Jesus instituted the Eucharist to make present his redeeming sacrifice down the ages, telling the Apostles: "Do this in remembrance of me" (*Lk* 22:19). From the earliest days, Christians lived out that commandment, gathering especially on Sunday, the first day of the week, for the "breaking of the bread", as the Eucharist was then called. (cf. *Acts* 20:7)

As the Israelites worshipped God for his loving kindness towards them, shown in the work of creation and especially in freeing them from slavery in Egypt, so Christians continued to worship him for everything God had done for them, especially through Jesus' death and resurrection, by which he redeemed them from the slavery of sin, death and the devil.

When we consider how good God has been to us in creating the world with all its beauty, in giving us life and faith, in redeeming us through the death of Christ on the Cross, in giving us the Church and the sacraments to help us along the way to eternal life, and in blessing us personally in so many ways, we should be eager to thank him by worshipping him through the Eucharistic sacrifice. After all, the word Eucharist comes from the word for thanksgiving.

And since the Mass is the most powerful prayer of the Church, being Christ's own sacrifice on the Cross offered to the Father, we go to Mass too to ask God for so many favours: for the Church and the Pope, for the world, for our country and for all our personal intentions.

At the same time we receive so much when we attend Mass. We pray along with the parish community, we hear the word of God in the readings, we benefit from the explanation of the readings in the homily, and above all we receive Christ himself in Holy Communion. Considering all this, we can surely spend one hour a week with God in Mass, remembering Jesus' words to the Apostles: "Could you not watch with me one hour?" (*Mt* 26:40)

Naturally, there can be reasons which excuse a person from

attending Mass. In addition to one's own illness and the care of infants, which are mentioned in the Catechism, other reasons might be the need to work at the times Mass is being celebrated, the fact that there is no Mass in the place where we are, the long distance we would have to travel to attend Mass, the need to care for someone who is sick or housebound, etc. We should always try to attend Mass but if we have missed it for a serious reason, we have not committed a sin.

678 Embryo adoption

A friend recently asked what I thought about allowing people to "adopt" unwanted frozen embryos stored in IVF clinics. I don't know anything about this. Can you fill me in?

The background is that in the In-Vitro-Fertilisation (IVF) process, multiple embryos are produced by uniting an egg and a sperm in a glass dish, only some of which are implanted in the woman's body. Some of the others are discarded because they contain faulty genes and others are frozen and kept in storage for future use, especially if the implanted embryos do not result in a pregnancy and birth of a child. As regards the morality of IVF, see my answer in *Question Time 3*, q. 407.

What can happen is that if the woman has a child or children with the implanted embryos or if for any other reason, including a marriage breakup, she does not want to use the other embryos, they remain frozen in storage. We should remember that an embryo is a human being in an early stage of development and it is entitled to all the care we would give to a baby or an adult.

According to figures released by the U.K.'s Human Fertilisation and Embryology Authority in 2015, over 3.5 million embryos were created in the U.K. from August 1991 to 2015. Of these, only 1.4 million were implanted, one sixth of which resulted in a pregnancy, 1.7 million were discarded unused and a further 23,500 were discarded after being taken out of storage. Some 840,000 were put into storage and some 5,900 were set aside for scientific research.

What is to be done with embryos which have been kept in storage and are unwanted? One solution which has been proposed is to allow couples to adopt an embryo or embryos and implant them in the woman's body in the hope that they will result in the birth of a child. In this way, the embryo has at least some chance of being born.

The Vatican's Congregation for the Doctrine of the Faith addressed the question in the Instruction *Dignitas personae* in December 2008. It said: "With regard to the large number of frozen embryos already in existence the question becomes: what to do with them? Some of those who pose this question do not grasp its ethical nature, motivated as they are by laws in some countries that require cryopreservation centres to empty their storage tanks periodically. Others, however, are aware that a grave injustice has been perpetrated and wonder how best to respond to the duty of resolving it" (n. 19).

After ruling out for obvious reasons using these embryos for research or for the treatment of disease, or allowing infertile couples to use them to resolve their infertility, the document makes reference to "embryo adoption": "It has also been proposed, solely in order to allow human beings to be born who are otherwise condemned to destruction, that there could be a form of 'prenatal adoption'. This proposal, praiseworthy with regard to the intention of respecting and defending human life, presents however various problems not dissimilar to those mentioned above. All things considered, it needs to be recognised that the thousands of abandoned embryos represent a situation of injustice which in fact cannot be resolved" (n. 19).

The Instruction quotes St John Paul II, who called for a halt to the production of human embryos, "taking into account that there seems to be no morally licit solution regarding the human destiny of the thousands and thousands of 'frozen' embryos which are and remain the subjects of essential rights and should therefore be protected by law as human persons" (Address, 24 May 1996; n. 19).

After the Instruction was made public, Archbishop Rino Fisichella, President of the Pontifical Academy of Life, said in a press conference that the new document was not ruling out embryo adoption altogether, but that the Vatican was moving towards that position because such adoptions involve prospective parents in an immoral process.

In fact, in the U.S., over one thousand babies have already been born through embryo adoption.

At present, Catholic ethicists are divided on the issue, including on whether infertile couples should be allowed to adopt an embryo. Although, in view of this statement of Archbishop Fisichella and the disagreement among ethicists, a couple would be free to adopt an embryo if they so desired, it would be better not to resort to this cooperation in an immoral process. Babies should be born as a result of an act of love between a man and a woman united in marriage.

Obviously, if the frozen embryos are not implanted in a woman, they would have to be thawed out and allowed to die. This is morally licit, since it is not necessary to resort to extraordinary means to keep a person alive.

679 When does the soul enter the body?

Can you please tell me at what stage the soul enters the body of a foetus? I am worried because my daughter has had several miscarriages and I am wondering whether there was a soul and whether, if so, the soul could go to heaven.

By way of background we should be aware of two truths. First, by the word "soul" in general we mean the life principle of a living thing. Every living being, whether a plant, an animal or a human being has a soul. It is the soul that gives unity to the being, and in philosophical terms it is called the "form" of the matter. Only in humans, however, is this soul spiritual, capable of understanding, thinking, loving, etc. And since the human soul has its own act of being, independently of the body, it continues to exist when the person dies.

Second, the human soul is created directly by God. In the words of the Catechism, "The Church teaches that every spiritual soul is created immediately by God – it is not 'produced' by the parents – and also that it is immortal: it does not perish when it separates from the body at death, and it will be reunited with the body at the final Resurrection" (*CCC* 366; cf. *CCC* 33).

As regards the history of the question, Aristotle (384-322 BC) taught that a human being first had a vegetative or plant soul, then a sensitive or animal soul and finally an intellective or human soul. For him, ensoulment, the entry of the human soul, took place forty days after conception for males and ninety days for females. It was believed at that time that only after this number of days was movement felt in the womb and so was pregnancy certain.

Among other early beliefs, Stoics maintained that the living animal soul was received only at birth through contact with the air and it was transformed into a rational soul at the age of fourteen. Epicureans and Pythagoreans believed that the soul began to exist at the moment of conception.

In the early Church Aristotle's view was accepted by many but the idea that the soul was infused at conception was also accepted as early as the third century and was confirmed by St Gregory of Nyssa in the fourth century. Later the Aristotelian view became more common, based on the belief that only the formed foetus possessed a human soul. St Augustine in the fifth century was of this opinion, although he did speculate about the possibility of the soul being present before that.

St Thomas Aquinas in the thirteenth century largely accepted the Aristotelian notion that the embryo first had a vegetative soul, then a sensitive soul and only after forty days an intellective human soul.

Jumping forward to the present, the Church has still not defined when ensoulment takes place. It remains an open question. The Congregation for the Doctrine of the Faith's *Declaration on Procured Abortion* (1974) says: "This declaration expressly leaves aside the question of the moment when the spiritual soul is infused. There is not a unanimous tradition on this point and authors are as yet in disagreement. For some it dates from the first instant; for others it could not at least precede nidation [implantation in the womb]. It is not within the competence of science to decide between these views, because the existence of an immortal soul is not a question in its field. It is a philosophical problem from which our moral affirmation remains independent for two reasons: 1) supposing a belated animation, there is still nothing less than a human life, preparing for and calling for a soul in which the nature received from parents is completed; 2) on the other hand, it suffices that this presence of the soul be probable (and one can never prove the contrary) in order that the taking of life involve accepting the risk of killing a man, not only waiting for, but already in possession of his soul" (footnote 19).

So while we cannot be absolutely sure when the soul is infused, we can assume that it is there very early on, even when there is an early miscarriage. As regards its salvation, the Catechism teaches: "As regards *children who have died without Baptism*, the Church can only entrust them to the mercy of God, as she does in her funeral rites for them. Indeed, the great mercy of God who desires that all men should be saved, and Jesus' tenderness toward children which caused him to say: 'Let the children come to me, do not hinder them,' (*Mk* 10:14) allow us to hope that there is a way of salvation for children who have died without Baptism" (*CCC* 1261).

And naturally, as the Vatican document on procured abortion says in number 2, since there is always the possibility that the human soul is present from the beginning, it would be a grave sin to take the risk and abort the child at any stage of the pregnancy.

680 Abortion and a woman's body

In recent, sometimes heated, conversations about abortion in our office, a feminist colleague argued that a woman has a right to do what she wants with her own body. I didn't know how to answer her. Can you help me?

I agree with your feminist colleague. A woman, and a man for that matter, has a right to do what she wants with her own body. Within limits of course. She cannot end her life, mutilate herself or do anything to harm her body or her health without good reason. Apart from that, it is her body and she can do with it what she wants.

But when it comes to having an abortion, it is not her own body. The foetus is someone else's body – her child's. While the foetus is completely dependent on the mother for the nine months it is in her womb, it is a separate individual, with its own body and soul, destined to grow up to have its own personality, temperament, gifts and talents, hair and eye colour, etc., all of which may be very different from those of its mother. In fifty per cent of cases it is of a different sex from that of the mother. As a separate individual, it has its own rights, including the right to life.

The Church has always maintained this. The Instruction *Donum vitae* of the Congregation for the Doctrine of the Faith (1987) stated: "Thus the fruit of human generation, from the first moment of its existence, that is to say, from the moment the zygote has formed, demands the unconditional respect that is morally due to the human being in his bodily and spiritual totality. The human being is to be respected and treated as a person from the moment of conception; and therefore from that same moment his rights as a person must be recognised, among which in the first place is the inviolable right of every innocent human being to life" (*DV* I, 1).

What is more, numerous studies have shown that when a woman has an abortion she not only kills her baby but she runs a high risk of harming herself as well. One of the largest studies ever undertaken was done in Finland by Gissler and colleagues and published in the *European Journal of Public Health* in 2005. It compared the causes of death of more than 1.2 million women over the years 1987 to 2000 in the twelve months following an abortion or giving birth. It found that the suicide rate within a year of having an abortion was on average 6.5 times higher than that after giving birth and the rate of accidental death was 4.5 times higher. For girls aged 15 to 24 the suicide rate was twelve and a half times higher than for girls who had given birth, for those aged 25 to 34 it was eight times higher and for those aged 35 and over it was three times higher. Interestingly, there were peaks in the suicide rate in the first two months after the abortion and again after seven or eight months, at about the time the child would have been born.

Another significant study was done in New Zealand by David Fergusson, a professor of psychiatry who described himself as a pro-choice atheist, and his colleagues, published in 2006. It followed over ten years a group of 500 women in Christchurch aged 15 at the beginning and 25 at the end, comparing those who had had an abortion with those who had an unwanted pregnancy but gave birth to the baby. The study found that those who had abortions had a thirty per cent higher rate of mental disorders, including depression, anxiety and substance abuse. In most cases the women had no problems before the abortion.

A similar study, done by Kaeleen Dingle and her colleagues at the Queensland University of Technology, was published in 2008. It followed 1200 girls over seven years from the age of 14 to 21, by which time 380 had become pregnant. Those who had abortions had more than twice the rate of alcohol abuse and 3.6 times the rate of illicit drug use compared with those who had given birth.

Moreover, numerous studies have shown a significantly higher incidence of breast cancer in women who have had an abortion. A study commissioned by the U.S. National Cancer Institute and published in 1994 showed a fifty per cent increase in breast cancer in women who had an abortion over other women who had been pregnant at least once and had given birth to the baby. In those who had the abortion before the age of 18 or after 30, the risk was double.

So a woman who has an abortion not only kills her baby but subjects herself to a higher risk of harming herself, both mentally and physically.

681 Abortion and the death penalty

I have always wondered why there is such a strong movement around the world against the death penalty and yet there is no such movement against abortion. Isn't this inconsistent?

It is inconsistent indeed. I do not have any definitive answer on why the world is so inconsistent on these issues – specialised surveys would be needed for that – but I can offer a few reflections.

First, we should look at the facts. As you say, in recent times there has been a strong movement against the death penalty all over the world. In 1989 there were 35 countries which did not have the death penalty and by 2017 the number had risen to 104. At present only 14 countries have the death penalty and retain the right to use it, while another 38 have it but do not use it. Most are in Africa, the Middle East and Asia.

Meanwhile, abortion is legal in practically the whole world. According to the United Nations' *World Abortion Policies 2013*, abortion is legal in 97 per cent of countries if the reason is to save a woman's life, in 68 per cent to preserve the woman's mental health, in 51 per cent in the case of rape or incest, in 50 per cent for foetal impairment, and in 35 per cent for economic or social reasons. Abortion merely at the request of the woman (abortion on demand) is allowed in 30 per cent of countries, including the USA, Canada, Australia, most European countries and China. Those countries are home to 42 per cent of the world's population.

A good way to see the inconsistency of these figures is to ask a group of people if they would be in favour of aborting the baby if a woman became pregnant as a result of rape. A large number would answer yes. If the same people were then asked if they would be in favour of putting the rapist to death, practically everyone would say no. But, one could tell them, the baby in the womb hasn't done anything wrong and yet you are in favour of killing it, while the rapist has committed a serious crime and you want to spare his life. Inconsistent indeed.

Why are so many people in favour of abortion and so few in favour of the death penalty? One answer is undoubtedly that abortion involves far more people and strikes closer to home. The World Health Organization estimates there are some 40-50 million abortions each year, or some 125,000 every day. Those are staggering figures, equivalent to the whole population of such countries as Spain, Colombia or South Korea being wiped out each year. By contrast, the number of executions is around 1,000 per year, excluding those in China and North Korea, which are a state secret.

When a woman is pregnant and does not want the baby, she will find any number of reasons to justify having an abortion, including pressure from the father of the child or from others close to her. Her thoughts will tend to revolve only around herself and her own needs and desires, blotting out the fact that she is terminating the life of her own child. If she does not have God in her life, having an abortion is all the easier.

The movement for women's rights, which is so strong today, justifies abortion as a woman's right, while ignoring the right to life of the baby, the most fundamental of all human rights. Indeed, the UN Universal Declaration of Human Rights of 1948 lists the right to "life, liberty and security of person" as the very first right. In abortion the right to life of the baby in the womb is sacrificed to the "right" of the mother to an easier life.

The push for the abolition of the death penalty, on the contrary, does not strike close to home and is couched in justifiably altruistic, noble concerns for the dignity of the criminal. In 2018 Pope Francis declared the death penalty morally inadmissible and ordered paragraph 2267 of the *Catechism of the Catholic Church* to be amended, to read in part: "Today, however, there is an increasing awareness that the dignity of the person is not lost even after the commission of very serious crimes... Consequently, the Church teaches, in the light of the Gospel, that the death penalty is inadmissible because it is an attack on the inviolability and dignity of the person, and she works with determination for its abolition worldwide."

Would that more people realised that abortion too is an attack on the inviolability and dignity of the person, in this case of an absolutely innocent and defenceless person, and that they had the same compassion for the unborn child as they have for the perpetrator of a serious crime on death row.

682 The Pope and the death penalty

I heard that Pope Francis has just declared the death penalty no longer admissible. Can he change Church teaching like this, so that what the Church has allowed from the beginning is now unacceptable?

For information, the new teaching came in a letter from the Congregation for the Doctrine of the Faith entitled "Letter to the Bishops regarding the new revision of number 2267 of the Catechism of the Catholic Church on the death penalty". Pope Francis, in an audience with the Secretary of the Congregation on 28 June 2018, approved the Letter and ordered its publication. This is thus a formal exercise of papal magisterium since the Catechism contains official Church teaching.

Can the Pope change a teaching of thousands of years so that the death penalty, which was allowed for all that time, is no longer admissible? In this case, because of substantial changes in a number of areas over the centuries, Pope Francis has now deemed it appropriate to offer this new development in the Church's teaching on the death penalty.

The Letter to the Bishops explains it like this: "If, in fact, the political and social situation of the past made the death penalty an acceptable means for the protection of the common good, today the increasing understanding that the dignity of a person is not lost even after committing the most serious crimes, the deepened understanding of the significance of penal sanctions applied by the State, and the development of more efficacious detention systems that guarantee the due protection of citizens have given rise to a new awareness that recognises the inadmissibility of the death penalty and, therefore, calling for its abolition" (n. 2).

In view of this the Letter goes on to say: "All of this shows that the new formulation of number 2267 of the *Catechism* expresses an authentic development of doctrine that is not in contradiction with the prior teachings of the Magisterium. These teachings, in fact, can be explained in the light of the primary responsibility of the public authority to protect the common good in a social context in which the penal sanctions were understood differently, and had developed in an environment in which it was more difficult to guarantee that the criminal could not repeat his crime" (n. 8). In summary, it is a matter of a development of doctrine, not a contradiction of previous teaching.

The Letter explains how St John Paul II himself had stated his desire to see the death penalty ended. In his *Christmas Message* of 1998 he expressed the wish that there would be throughout the world a "consensus concerning the need for urgent and adequate measures … to end the death penalty." The following month on 23 January in a homily in Guadalupe, Mexico, he said: "There must be an end to the unnecessary recourse to the death penalty." A few days later on 27 January in St Louis, USA, he repeated it: "A sign of hope is the increasing recognition that the dignity of human life must never be taken away, even in the case of someone who has done great evil. Modern society has the means of protecting itself, without definitively denying criminals the chance to reform. I renew the appeal I made most recently at Christmas for a consensus to end the death penalty, which is both cruel and unnecessary."

Pope Benedict XVI too called "the attention of society's leaders to the need to make every effort to eliminate the death penalty" (Apostolic Exhortation *Africæ munus* (2011), n. 83). And Pope Francis himself in his *Letter to the President of the International Commission Against the Death Penalty* (20 March 2015) wrote that "today capital punishment is unacceptable, however serious the condemned's crime may have been" and that the death penalty, regardless of the means of execution, "entails cruel, inhumane, and degrading treatment."

In continuity with this magisterium of recent Popes the Church now declares that, taking into account the new understanding of punishments as "oriented above all to the rehabilitation and social reintegration of the criminal" and that "modern society possesses more efficient detention systems, the death penalty becomes unnecessary as protection for the life of innocent people" (Letter, n. 7).

The new text of paragraph 2267 of the Catechism will read: "Recourse to the death penalty on the part of legitimate authority, following a fair trial, was long considered an appropriate response to the gravity of certain crimes and an acceptable, albeit extreme, means of safeguarding the common good. Today, however, there is an increasing awareness that the dignity of the person is not lost even after the commission of very serious crimes. In addition, a new understanding has emerged of the significance of penal sanctions imposed by the state. Lastly, more effective systems of detention have been developed, which ensure the due protection of citizens but, at the same time, do not definitively deprive the guilty of the possibility of redemption. Consequently, the Church teaches, in the light of the Gospel, that the death penalty is inadmissible because it is an attack on the inviolability and dignity of the person, and she works with determination for its abolition worldwide."

This is an important and welcome development of the Church's teaching on this question, to be embraced by all, especially leaders of nations.

683 What is euthanasia?

I was talking recently with friends about the euthanasia bill soon to be debated in our state parliament and one said she didn't understand why we shouldn't let a suffering person die if that is what they want. Also, we were wondering what is and what is not euthanasia.

First we should understand what we mean by euthanasia. The word comes from the Greek and means good or happy death. Pope St John Paul II, in his encyclical *Evangelium vitae* (1995), defined euthanasia as "an act or omission which, of itself and by intention, causes death with the purpose of eliminating all suffering" (*EV* 65) That is, euthanasia is the killing of an innocent human person, as is murder, but with the particular aim of eliminating the person's suffering.

In his encyclical Pope John Paul confirmed that "euthanasia is a grave violation of the law of God, since it is the deliberate and morally unacceptable killing of a human person. This doctrine is based upon the natural law and upon the written word of God, as transmitted by the Church's Tradition and taught by the ordinary and universal Magisterium. Depending on the circumstances, this practice involves the malice proper to suicide or murder" (*EV* 65).

The *Catechism of the Catholic Church* too is very clear on this, saying that euthanasia "constitutes a murder gravely contrary to the dignity of the human person and to the respect due to the living God, his Creator. The error of judgment into which one can fall in good faith does not change the nature of this murderous act, which must always be forbidden and excluded" (*CCC* 2277). While it is always acceptable and indeed advisable to do everything possible to reduce a person's suffering, it is not lawful to achieve this by ending the person's life. God, after all, is the master of life and it is up to him to decide when the person is ready to die. We can kill an animal that is suffering, because it is only an animal, but not a human person made in the image and likeness of God.

We should not forget the reality of purgatory and the pain, always likened to fire, that the souls suffer there at the same time as they are exceedingly happy, because they are being purified for heaven. For all we know, if we end someone's life prematurely through euthanasia, we may very well not be ending their suffering at all but rather plunging their soul into even greater suffering in purgatory. God may have wanted them to suffer a little longer here on earth so that he could take them straight to heaven. We must let God decide when it is time for someone to die.

Meanwhile we should do everything possible to reduce the person's suffering through palliative care, which usually involves the use of morphine or some other drug. Even though this may shorten the person's life and diminish their degree of consciousness, this is not euthanasia but rather good patient care (cf. *CCC* 2279). Nonetheless, the person should be kept conscious until they have fulfilled their moral and family duties and have had the opportunity to prepare themselves spiritually for their definitive encounter with God (cf. *EV* 65). And always the ordinary care owed to a sick person must be continued, including the provision of food and water.

Also, it is not euthanasia to discontinue certain procedures that prolong the life of the person when it is clear that they are not achieving their aim or that they are burdensome to the person, dangerous or disproportionate to the expected outcome. As the Catechism explains, "Here one does not will to cause death; one's inability to impede it is merely accepted. The decisions should be made by the patient if he is competent and able or, if not, by those legally entitled to act for the patient, whose reasonable will and legitimate interests must always be respected" (*CCC* 2278). For example, it is acceptable to disconnect life support when it is clear that without it the person would die anyway from their underlying condition.

Likewise, it is permissible to forgo certain forms of treatment if they cannot bring about a cure but will only prolong the person's suffering. This includes chemotherapy and radiotherapy and any other form of treatment that offers no hope of a cure.

In the advanced world we have excellent palliative care and this normally makes the person sufficiently comfortable so that there is no desire for euthanasia. But even when the person is suffering considerably, we cannot resort to euthanasia to end their suffering.

684 Arguments against euthanasia

I want to write to my local member to express my views on a euthanasia bill before the New South Wales state parliament and would be grateful if you could give me some arguments to use.

It is very important that we do all we can to avoid euthanasia, or assisted suicide, being legalised in this country. The implications are enormous. Pope St John Paul II said of euthanasia in his encyclical *Evangelium vitae*, "Here we are faced with one of the more alarming symptoms of the 'culture of death', which is advancing above all in prosperous societies, marked by an attitude of excessive preoccupation with efficiency and which sees the growing number of elderly and disabled people as intolerable and too burdensome" (*EV* 64). In this column I will give six arguments in answer to your question and in the next a few more.

First, the bill before the New South Wales parliament allows anyone over the age of 25 suffering considerable pain to be assisted to end their life if two doctors certify that the person has an illness or condition such that they will die within a year. We all know people who tell us that years ago they were given a few months to live and now they are completely healthy. If they had chosen to end their life when they were sick, what a great loss it would have been to them, their families and friends! Mistakes can be made about life expectancy. Legalised euthanasia will only multiply them.

Second, allowing euthanasia sets a double standard about how a society values life. On one hand we rightly deplore the ending of life by suicide, especially when it is done by a young person, and we go to great lengths to prevent people taking their own life. But on the other we legalise euthanasia so that we can assist others to end their life. What message are we sending to those who want to commit suicide? Do we value life and deplore suicide or not?

Third, legalised assisted suicide can lead to an increase in the general suicide rate. Once assisted suicide has received social acceptability by being legalised, it can lead people not suffering from a terminal illness to end their life. This is borne out in the U.S. state of Oregon, the first state to legalise assisted suicide, where the general suicide rate is 40 per cent higher than the average in the U.S. Do we want that to happen in this country?

Fourth, and following on from this, once we open the door to legalised killing the push will come to open it ever wider. For example, why should a 25 year-old suffering from the pain of cancer be able to have a doctor assist him to end his life when another 25 year-old suffering from the perhaps greater pain of depression or crippling osteoarthritis cannot? After all, the first person's pain will presumably end within a year from the terminal illness whereas the others' will be ongoing, perhaps for many years. The law is clearly discriminatory. We should not open the door at all.

Fifth, assisted suicide is not mercy. It is not a humane response to suffering. As St John Paul II wrote in *Evangelium vitae*, "Even when not motivated by a selfish refusal to be burdened with the life of someone who is suffering, euthanasia must be called a false mercy, and indeed a disturbing 'perversion' of mercy. True 'compassion' leads to sharing another's pain; it does not kill the person whose suffering we cannot bear. Moreover, the act of euthanasia appears all the more perverse if it is carried out by those, like relatives, who are supposed to treat a family member with patience and love, or by those, such as doctors, who by virtue of their specific profession are supposed to care for the sick person even in the most painful terminal stages" (*EV* 66).

Sixth, medical professionals are trained to heal and to preserve life, not to end it. The Hippocratic Oath, taken by doctors as early as the fourth or fifth century BC contained the statement, "I will use treatment to help the sick according to my ability and judgment, but never with a view to injury and wrong-doing." The last phrase is often shortened to "First, do no harm." Euthanasia causes the greatest possible harm. It goes against everything doctors stand for. We shouldn't expect doctors to use their skill to end the life of their patient.

In view of all this, we should do everything to resist the legalisation of assisted suicide.

685 More arguments against euthanasia

Apart from what you have written in past columns, what other arguments are there against legalising assisted suicide in this country?

In my last column I wrote that doctors are trained to heal and to preserve life, not to end it. Giving someone a drug to end their life goes against everything doctors are trained to do and many suffer emotionally from having cooperated in it. A survey of doctors who had participated in euthanasia or assisted suicide in the U.S. found that 24 per cent regretted doing so and 16 per cent said the emotional burden of having participated adversely affected their practice. In a survey of Oregon physicians in 1995, more than 50 per cent stated that they would not provide a lethal prescription if physician-assisted suicide were legal. It is no wonder the Australian Medical Association and the World Medical Association say that doctors should not be involved in assisted suicide.

Likewise, family members who offer the lethal drug and then watch their relative die can suffer greatly. It is one thing to accompany someone who is dying of natural causes, including someone who experiences great pain; it is quite another to give them the means to end their own life. Being the nominated person who obtains the lethal medication from the pharmacy and gives it to their loved one – often a very close relative – is nothing like giving that person a pain killer. It is giving them what will end their life. It is understandable that this can lead to feelings of guilt, remorse, and even depression and post-traumatic stress disorder. If caring for a dying person can cause stress and anxiety, helping that person to commit suicide will do so all the more.

What is more, the lethal drug may not always lead to a quick and peaceful death. Evidence from overseas has shown that the person taking the drug may suffer such complications as vomiting, seizures, failure to enter a coma and a lengthy process of dying. The longest death recorded in Oregon, where assisted suicide has been legal since 1997, is 104 hours, or just over four days. If a doctor is not present when the person takes the lethal substance, it would be traumatic in the extreme for the family to deal with these complications until their loved one finally dies.

Then too, and very importantly, legalising euthanasia will put pressure on many people to end their lives prematurely. Elderly people in a nursing home, for example, may feel pressure to end their lives so that the money they leave their loved ones will not be diminished unduly by the considerable expense of staying alive. Or they may simply feel they are a burden on their family and should "do the right thing" and end their life. This would be tragic. The more assisted dying becomes commonplace and people choose to end their life prematurely for the sake of their family, the more pressure will be experienced by others to do the same thing.

An added consequence of choosing to end one's life in accordance with the proposed law is that insurance companies may not pay out on a life insurance policy. At present they often do not pay out when the person has committed suicide and they may very well choose to do the same when a person has ended their life under the proposed legislation. Even though the cause of death is recorded as the underlying condition that led to the person choosing to end their life, the insurance company may still regard it as suicide.

Finally, it is often the family members and friends of the dying person who experience the great suffering of caring for him or her and are happy for their loved one to end their life. What most dying people want is company, compassion, to know that they are loved, not a quick end to their suffering. We in this country are not used to seeing people suffer, as are people in most developing countries where there is far more suffering than here and where palliative care is nowhere near as good. Yet in those countries there is not the widespread call for euthanasia that there is in the developed world.

Dr Brian Pollard, who set up the first palliative care unit in New South Wales says that in all his years of looking after dying people he never had a request for euthanasia from a patient. He did have requests from family members who, he says, seemed to be saying, "Could you please put him or her out of our misery?" If we learn to show more compassion, perhaps we can reduce greatly the requests for assisted dying.

686 The slippery slope of euthanasia

I sometimes hear about the dangers of the slippery slope down which the practice of euthanasia can slide if it is approved. Is this a real danger?

The slippery slope is indeed a real danger with euthanasia. The way it works is simple. The initial legislation can be tightly worded with strict conditions under which euthanasia is allowed to be practised, but then gradually the interpretation of the law is extended in fact by medical practitioners and the general public to situations never envisioned in the law. Also, public pressure can give rise to an extension of the law itself over time. In any case, progressively more and more people end their lives by euthanasia.

For example, although the 2002 law in the Netherlands allowed euthanasia when the suffering was unbearable with no prospect of improvement, little by little this was extended to include psychological suffering. An article in the *Journal of the American Medical Association Internal Medicine* in August 2015 reported that in the Netherlands in one year 6.8 per cent of people who died from euthanasia or physician-assisted suicide did so because they were tired of living. Similarly, 49.1 per cent characterised part of their suffering as loneliness. In 2012 42 people were euthanased in that country for early dementia and 13 for psychiatric conditions. What is more, 53.7 per cent of approved requests for euthanasia were from people over 80 years of age, as if old age itself might be considered a form of suffering.

In Belgium in 2013 people were allowed to list tiredness of life as a reason for requesting euthanasia. Also in that country was the high profile case of 45-year-old deaf identical twins who were euthanased when their eyesight began to fail, and of a woman who had anorexia and opted to have her life ended after being sexually abused by the psychiatrist who was supposed to be treating her. Other reasons for euthanasia there have included autism and chronic fatigue syndrome. The slope is slippery indeed.

An article in the prestigious *New England Journal of Medicine* in 2005 reported that over a seven-year period 22 newborn babies with spina bifida and/or hydrocephalus were put to death by lethal injection in the Netherlands, despite it being illegal. It is estimated that some 15 to 20 newborn babies with birth defects are killed each year in that country. This is infanticide at its worst but a natural progression of the culture of death that begins when euthanasia is legalised.

In the state of Oregon, where assisted suicide was first legalised in the U.S., there have been two well publicised cases of people with cancer who were told that the Oregon Health Authority would not pay for their chemotherapy but would readily pay for their assisted suicide, which was of course much cheaper. This is utilitarianism at its worst. Do we want that to happen in this country?

Then too the number and proportion of people dying from euthanasia is constantly increasing in countries where it is legal. In 2012 one in every 30 deaths in the Netherlands was a result of euthanasia, and children as young as 12 can now request it. In Flanders, Belgium, where in 2007 one in every 53 deaths was by euthanasia, in 2013 this had risen to one in every 22. In Switzerland, where assisted suicide is legal, the number of deaths increased from 43 in 1998 to 297 in 2009. Among the conditions of these people were arthritis, blindness, spinal injury, diabetes and mental illness.

What is happening is that people see practically any form of suffering as unbearable and they want to be freed from it by ending their life. Yet suffering in its various forms is a normal part of life for everyone, and Christ taught us by his own suffering and death on the cross that it can have great meaning and value. But when God is pushed out of the life of more and more people, as is happening today in the Western world, a painless end to suffering seems the only solution.

So yes, the slippery slope of euthanasia is real, especially in an increasingly godless world unused to suffering. We should do everything possible to avoid legalising euthanasia and putting ourselves at the top of the slope.

687 Involuntary euthanasia

I understand that in the Netherlands and other countries the legalisation of euthanasia has led to people being put to death without their consent. Is this a reality and could it happen here?

The situation you describe is most certainly a reality in the Netherlands and is a natural progression of the culture of death described by Pope St John Paul II. When human life is not valued in itself, no matter what the age or state of health or mental capacity of the person, the killing of those considered to be a burden or whose life is "not worth living" is a natural consequence. Let us examine what has happened in the Netherlands, using a well-documented report from the U.S.-based Patients Rights Council.

By way of background, although the Netherlands passed a law legalising euthanasia as late as 2002, before that several court decisions held that doctors who killed their patients or helped them kill themselves would not be prosecuted as long as they followed certain guidelines. The doctors were to inform the authorities of all cases in which they intervened and these were summarised in three official government reports for the years 1990, 1995 and 2001 known as Remmelink Reports, named after the Attorney General of the High Council of the Netherlands who headed the study committee. It should be said that many cases of euthanasia were not reported at all, since doctors attributed these deaths to "life terminating treatment" in order not to classify them as euthanasia.

Some of the findings are disturbing, revealing the frequency of euthanasia practised without the patient's consent. For example, in the report for 1990, 1041 people, an average of three per day, died from involuntary euthanasia, practised without the patient's knowledge or consent. Fourteen per cent of these patients were fully competent, 72 per cent had never given any indication that they would want their lives terminated, and in 8 per cent of cases, doctors performed involuntary euthanasia despite the fact that they believed alternative options were still available.

In addition, 8100 patients died as a result of overdoses of pain medication, given not for the primary purpose of controlling the pain but to hasten the patients' death. In 61 per cent of these cases the intentional overdose was given without the patient's consent. Overall in 1990, physicians deliberately and intentionally ended the lives of 11,840 people by lethal overdoses or injections, representing 9.1 per cent of all deaths that year. The majority of all euthanasia deaths were involuntary. In 45 per cent of cases of involuntary euthanasia carried out in a hospital, the patients' families had no knowledge that their loved ones' lives were deliberately terminated by doctors.

The most frequently cited reasons for ending the lives of patients without their consent were "low quality of life", "no prospect for improvement" and "the family couldn't take it anymore". What is sad is that euthanasia was practised with little or no effort to help the patients through palliative care.

In 1988 the British Medical Association released the findings of a study on Dutch euthanasia which found that palliative care in the Netherlands was very poorly developed. In mid-1990, for example, there were only two hospice programs in the whole country and the services they provided were very limited. When euthanasia is an accepted solution to pain and suffering, there is little incentive to develop adequate palliative care programs.

With so many cases of involuntary euthanasia, as early as 1990 the Dutch Patients' Association, a disability rights organisation, began handing out cards which state that if the signer is admitted to hospital, "no treatment be administered with the intention to terminate life."

What is ironic and sad is that during World War II the Netherlands was the only occupied country whose doctors openly defied an order to participate in the German euthanasia program. The German officer who gave the order was later executed for war crimes. This led British journalist Malcolm Muggeridge to write in an essay entitled "The Humane Holocaust" that it took only a few decades "to transform a war crime into an act of compassion."

688 Euthanasia in Australia

I was recently talking with a nurse who confided that she had been asked to give an elderly patient a dose of morphine that she judged would kill the patient and she refused. Is it possible that euthanasia is already being practised in this country?

Over the years I too have heard of cases like the one you describe, leading me to ask the same question. What you are describing is involuntary euthanasia, where the patient has not requested it and yet it is practised not only immorally but illegally. Is this practice going on in Australia today, when voluntary euthanasia is not yet legalised? The answer is unfortunately yes.

The facts are detailed in an article by Helga Kuhse, Peter Singer, Peter Baume and others published in the *Medical Journal of Australia* in 1997. The article is based on a postal survey conducted by the authors in 1996 of a random sample of medical practitioners from all Australian States and Territories selected from medical disciplines in which the doctor had opportunities to make medical end-of-life decisions. The questionnaire was sent to 3000 practitioners and the response rate was 64 per cent. The questionnaire was based on one used in the Netherlands and had the same 24 items. The responses were of course anonymous since the Australian practitioners would have been liable to prosecution for their actions in ending the life of their patients. The idea was to compare the responses of Australian doctors with those of their Dutch counterparts., and the results were alarming. What follows is taken from that article, often word for word.

In summary, an estimated 1.8 per cent of all Australian deaths in 1996 were the result of euthanasia, including 0.1 per cent of physician-assisted suicide. This compares with 1.7 per cent of euthanasia deaths and 0.2 per cent of physician-assisted suicide in the Netherlands as detailed in the Remmelink Report for 1990.

An estimated 3.5 per cent of all deaths in Australia involved termination of the patient's life without the patient's explicit request. This compares with 0.8 per cent of such deaths in the Netherlands in 1990, in violation of the guidelines for euthanasia in that country.

In 30 per cent of all Australian deaths, a medical end-of-life decision was made with the explicit intention of ending the patient's life, of which only 4 per cent were in response to a direct request from the patient. Overall, Australia had a higher rate of intentional ending of life without the patient's request than the Netherlands.

An estimated 24.7 per cent of all Australian deaths involved a decision not to treat with the explicit intention of not prolonging life or of hastening death. Of these, less than one-tenth (or 2.2 per cent of all Australian deaths) were in response to an explicit request from the patient, and in most cases (22.5 per cent of all Australian deaths) there was no explicit request from the patient.

Therefore, in 14.3 per cent of all Australian deaths, the death was preceded by a medical decision to withhold or withdraw treatment with the explicit intention of not prolonging life or of hastening death, despite the fact that the decision was not based on an explicit request from a patient.

In 6.5 per cent of all Australian deaths, doctors prescribed opioids (morphine or a comparable drug) with a dual intention: in part, to alleviate pain and symptoms and, in part, to hasten death. Drug doses were large enough to have, in the judgment of the respondent and with regard to the particular death, a life-shortening effect.

The authors of the Australian article conclude that "Australian law has not prevented doctors from practising euthanasia or making medical end-of-life decisions explicitly intended to hasten the patient's death without the patient's request."

One can only conclude that if euthanasia without the patient's request was already being practised in this country twenty years ago when euthanasia was strictly illegal, the frequency would undoubtedly only increase if it were legalised. It is one more strong reason not to legalise this practice, which is a clear manifestation of the culture of death warned about by St John Paul II.

689 Attending a person dying by assisted suicide

I read recently that a Vatican Archbishop said he would hold the hand of a person dying by assisted suicide and later I saw criticism of the Archbishop's position. I am confused and would be grateful for clarification of what can be done in these cases.

This is an issue which is very close to home. With more states legalising assisted suicide in this country, it is only a matter of time before priests will have to decide what to do when a Catholic family approaches them about a family member who has chosen to end his life in this way.

The matter hit the news when Archbishop Vincenzo Paglia, president of the Pontifical Academy for Life, in a press conference on 10 December 2019 was asked to comment on guidelines issued by the Swiss bishops that directed that pastoral caregivers should not be present during a person's death by assisted suicide. He responded: "Let go of the rules. I believe that no one should be abandoned. To accompany, to hold the hand of someone who is dying, is something that every believer must promote as they must promote a culture that opposes assisted suicide."

A clearer comment on the issue was given later by Cardinal Willem Eijk of Utrecht, in the Netherlands. He told Catholic News Agency CNA that "a priest must clearly say to those who opt for assisted suicide or euthanasia that both of these acts violate the intrinsic value of human life, that is a grave sin." This echoes the Catechism's teaching that suicide is "gravely contrary to the just love of self" (*CCC* 2281).

Thus if a priest or any other Catholic is approached by a person considering assisted suicide, even if the person is in great pain, they should encourage the person to entrust himself to the mercy of God, obtain good palliative care to lessen the pain, and not risk his eternal salvation by committing the grave sin of ending his life. As the Catechism says, "We are stewards, not owners of the life God has entrusted to us. It is not ours to dispose of" (*CCC* 2280).

Cardinal Eijk went on to say that a priest cannot be present when assisted suicide is carried out as this would imply that he saw nothing wrong with the decision, which is gravely sinful. This too, echoes the Catechism, which teaches: "Voluntary cooperation in suicide is contrary to the moral law" (*CCC* 2282). The mere presence of a priest who does nothing to stop a person taking a drug to end his life is a form of voluntary cooperation by implicit consent, which can encourage the person to go through with the suicide.

As regards whether the priest can administer the sacraments of penance and anointing of the sick before the person takes the drug to end his life Cardinal Eijk made clear that he cannot. The sacraments can only be administered to persons with the proper dispositions and here the person is clearly not sorry, since he is freely and knowingly choosing to end his own life, thereby committing a grave sin. Although the Cardinal did not say so, the priest could certainly go to the home of the person and try to dissuade him from committing suicide.

Also, if the priest were called to the home after the person had taken the drugs and was still alive, he could certainly go and try to elicit some expression of repentance, in which case he could give the sacraments. And he could stay there and even hold the hand of the person, praying that he would have the grace to repent before rendering up his soul.

As regards celebrating the funeral, great care must be taken. In the case of assisted suicide the person will often be more in his right mind, and therefore more responsible before God, than a person suffering from severe depression who ends his life by suicide. Celebrating the funeral in this case could imply that the priest sees nothing wrong with what the person has done.

But since the Church now acknowledges that "grave psychological disturbances, anguish, or grave fear of hardship, suffering, or torture can diminish the responsibility of the one committing suicide" (*CCC* 2283), and since it is always possible that the person may have been given a light from God at the last moment to repent, the priest could often give the person the benefit of the doubt and celebrate the funeral. It would be important then to make clear to those present the Church's opposition to assisted suicide but at the same time to ask them to pray for the eternal salvation of the person's soul.

690 The origins of gender theory

I am in my seventies, so I may be out of touch, but I don't understand why for the last few years there is such a push for gender theory, or whatever they call it. This was never an issue when I was growing up or even twenty years ago. Where did it come from?

I think we are all asking that question. Why is it that suddenly there is this big push for gender to be what we make of it, not what we are born with? When a baby is born, even today the first question of the parents is "Is it a boy or a girl?" Who is pushing the gender fluidity ideology, which argues that we decide our own gender?

German writer Gabriele Kuby, in her book *The Global Sexual Revolution*, offers an insightful analysis of the history of the question, which is of fairly recent origin. She goes back to the French radical feminist Simone de Beauvoir, who in the 1960s made the seminal statement, "One is not born, but rather becomes, a woman."

It was the beginning of the effort to deconstruct the binary sexual identity of human beings as either male or female. One of the ploys was the introduction of the word "gender" to replace "sex" as the descriptor of whether one is male or female. We are all familiar with filling out forms where we are asked to tick a box identifying our sex as either "M" or "F". I recently saw the success of this movement when I filled out a form that had a third box labelled "Other". What other sex is there? If sex is universally considered to be male or female, gender is now being presented as something fluid, with many variations. It is what we want it to be, they say. So we now have LGBTI: lesbian, gay, bisexual, transsexual and intersexual. And sometimes Q: queer.

According to Kuby, the pioneer of gender theory is Judith Butler, a lesbian born in the United States in 1956 of Jewish academic parents of Hungarian-Russian origin. With a doctorate from Yale University in 1984, in 1990 she published *Gender Trouble: Feminism and the Subversion of Identity*, which is considered the fundamental work on gender ideology. In the foreword to the book she pulls no punches about her intention: "What best way to trouble the gender categories that support gender hierarchy and compulsory heterosexuality?"

As a post-structuralist philosopher, she has developed a complicated theory that invents a new language intended to shake the foundations of the human order through "subversive confusion and multiplication of gender identities." In simple terms, there are no such beings as "men" and "women". One's sex is a fantasy, something we only believe because we have heard it repeated so often.

Gender, according to Butler, is not associated with biological sex, which plays absolutely no role and arises only because it is created by language, and because people believe what they constantly hear. In Butler's view, gender identity is free-flowing and flexible. Her goal is the dissolution of sexual identity altogether because only then will the individual be emancipated from the dictatorship of nature and have complete freedom of choice, the ability to reinvent oneself at any time.

For Butler, the illusion or "phantasm" of two sexes is created by the incest taboo and by words like "man" and "woman", "father" and "mother", which must be eliminated in favour of free self-invention. Even marriage and family, sexuality and fertility are not considered natural, and since they establish the domination of men over women and of heterosexuality over all other forms of sexuality they must be destroyed at their roots.

One would think a theory so radical and contrary to common sense, to the natural order, and to the good of the family and society would be ridiculed and consigned to the rubbish bin. Yet Butler received a Guggenheim Fellowship in 1999, a Rockefeller Fellowship in 2001 and, in addition to other prizes, in 2008 the Andrew W. Mellon Award with a $1.5 million grant for teaching and research! Since 2012 she is a visiting professor at Columbia University.

In little over twenty years, gender theory has become extremely influential, having been embraced by governmental bodies and taught in numerous universities as gender/queer studies. It is the underlying theory of the Safe Schools program here in Australia.

691 Gender theory and the Yogyakarta Principles

I read somewhere about the Yogyakarta Principles in connection with gender theory. What are they?

An influential document setting out the gender ideology agenda for worldwide adoption was framed in Yogyakarta, Indonesia, in 2007 and has come to be known as the Yogyakarta Principles. The 29 principles are a detailed manual for implementing gender ideology, including free choice of gender, sexual orientation and identity.

Who formulated these principles? According to Gabriele Kuby, in her book *The Global Sexual Revolution*, it was a group of self-proclaimed "renowned human rights experts" who in reality had no official authorisation or legitimation. They were obviously LGBTI activists. To give their document a semblance of authority the "experts" presented it to the public at the UN building in Geneva. The principles are a "new tool for activists" and are accompanied by a 200-page handbook with a set of instructions for translating the principles into political action.

The document's key concepts are "sexual orientation" and "gender identity". "Sexual orientation" is defined in the Preamble as referring to "each person's capacity for profound emotional, affectional and sexual attraction to, and intimate and sexual relations with, individuals of a different gender or the same gender or more than one gender." As Kuby points out, the definition does not exclude any type of sexual activity, including paedophilia, incest, polygamy, polyandry, polyamory (sex with more than one person) and bestiality.

"Gender identity" refers to "each person's deeply felt internal and individual experience of gender which may or may not correspond with the sex assigned at birth, including the personal sense of the body (which may involve, if freely chosen, modification of bodily appearance or function by medical, surgical or other means) and other expressions of gender, including dress, speech and mannerisms."

The second of the principles declares that no one is to be

discriminated against on the basis of sexual orientation or gender identity "whether or not the enjoyment of another human right is also affected." This is alarming. Human rights that might be affected, like freedom of speech and freedom of conscience, are to be subordinated to the right to sexual orientation and gender identity. It would be considered discrimination, for example, to teach or raise children to believe that the purpose of sexuality is love between a man and a woman for the procreation of children. We saw an example of this in Australia when Archbishop Julian Porteous of Hobart was accused of discrimination for simply proclaiming publicly the Church's constant teaching on traditional marriage.

Whereas sciences such as biology, medicine, psychology and sociology teach that there are specific differences between men and women, to the point where each and every cell of a person's body is either masculine or feminine, the Yogyakarta principles make sexual identity depend on feelings and emotions, which are inherently unstable and subject to change. The Preamble to the principles actually states that all claims of inalienable differences between men and women are based on "prejudices and stereotyped roles for men and women" which the principles are intended to wipe out.

Each of the 29 principles is introduced by a general statement and is followed by demands that all countries must enforce. These include ensuring that all state-issued identity papers which indicate a person's sex/gender reflect the person's profound self-defined gender identity. States are also to respect and legally recognise each person's self-defined gender identity.

The principles demand that all countries take totalitarian measures to change their constitutions, laws, social institutions, education systems and their citizens' basic attitudes in order to enforce and legally compel acceptance and privileged status for homosexuality and other non-heterosexual identities and behaviours. Among the countries that have already jumped on the Yogyakarta bandwagon are Germany, Denmark, the Netherlands, Norway, Sweden, Switzerland, the Czech Republic, Argentina, Brazil and Uruguay. We have entered a truly brave new world.

692 The power of the gender movement

I am more and more intrigued by the influence of the gender ideology movement in our society. Is it just a case of a small number of people making a big noise, or are there some powerful organisations behind it?

There are some very powerful organisations behind the movement. Those experiencing gender dysphoria and adopting lesbian, gay, bisexual, or transgender lifestyles represent a very small minority in any country, perhaps some two to three per cent of the population. But they wield a vastly disproportionate influence, as we see in Australia in such causes as the legalisation of same-sex marriage and the adoption of the *Safe Schools* program.

As I have written before, the writings of Judith Butler, with her book *Gender Trouble: Feminism and the Subversion of Identity* in 1990, and the framing of the Yogyakarta Principles in 2007 were important milestones in the rise of gender ideology. But only a handful of people were involved in those efforts. Yet Butler received a Guggenheim Fellowship, a Rockefeller Fellowship and, in addition to other prizes, the Andrew W. Mellon Award with a $1.5 million grant for teaching and research. Powerful organisations were indeed influential in getting her ideas into the public sphere.

And the UN provided a launching pad for the Yogyakarta Principles and assisted in their implementation. The framers of the Principles listed at the end of their document sixteen "additional recommendations" for implementing the cultural revolution based on the Principles. Specifically, they sought the contribution of the UN High Commissioner for Human Rights, the UN Human Rights Council and the Treaty-Monitoring Bodies, as well as of numerous other intergovernmental and state bodies, including courts, professional bodies, the educational sector, the media, etc.

In addition to the United Nations, the European Union has also contributed substantially to the LGBTI cause. According to Gabriele Kuby in her book *The Global Sexual Revolution*, hundreds of millions of dollars flow to the LGBTI cause through official UN and EU sub-organisations and private foundations, including the Rockefeller, Ford, and Bill and Melinda Gates Foundations. This is presented as part of their official budgets. The International Lesbian, Gay, Bisexual, Trans and Intersex Association (ILGA) is more than 60-per cent funded by the European Commission, with additional contributions from billionaire George Soros and two other large donors.

By the way, the European Commission also regularly uses tax money to fund projects of the world's two largest abortion providers, Marie Stopes International and International Planned Parenthood. The Commission's contribution is labelled "sexual and reproductive health", even through the EU's definition of this term explicitly excludes abortion.

The *Activist's Guide* which accompanies the Yogyakarta Principles recommends that, in pursuing a legal strategy to protect the human rights of LGBTI people, activists should "engage with the UN system, via the Universal Periodic Review, shadow report to treaty bodies, in coalition with others, making contact with Special Rapporteurs, etc." The underlying assumption is that the UN system is favourable to the LGBTI cause, as indeed it is. Legal cases are then brought to the European Court of Human Rights and the European Court of Justice with the hope of finding a sympathetic judge. Numerous cases have been taken to those courts in recent years.

What is more, the LGBTI movement has succeeded in having research into the causes of homosexuality and treatment for those seeking to change their same-sex orientation regarded as "discrimination". In 2012 California became the first U.S. state to ban therapy for minors seeking to change their unwanted homosexual orientation, and the following year New Jersey did the same. This is an unbelievable violation of an individual's right to treatment for an unwanted condition, and of professional bodies' freedom to conduct research and use their skills to help those seeking their assistance.

Yes, powerful organisations have been involved in the success of the gender theory cause.

693 The European Union and the gender ideology movement

I was surprised to read in one of your columns of the European Union's backing of the gender ideology movement. When I think of the deep Catholic roots of Europe I was amazed and somewhat alarmed. Can you tell me more?

The first thing to say is that Europe has lost a great deal of its Catholic, or even Christian, identity and your question reveals that. At the same time Australia too has lost much of its Christian identity, as seen recently in the legalisation of same-sex marriage and of abortion and euthanasia in some jurisdictions, the introduction of the Safe Schools program, etc.

The European Union's involvement in promoting gender ideology is extensive and truly alarming. Gabriele Kuby, in her book *The Global Sexual Revolution*, describes it in detail. While the Treaty which established the European Union says that the issues of marriage and family are reserved to the member states, the EU wields a huge influence in those areas.

For example, the International Lesbian, Gay, Bisexual, Trans and Intersex Association (ILGA), which organises gay pride manifestations around the world and was denied accreditation at the UN, receives almost seventy per cent of its funding from EU taxes, yet somehow retains its status as an independent non-governmental organisation claiming to represent the interests of civil society. I dare say there are many citizens of EU countries who would be horrified to know that their taxes are being used to support that group, just as we would be in this country if the government were using our taxes to fund causes such as this. The ILGA is involved in continuous lobbying for legal reforms leading to the adoption of same-sex "marriage" laws in the member states, and it promotes initiatives which would be illegal in many of those countries.

Through "civil dialogue", the ILGA, like other non-governmental organisations, is integrated into the legislative process and then, through "community action programs" funded with millions of euros from the EU, implements its policies in the various member states.

The LGBTI lobby organisations are by far the strongest lobby groups in the European Parliament. While only some two per cent of the population is homosexual, twenty per cent of the members of the European Parliament form part of the European Intergroup on LGBT Rights, which endeavours to influence the lawmaking process in favour of those rights.

Another body financed with millions of euros from the EU is the European Youth Forum (EYF), which campaigns in Europe and internationally for youth empowerment, gender equality and safe sex. It collaborates with abortion organisations like International Planned Parenthood and Marie Stopes International.

When the Lithuanian parliament passed an amendment to the youth protection act that opposed "promotion of homosexual relationships" on the grounds that "homosexual, bisexual and polygamous relationships damage the physical and mental health of youth", the European Parliament in 2009 passed two resolutions challenging the democratic decision of that parliament. The decision was changed. It is but one example of the EU putting pressure on member states in an area which is left to those states.

The EU's Fundamental Rights Agency founded in 2007 has an annual budget of 20 million euros with such aims as battling homophobia and discrimination based on sexual orientation. Its director, Michael O'Flaherty, appointed in 2016, is a former Catholic priest who was the main author of the Yogyakarta Principles which set the agenda for the LGBTI movement. He campaigns for the legalisation of same-sex "marriage", the choice of one's gender, abortion as a human right, the criminalisation of "hate speech" and the restriction of free speech.

Over the years the EU parliament has passed resolutions urging member states and prospective members to change restrictive homosexuality laws; legalise abortion; prosecute discrimination against lesbian, gay, bisexual and transgender people; legalise same-sex "marriage", etc.

All in all, it highlights the need for all of us to be more active in living our faith and in promoting Christian values in public life lest we too go down that track.

694 Safe Schools and Gender Dysphoria

I understand the Safe Schools program will be mandatory in all state schools in Victoria from 2018 on and this worries me, since it celebrates transition of children to a different gender. Am I right to be worried or am I just old fashioned?

You have every right to be worried since the program does indeed celebrate, and thereby encourage, the transition of children to a different gender.

As I wrote in an earlier column Roz Ward, a co-founder of the program, stated that Safe Schools is not an anti-bullying program but rather about the promotion of sexual and gender diversity. It was written by activists with the express aim of transforming society and it sexualises children from a young age, teaching them how to masturbate, engage in oral and anal sex, use contraception, etc. The children are told not to talk about this outside the classroom.

To assist children who feel they belong to a different gender, South Australia already has a mandatory policy for all state schools to allow students to choose the bathroom, uniform, sporting team and sleeping quarters which correspond to their chosen gender identity, without the consent, consultation or even notification of their parents.

How big an issue is gender transition in terms of the numbers of people involved? Not big at all. Current data in the most liberal and accepting parts of the world suggest the percentage of transgendered people (very broadly defined to include cross-dressers, gender fluid persons, etc.) might be as high as 0.5 per cent, or one in 200, or as low as 0.1 per cent, one in 1000. At the same time, it is certain that any program in schools that celebrates and thereby encourages children to change their gender can only increase these numbers.

This is dangerous. Why? Because according to the *Diagnostic and Statistical Manual* (DSM-5) of the American Psychiatric Association, as many as 98 per cent of gender confused boys and 88 per cent of girls will accept their biological sex by late adolescence. To encourage them to change their gender when they are young would thus make it harder for them to accept their biological sex later.

When a young person believes he or she is of the opposite sex to that of their birth, they are suffering from a mental disorder which DSM-5 recognises as Gender Dysphoria (GD). What the child needs is psychological or psychiatric help, not encouragement to change their sex. If a child is suffering from anorexia or depression, we don't encourage them to eat less or end their life, and we shouldn't encourage someone suffering from GD to change their sex, but rather counsel them to accept it.

What is more, a report by the American College of Pediatricians in June 2017 says that the effects of taking cross-sex hormones (testosterone and oestrogen) and sex reassignment surgery to aid gender transition can be severe. The rate of suicide in Swedish adults who used these means was nearly twenty times higher than in the rest of the population and 62 per cent of male-to female transgender persons and 55 per cent of female-to-male persons suffered from depression, much higher than in the rest of the population. In the U.S. a survey conducted by the National Gay and Lesbian Task Force and National Center for Transgender Equality found that 41 per cent of transgender persons had attempted suicide, vastly exceeding the 4.6 per cent in the overall U.S. population.

Also, pre-pubescent children with gender dysphoria may be

given puberty blockers and they will require cross-sex hormones in later adolescence to continue to live in accordance with the opposite gender. As a result they will become sterile and never able to conceive any genetically-related children even via artificial reproductive technology. What is more, cross-sex hormones are associated with such dangerous health risks as cardiac disease, high blood pressure, blood clots, stroke, diabetes and cancer. To give these treatments to children who are too young to give valid informed consent, is nothing short of child abuse.

In summary, encouraging gender transition in children is negligent and dangerous in the extreme.

695 Pope Francis and gender ideology

As a parent I am very concerned about the approach taken in some of our schools, even Catholic ones, to children uncertain of their gender. Has the Pope said anything about this?

Pope Francis has spoken and written about this issue many times and it is good that we be aware of what he has said. What is more, in February 2019 the Vatican's Congregation for Catholic Education issued an important document on the question for the benefit of Catholic schools and other educational institutions. I will write about it in my next column.

One of the strongest statements of Pope Francis comes in his Apostolic Exhortation *Amoris Laetitia* (2016), where he speaks of gender theory, which "denies the difference and reciprocity in nature of a man and a woman and envisages a society without sexual differences, thereby eliminating the anthropological basis of the family. This ideology leads to educational programs and legislative enactments that promote a personal identity and emotional intimacy radically separated from the biological difference between male and female. Consequently, human identity becomes the choice of the individual, one which can also change over time" (*AL* n. 56).

Elsewhere in that same document he writes that "the young need to be helped to accept their own body as it was created, for thinking that we enjoy absolute power over our own bodies turns, often subtly, into thinking that we enjoy absolute power over creation... Sex education should help young people to accept their own bodies and to avoid the pretension to cancel out sexual difference because one no longer knows how to deal with it" (*AL* n. 285).

In a closed-door session with the bishops of Poland during a visit there in July 2016, Pope Francis said: "Today, in schools they are teaching this to children – to children! – that everyone can choose their gender." The Pope blamed what he called "ideological colonising" backed by "very influential countries" which he didn't identify, adding: "this is terrible." He told the bishops he had spoken about the issue with Emeritus Pope Benedict XVI, who said: "Holiness, this is the epoch of sin against God the Creator." Pope Francis commented: "He's intelligent! God created man and woman, God created the world this way, this way, this way, and we are doing the opposite."

In an extensive interview with French journalist Dominique Wolton entitled *Politics and Society: Conversations with Dominique Wolton,* Pope Francis said: "It's true that behind all this we find gender ideology. In books, kids learn that it's possible to change one's sex. Could gender, to be a woman or to be a man, be an option and not a fact of nature? This leads to this error."

In his encyclical *Laudato si'* (2015) he spoke of a "human ecology" that respects "our dignity as human beings" and the necessary relationship of our life to the "moral law, which is inscribed into our nature" (nn. 154-155).

In November 2014, in an address to the International Colloquium on the Complementarity Between Man and Woman sponsored by the Congregation for the Doctrine of the Faith, Pope Francis spoke of the importance of the family formed by a man and a woman for the proper development of children: "Children have a right to grow up in a family with a father and a mother capable of creating a suitable environment for the child's growth and emotional development. This is why, in the Apostolic Exhortation *Evangelii Gaudium*, I stressed the 'indispensable' contribution of marriage to society, a contribution which 'transcends the feelings and momentary needs of the couple'" (*EG* n. 66).

And in July 2010, when he was still Archbishop of Buenos Aires and the Argentine parliament was debating a bill to legalise same-sex "marriage", he wrote a letter to four monasteries of contemplative nuns in the country asking them to pray that the bill would be defeated. In it he stated: "At stake is the identity and survival of the family: father, mother and children. At stake are the lives of many children who will be discriminated against in advance, and deprived of their human development given by a father and a mother and willed by God. At stake is the total rejection of God's law engraved in our hearts. Let us not be naive: this is not simply a political struggle, but it is an attempt to destroy God's plan. It is not just a bill (a mere instrument) but a 'move' of the father of lies who seeks to confuse and deceive the children of God."

696 Vatican document on gender theory

I have seen several references to a recent Vatican document on gender theory but don't know anything about it. Can you help me?

The document to which you refer, *"Male and female he created them" – towards a path of dialogue on the question of gender theory in education,* was issued on 2 February 2019 by the Vatican's Congregation for Catholic Education. It intends to offer reflections on the issue to guide and support those working in the education of young people. It is a timely contribution since gender theory has taken the world by storm and has made considerable inroads in schools in this country.

What is gender theory? Quoting Pope Francis' Apostolic Exhortation *Amoris Laetitia* (2016), the document says that gender theory "denies the difference and reciprocity in nature of a man and a woman and envisages a society without sexual differences, thereby eliminating the anthropological basis of the family". The Pope goes on to say that this ideology "leads to educational programmes and legislative enactments that promote a personal identity and emotional intimacy radically separated from the biological difference between male and female. Consequently, human identity becomes the choice of the individual, one which can also change over time" (*AL* 56).

The first part of the document is structured on the basis of three guiding principles to be borne in mind: to listen, to reason and to propose. In this column I will deal with this part of the document and in the next with the remainder, highlighting some of the key ideas.

The first outlook needed in dialogue with others is *listening*. Here we see how proponents of gender theory hold that a person can decide or choose their own gender, independent of their biological sex, and that this choice is fluid and can change over time. As is obvious, this view is contrary to biological reality and to the nature of marriage between a man and a woman through which children come into the world. Nonetheless, we can agree that there should be no unjust discrimination against those who hold to gender theory or who freely choose to change their gender.

Critiquing gender theory, the document notes that the theory is based on a dualistic view of the human person, with the body completely separate from the soul and the will being absolute and able to manipulate the body as it pleases. This is contrary to reality where, in the words of the Second Vatican Council, "though made of body and soul, man is one" (*GS* 14).

This in turn leads to relativism, in which everything is of equal value, without any real order or purpose. The basis of the family, formed by a man and a woman united in marriage with their children, is thus emptied of meaning.

The second guiding principle is *reasoning*. Reason shows that the sexual difference between men and women can be demonstrated scientifically by the fields of genetics, endocrinology and neurology. It is not a social construct, something invented by man that can be changed or disregarded, but rather something deeply ingrained in the biology of the individual, indeed at the level of the cells. Every cell in a male has the XY chromosome and every cell in a female has the XX chromosome. This stamps a person as male or female, with all the attendant characteristics that follow from their biological sex.

Moreover, the document notes that terms like "intersex" and "transgender", in a self-contradictory way, actually presuppose the very sexual difference that they propose to deny. Thus, for example, a boy wanting to be a girl or a woman wanting to be a man are in fact admitting the existence and desirability of being female or male.

The third principle is *proposing*. Here the Church proposes an educational program based on a proper anthropology, according to which "man too has a nature that he must respect and that he cannot manipulate at will" (Pope Benedict XVI, Address 22 Sept. 2011). This nature is seen in the book of *Genesis* which says that "male and female he created them" (*Gen* 1:27). The denial of this duality not only erases the vision of human beings as the fruit of an act of creation but creates the idea of the human person as a sort of abstraction who chooses for himself what his nature is to be, thereby undermining the basis of the family. Also, only in accepting one's masculinity or femininity can one recognise his or her identity in an encounter with someone who is different.

697 More on the Vatican document on gender theory

You began an interesting commentary on the Vatican document on gender theory and promised to continue. What else does the document say?

After discussing the three guiding principles of listening, reasoning, and proposing, which I treated last week, the document *"Male and female he created them" – towards a path of dialogue on the question of gender theory in education* goes on to give criteria to the different groups involved in education.

The first of these is the family, the natural place for the relationship of complementarity between man and woman to find its fullest realisation. The family is a natural unit and is the first one responsible for the education of its children. The document insists on two fundamental rights in this regard.

The first is the family's right to be recognised as the primary environment for the formation of children, including their sexual and affective education. This is fundamental in Australia, where programs like Safe Schools seem to take this right away from parents and transfer it to schools, in the event that a child wishes to adopt a different gender and the parents are opposed to this transition.

The second right is that of children to grow up in a family with a father and a mother where the masculinity and femininity of the father and mother help the child grow in affective maturity. This too is fundamental in this country, where same-sex "marriage" has been legalised and where other types of relationships deny children the complementary roles of a father and a mother.

The document next addresses the school, which educates children in a role subsidiary to that of the family. The goal of the Catholic school is the promotion of the human person, and the person finds the fullness of the truth about man in the person of Jesus Christ. The document stresses that the school is to dialogue with the family and respect the family's culture, listening to its needs and expectations. The school should help children grow in affectivity and develop a critical sense in dealing with such issues as the flood of pornography and the overload of stimuli that can deform sexuality.

As regards society as a whole, the document mentions that the educational process should give a perspective on the situation of contemporary society, where the culture of marriage is in decline. There should be an educational alliance between family, school and society but this alliance, the document says, is in crisis. All participants in education are to carry out their responsibilities in the name of the parents and with their consent.

The document next addresses formators, those who contribute to the formation of the students in various ways. They can have a strong influence on their students, and for this reason they should have not only professional qualifications but also cultural and spiritual preparedness. They should always endeavour to give their students good example since, in the words of Pope Paul VI, "modern man listens more willingly to witnesses than to teachers, and if he does listen to teachers, it is because they are witnesses" (*EN* 41). Educators should be especially prepared regarding the issue of gender theory and regarding current and proposed legislation in this matter. And they should develop new teaching materials that offer a sound vision of the human person to counter materials that give a partial or distorted vision.

In its conclusion, the document says that the path of dialogue, which involves listening, reasoning and proposing the Christian vision, is the most effective way to bring about a positive transformation of concerns and misunderstandings in the area of gender theory. This culture of dialogue does not contradict the legitimate aspirations of Catholic schools to maintain their own vision of human sexuality, in keeping with the right of families to base the education of their children on a proper anthropology of the person's true identity. And a democratic state cannot reduce the range of education on offer to a single school of thought, especially in relation to this extremely delicate subject, which is concerned with the fundamentals of human nature and with the rights of parents to choose freely an educational model that accords with the dignity of the human person.

698 The attack on the family

A friend says she thinks the push for same-sex "marriage" and the acceptance of the LGBTI agenda have as a more sinister aim the destruction of the family itself. Is this over the top?

It is not over the top at all. Obviously, the family composed of a father and a mother and their children is so grounded in human nature that it will be here for all time, as it has been since Adam and Eve. To attempt to undo something as natural and fundamental to human well-being as the family is to attempt the impossible. But the attack on marriage and the family is real and it has been with us for a long time, even if it has reached its present intensity only in recent times.

To understand the depth of the attack it is helpful to trace its origins in history. In doing so I will use primarily the wonderful book *The Global Sexual Revolution* by Gabriele Kuby, in the updated and revised edition published in 2017 by Parousia Media. The book is a masterful treatise on the background and insidiousness of the global sexual revolution, which has such aims as the legalisation of same-sex "marriage", the implementation of educational tools like Safe Schools and ultimately the destruction of the family as we know it. I will use the book to answer your question in the next two columns.

A major contribution to the attack on the family comes from the nineteenth-century Germans Karl Marx and Friedrich Engels, and of course from their Marxist followers today, one of whom, Ros Ward, is one of the writers of the Safe Schools program. Marx and Engels began with an even more general and fundamental attack on religion and morality. Marx wrote in the *Manifesto of the Communist Party* in 1848: "Communism abolishes eternal truths, it abolishes all religion and all morality, instead of constituting them on a new basis; it therefore acts in contradiction to all past historical experience."

As regards the family, Marx and Engels wrote: "The secret to the Holy Family is the earthly family. To make the former disappear, the latter must be destroyed, in theory and in practice" (*Gesamtausgabe*, vol. 3, 6). This is strong and alarming language.

Engels saw the relationship of husband and wife in monogamous marriage as the first example of the opposition of the sexes: "The first class antagonism appearing in history coincides with the development of the antagonism of man and wife in monogamy, and the first class oppression with that of the female by the male sex" (*The Origin of the Family, Private Property and the State* (1884)). He added that the monogamous nuclear family only emerged with capitalism, since before that traditional tribal societies were classless and practised a form of primitive communism in which there was no private property, nor were there husbands and wives but rather groups of men and women and their children living together with no restrictions on their sexual relationships with each other. This is of course arrant nonsense.

Engels went on to say that with the rise of capitalism and the monogamous family, the bourgeoisie could pass their wealth on to their children, rather than sharing it with the masses of the proletariat, thus fostering and perpetuating inequality. Also, in the family children were taught to obey their parents in a hierarchical society, something antithetical to the socialist ideal of the classless society. Clearly, the family had to be destroyed.

Another extremely influential contributor to the LGBTI ideology was the German Marxist psychoanalyst Wilhelm Reich (1897-1957). In 1936 he wrote *The Sexual Revolution* in which he argued that the sexualisation of the masses, particularly of children, was the way to true liberation and the classless society, and that "compulsory marriage" and the "compulsory family" had to be destroyed. He wrote: "The patriarchal family is the structural and ideological breeding ground of all social orders based on the authoritarian principle." Reich considered sexually active children as natural revolutionaries who rebel against all authority, including that of their parents, and he promoted masturbation and sexual promiscuity starting at puberty to release young people from their family ties and thus undermine the family. The Safe Schools program teaches all of this!

These thinkers set the platform for what we are witnessing today in the sexual revolution and the effort to destroy the family. We must be on guard and resist it at all costs.

699 More on the attack on the family

You said you were going to continue your interesting report on the historical background of the attack on the family. What other elements are there in this history?

Once again I will draw on Gabriele Kuby's fascinating book *The Global Sexual Revolution*.

One of the important influences in the attack on morality and the family was the psychology of behaviourism, pioneered by John Watson with his book *Behaviorism* in 1914. This approach sees man as little more than a higher ape who can be programmed to behave in a predictable way by various positive and negative stimuli. With his book *Psychological Care of Infant and Child* in 1928 Watson sought to replace parental love and traditional standards of childrearing with "scientific" behaviour control.

This in turn led to the idea of social engineering, with people like Edward Bernays, an atheist, endeavouring to influence popular thinking without the people being aware of it. *Life* magazine listed him as one of the one hundred most influential people of the twentieth century. In his book *Propaganda* in 1928 he wrote: "The conscious and intelligent manipulation of the organized habits and opinions of the masses is an important element in democratic society. Those who manipulate this unseen mechanism of society constitute an invisible government, which is the true ruling power of our country." While this may sound alarming, how else can we explain how the LGBTI lobby, which represents a tiny per cent of the population, has come to dominate the social agenda in Australia today? Obviously, with the help of the media.

E. Michael Jones, in his book *Libido Dominandi – Sexual Liberation and Political Control* (St Augustine's Press, 2000) explains how this works: "The goal of secularization was the reduction of all of life's imperatives to 'opinions', which is to say not the expression of moral absolutes or divine law. Once this 'secularization' occurred, the people who controlled 'opinions' controlled the country." We see this happening around us. Moral absolutes like sexual morality, the sanctity of life and the nature of marriage are reduced to opinions, opening the way to sexual promiscuity and the legalisation of euthanasia and same-sex marriage.

Another important contributor to the destruction of sexual morality and the family was Alfred Kinsey, the "father of sexology", with his books *Sexual Behavior in the Human Male* (1948) and *Sexual Behavior in the Human Female* (1953). Even though his statistics were later shown to be flawed, he succeeded in undermining the "repressive" sexual heritage of Judeo-Christian culture, claiming that the laws that had protected families, women and children were relics of a hypocritical morality that no one adhered to and that stood in the way of the blessings of a "sexually enlightened and honest era." In the first two months after publication his first book sold 200,000 copies and convinced Americans that it was "normal" to engage in premarital sex, get divorced, indulge homosexual tendencies and view pornography. We see how widespread these ideas and practices are today.

Kuby comments that the rise of no-fault divorce, the legalisation of abortion, extramarital sex, cohabitation, and toleration of fornication, sodomy, homosexuality, divorce, and prostitution "had the effect Kinsey was looking for: disintegration of families, absent fathers, the explosive spread of sexually transmitted diseases, and an emotionally traumatized youth" (p. 33).

Another important figure was John Money, a psychiatrist at Johns Hopkins Hospital in Baltimore. He played a key role in gender ideology, which promoted free choice of one's gender, and in the 1960s he opened the Gender Identity Clinic, the first clinic for sex change operations.

And then Simone de Beauvoir, with the publication of *The Second Sex* in 1949, launched the radical feminist agenda in a major way, arguing that women should break free from the shackles of male domination, as well as from motherhood, and should indulge themselves in "liberated sexuality." To that end contraception and abortion were essential. Her radical feminist agenda included the rejection of sexual morality, motherhood and family, with abortion as a woman's right, the career woman as the only role model, and a power struggle against men.

700 Still more on the attack on the family

I have been reading with interest your articles on the background to the attack on the family. What other elements are there?

Gabriele Kuby, in her book *The Global Sexual Revolution*, gives great importance to the Frankfurt Institute for Social Research, founded in 1923 to conduct research into scientific Marxism. Its *Journal of Social Research* was the most important platform for such Marxists as Max Horkheimer, Theodor Adorno, Erich Fromm and Herbert Marcuse. The Frankfurt School sought to merge Marxist theory with Freudian psychoanalysis in order to transform society on Marxist principles, including the abolition of private property, the destruction of religion and the destruction of the family.

When the Nazis closed the Institute in 1933 it eventually found a home in Columbia University in New York and it was there that Adorno and others began their research into the "authoritarian personality", which is brought about by the "authoritarian family" and is potentially fascist, legitimising the Marxists' effort to destroy the family. After the war, in 1946, the University of Frankfurt brought the Institute back to that city, where it collaborated closely with the Socialist German Student League, one of whose most prominent leaders was Rudi Dutschke. The league spawned the Red Brigades which were responsible for violent protests against the Vietnam War. Among their slogans were "Destroy what is destroying you!", "Battle the bourgeois nuclear family!", and "If you sleep with the same one twice, you're a slave of bourgeois vice!" Some of the Frankfurt School's writers blamed the Holocaust on Germans' authoritarian mentality, leading to the conclusion that the family had to be destroyed if Germans were to be re-educated.

In order to destroy the authoritarian mentality and the family that had engendered it, Herbert Marcuse, in his book *Eros and Civilization* (1955), sought to merge Marxist thought and Freudianism, proposing that society would be less repressive if eros, the sex drive, were given free rein. In two communes in Berlin which came into existence at that time, "liberated sexuality" free of such evils as "compulsory marriage", the taboo against incest and the prohibition of paedophilia was openly practised and glorified by the media. Sex with anyone was promoted – in front of children, with children and among children. As is obvious, all of this was leading to the breakdown of traditional values of marriage, parent-child relationships, and sexual morality.

The next step was the portrayal of more and more sex in the media and cinema. It began with the downfall of the Motion Picture Production Code, a voluntary code agreed upon by movie producers in 1930, one of the principles of which was that entertainment should "improve the race, or, at least, to recreate and rebuild human beings". In its General Principles it stated that entertainment "enters intimately into the lives of men and women and affects them closely; it occupies their minds and affections during leisure hours, and ultimately touches the whole of their lives. A man may be judged by his standard of entertainment as easily as by the standard of his work. So correct entertainment raises the whole standard of a nation." How good is that?

Over the years producers pushed the boundaries of the Code until in 1968 it was replaced by the present Code, which classifies films to warn the viewer of potentially harmful content, including the "R" and "X" classifications, where sex is explicitly portrayed. This was accompanied by the opening of sex shops, the arrival of magazines like *Playboy* in 1959 and a host of other increasingly pornographic publications. The advent of television brought more and more sexually explicit films and other programs over the years. The 1960s saw the rise of the hippie culture, with its rock music, psychedelic drugs and sexual promiscuity. In the 1990s the arrival of the internet brought the availability of pornography on an unprecedented scale.

All of this, along with the feminist creed that women who were wives and mothers were oppressed and inferior, brought "sexual liberation" into everyday life and led to increasing promiscuity, the breakdown of marriages, the introduction of no-fault divorce and the social acceptability of extramarital affairs and of divorce. Marriage was and is truly under attack.

701 Defending family values

With the legalisation of same-sex "marriage" imminent, I am afraid that many of the family values we hold dear will come under attack. Are these fears justified and is there anything we can do about it?

I think there is no question but that many of the values we hold dear are already under attack. The attack is coming not so much from the same-sex couples who can now have their union recognised as from the LGBTI lobby that has come to dominate the social agenda in recent times. Even though these gender activists represent a tiny minority of the population they have wielded an enormous influence in the national discourse.

One of the great influences is in the use of language, through which we understand reality. By changing the meaning of words, our concepts are gradually altered and we lose sight of what mankind has understood for millennia. Apart from the definition of "marriage", which has now been given a totally different meaning, consider, for example, the word "family". This word has always meant what the *Catechism of the Catholic Church* defined as "A man and a woman united in marriage, together with their children" (*CCC* 2202). The Catechism goes on to speak about the importance of this understanding: "This institution is prior to any recognition by public authority, which has an obligation to recognize it. It should be considered the normal reference point by which the different forms of family relationship are to be evaluated" (*ibid*).

With the approval of same-sex "marriage" and the desire of same-sex couples to have children, the word "family" will inevitably be extended to include these couples and any children they may have by adoption, in-vitro fertilisation, artificial insemination, etc. Of course the word "family" can also be used to speak of a spouse and his or her children when the other spouse has died or left, a mother who was never married and her children, etc., but we should always remember, as the Catechism says, that the normal reference point must always be a man and a woman united in marriage and their children.

Even words like "father" or "mother", whose meaning is engraved indelibly on the minds of all those who grew up in a natural family, will now become perverted. What is to prevent a woman in a lesbian relationship from calling herself the father, alongside the other woman who assumes the role of mother, or a man in a gay relationship calling himself the mother? Every child, no matter how they came into being, has a biological father and mother, but this will be lost on many in our brave new world.

Since children of same-sex couples will most often not know who their biological father or mother is, it will more and more be considered offensive for children in a school to talk about their father or mother. Scotland's National Health Service has already banned the use of the words "Mom" and "Dad" in kindergarten, because they discriminate against same-sex parents. God help us, when the first words a child learns to say, "Dada" and "Mama", are no longer acceptable. This has also been seen in the effort by some to ban the celebration of Fathers' Day and Mothers' Day so that we can no longer have a day to honour our fathers and mothers.

Some are even beginning to say we shouldn't use words like "boy" and "girl", since they might offend someone who is unsure of their gender.

And then those forms we have all filled out where we are asked to indicate our gender and we were given only two options, M and F, may be a thing of the past too. It seems the German High Court has recently handed down a decision according to which there are now to be three genders, with the third not yet given a name. Where are we going? When a baby is born there is only one question the parents ask: "Is it a boy or a girl"?

And of course in order not to offend people in same-sex relationships who have a baby, the birth certificate may no longer ask for the names of the father and mother, but rather for Parent 1 and Parent 2.

We Christians should fight and fight hard to resist these impositions on our use of traditional language, which is based on human nature and has stood the test of time.

702 Safe Schools and same-sex marriage

People talk about the Safe Schools program somehow coming into our schools if same-sex marriage is legalised. Is this possible and what is so bad about Safe Schools?

The mandating of the Safe Schools program following the legalisation of same-sex marriage is a distinct possibility. The program aims to educate children in gender theory, teaching them that we are not male or female, as we have always thought, but rather we are somewhere on a gender spectrum with some sixty-three – yes sixty-three! – genders. After all gender, according to this program, is just a social construct, it is what we make of it, what we want to be.

The LGBTI lobby has the two goals of changing the Marriage Act so that marriage can be between two people of any sexual orientation, and then to have the Safe Schools program adopted everywhere so that children will understand that homosexuality is perfectly normal, as are other gender choices.

While it is often presented as an anti-bullying program, the co-founder of the program, Roz Ward, has stated that Safe Schools is not an anti-bullying program but about the promotion of sexual and gender diversity. It was written by activists with the express aim of transforming society. Safe Schools proposes a radical reform of the whole curriculum to include gender theory content in all subjects, even maths and history. Let us be clear that gender theory is no more than a theory, with no scientific foundation.

Safe Schools in fact sexualises children from a young age. It teaches them how to masturbate, how to engage in oral and anal sex, how to use contraception, etc. What is worse, the children are told not to talk about this outside the classroom. Schools are not required to notify parents that the program is being used in their children's school nor are the parents required to give consent to their children attending the classes.

A Victorian mother recently looked into the program after her children told her what they were learning in school. When she objected to the principal, she was told of the "whole school" approach and she had no choice but to withdraw her children from the school. After researching the program thoroughly, she was so horrified by what she found that she posted a video on social media to alert others to its dangers. The video, which can be seen on the Coalition for Marriage website, has had over four million viewers.

Ten years ago one would never have thought this type of material could be taught in Australian schools, yet now it is here. Not only are children taught sexually explicit material in the classroom, but in South Australia there is a mandatory policy for all state schools to allow students to choose the bathroom, uniform, sporting team and sleeping quarters which correspond to their chosen gender identity without the consent, consultation or even notification of their parents.

In other countries where same-sex marriage has been legalised, programs like Safe Schools have become compulsory, at least in all state schools. In Canada, which introduced same-sex marriage in 2005, parents cannot remove their children from the classes, and the courts have sided with the schools on this.

For example, in 2016 Steve Tourloukis of Hamilton, Ontario, sought to have his children in Grades 1 and 4 removed from classes which presented homosexuality as normal. The school refused on the grounds it was impractical because LGBTI issues were embedded throughout the curriculum, and the school considered the ability to opt-out to be a form of "bullying." An Ontario Superior Court justice, while acknowledging it was a significant infringement of his parental rights, denied his request and sided with the school.

It is not inconceivable that this form of "bullying" of parents by schools and the courts could become a reality in Australia if same-sex marriage is legalised. Safe Schools would first be introduced in state schools where the government endorsed it, but it could be mandated in Catholic and other independent schools as well. If a school refused to use it, the authorities could refuse to register the school or to fund it with state funds. The brave new world about which I have been writing may be just around the corner.

SPECIFIC MORAL ISSUES 227

703 More about Safe Schools

I have been discussing the Safe Schools program with my friends and we don't know much about it. Can you alert us to some of the dangers?

I will take most of my material from a report on Safe Schools on the Australian Christian Lobby website by Dr Elisabeth Taylor, Director of Research for that organisation. Dr Taylor has a PhD from Cambridge University and her report is frankly alarming.

In order that LGBTI children can feel safe and included in school and in society, the Safe Schools program proposes to educate all children in a new understanding of gender and sexuality, in what is called "queer theory". According to this theory, we should not consider heterosexuality – that boys are naturally attracted to girls and vice versa – as normal nor that society is divided into males and females, since this discriminates against the sexually diverse. The program is, in Taylor's words, nothing short of "a vehicle for social transformation". It is social engineering, pure and simple. It challenges all the traditional assumptions of gender, sexuality and the institutions that are built on these, such as marriage and the family. What is more, the program has been accepted by governments without any consultation with the community.

The *All of Us* booklet, which contains the lesson plans, uses ridiculously exaggerated statistics on which to base the need for the program, quoting "international research", but the research does not support the statistics. The booklet says that around one in ten people are same sex attracted, up to one in twenty-five are transgender or gender diverse and around one in sixty are born with intersex bodies. The reality is that only between one and three per cent of people are same sex attracted, about one per cent are transgender, and only one in 1500 to 2000 are intersex, with ambiguous genitalia.

In other words, the very need for the Safe Schools program is undermined by these false statistics, since the number of LGBTI students is much smaller than alleged. Any school, with the anti-bullying policies it already has in place, can adequately provide for these students so that they do not feel marginalised or discriminated against, just as schools provide for students of other minority groups who may be bullied, including those of different races and religions, and individuals who stand out for various reasons. But this of course would not satisfy the aim of total social transformation which the authors of the program set out to achieve.

A serious flaw in the Safe Schools approach to gender fluidity is to affirm or celebrate in school a student's feeling that he or she is same-sex attracted, or should be of a different gender. An ongoing longitudinal study of 12,000 students in the U.S., beginning when they were in years 7-12, found that over 70 per cent of those who manifested same sex or both sex attraction in school identified as exclusively heterosexual thirteen years later. Thus to celebrate and encourage a sexual identity that is not yet determined is at best problematic and at worst positively harmful.

One of the worst features of Safe Schools is to take away from parents their rights and duties with respect to their children. This happens in the first place when the school takes upon itself the right to impart sex education, with explicitly graphic material devoid of any moral consideration, an education with which the parents might be in total disagreement. Moreover, because this material is taught across the whole curriculum, the parents cannot withdraw their children from the classes.

Even more alarming is Safe Schools instructing schools to provide support for students to affirm their self-declared gender identity without the need for psychological or medical advice and even without the knowledge or consent of the parents. What is more, parents who refuse to affirm the transgender identity of their child may be reported to the authorities as putting their child at risk of harm, as being abusive. Parents' rights have been taken over by the state.

And what to say of the policy of allowing boys who now identify as girls to use girls' toilets, change rooms and sleeping quarters on camps? Teachers or girls who object could be regarded as guilty of discrimination and disciplined accordingly.

This program is positively dangerous and must be resisted at all costs.

704 Attending same-sex "weddings"

I have always been close to my sister who has same-sex attraction and has lived with her partner for several years. Now she has done what I always feared: invite me to her wedding. As much as I disagree with it, I really feel I should attend to keep up our relationship. Can I do this?

In the few months since same-sex marriage became legal in Australia I have already been asked this question several times. The question has always been accompanied by a considerable amount of anguish, as if the person were saying, "I really disapprove of same-sex relationships but because of my close relationship with the person I feel I have to attend." It is a classic dilemma.

Added to the problem in this case is the fact that two persons in a same-sex relationship are living in a state of sin since any sexual acts between them are grievously sinful. How can one celebrate with them the formalisation of a sinful relationship? I addressed the question of attending "garden" weddings some years ago (cf. J. Flader *Question Time 2*, q. 248) and what I wrote there can be applied to the present case, although with some obvious differences.

There are two strong goods at stake and choosing between them inevitably leaves one of them wounded. The two goods are of course respect for the truth about Christian marriage and sexuality on one hand, and love for one's family and friends on the other.

Attending a gay wedding is an instance of what is called "cooperation in sin". Because marriage in God's plan is between a man and a woman and because two people of the same sex having sexual relations with each other are committing a grave sin, a gay wedding is intrinsically wrong, unlike, for example, the garden wedding of two unmarried persons of opposite sex. Hence the reasons for attending must be proportionately more serious.

As we know, according to traditional Catholic moral theology, one should ordinarily not cooperate in the wrongful deeds of another, but there may be circumstances in which one may do so.

First, one may never cooperate *formally*; that is, agreeing with and accepting the sin. This would be the case of someone who saw nothing wrong with a gay couple living together and getting married. If the person disagrees with the sin, but feels he or she should attend the wedding, the cooperation is called *material*.

Second, one can cooperate materially only if there is a proportionate reason to do so. And the more *proximate*, as distinct from *remote*, the cooperation is, the stronger the reason one needs to justify cooperating. For example, the celebrant, the best man and the maid of honour cooperate more proximately or closely than those who merely attend. Without their cooperation the wedding might not go ahead, because a celebrant and two witnesses are necessary for the civil validity of a marriage. Normally, one should not participate with this close degree of cooperation. Those who merely attend the wedding are cooperating more remotely, since even if they do not attend, the wedding will still go ahead.

In the case of a same-sex "wedding", given the immorality of the relationship that will follow it, it would always be advisable to avoid attending, no matter how close one's relationship with the persons. To attend would imply that one was in some way accepting of this new step in their lives, and it would also send a signal to others that one accepted it.

How should you go about explaining to your sister this course of action? To begin with, she undoubtedly knows already that you disapprove of her same-sex relationship, even though at the same time you still love her. So it may not come as a surprise that you now tell her that, in spite of your love for her, you cannot in conscience attend her ceremony, which is not a true marriage. You assure her that you will always love her and that you will treat her partner cordially too, and that you know that this will undoubtedly cause her pain, as it does you.

You might also say that, although you do not agree with what she is doing, you respect her choice, and therefore you hope she will respect your choice too. This may cause tension in your relationship, but this will heal over time, especially if you continue to show that you care about her and her welfare.

It can happen too that different members of the same family adopt different approaches to this situation, with some saying they will not attend the ceremony and others being willing to do so. If this happens and there are others who side with you, it makes your decision easier for your sister to understand. What is important in this case, is for the family to remain united in spite of their differences over this particular matter.

Might there be a situation in which one feels she has no choice but to attend in order to avoid causing irreparable harm to a relationship? Possibly, but every effort should be made to avoid doing so, and these cases should be exceedingly rare. After all, the good of respect for God's plan for marriage takes precedence even over that of human relationships. Jesus said, "He who loves father or mother more than me is not worthy of me; and he who loves son or daughter more than me is not worthy of me" (*Mt* 10:37).

705 *Humanae Vitae* revisited

I have read in recent months about the commemoration of the fiftieth anniversary of the encyclical Humanae vitae *by Pope Paul VI. What was so important about that encyclical?*

Pope Paul VI's encyclical *Humanae vitae* was a truly monumental work. To recall the background, in the 1960s the oral contraceptive pill began to appear on the market and it soon became widely used, including by many Catholics.

Pope Paul had instructed the bishops in the Second Vatican Council (1962-65) not to discuss the issue of contraception. Meanwhile he awaited the report of a commission of bishops, theologians, doctors and married couples appointed by Pope John XXIII to advise him on the matter. The world waited with bated breath for his ruling. Many were hoping he would approve the pill and open the way to a reliable method of birth control while others expected him to uphold the traditional teaching that the use of contraception was never permitted.

Finally, on 25 July 1968 he issued *Humanae vitae,* reaffirming the traditional teaching, and all hell broke loose. Journalists quickly seized on the few lines which banned contraception and pilloried the encyclical, and soon a large group of theologians from around the world signed a letter of protest to the Pope. At the same time a great number of bishops, theologians and married people applauded the Pope for reaffirming what they had always believed and lived. For years afterwards reference was made in the media to "the encyclical", as if it were the only one ever written.

Pope Paul VI was truly courageous in writing *Humanae vitae.* He mentioned at the beginning that there were changes in society that argued in favour of contraception: the growing worry about rapid population growth, the difficulty of raising a large family in times of financial and housing stress, the growing role of women in society, etc. He alluded too to the fact that the conclusions of the commission favoured allowing the use of contraception and that the commission itself was divided on the issue (cf. *HV* 6). Among those on the commission was Cardinal Karol Wojtyla, the future Pope St John Paul II, who was of course opposed to the use of contraception.

Pope Paul knew that his encyclical would give rise to a storm of protest and controversy, even within the Church. It did. But, as he wrote at the beginning, he "prayed constantly to God" and gave his reply "by virtue of the mandate entrusted to us by Christ" (*HV* 6).

He knew that the Church had always opposed the use of contraception, as had all Christian denominations until 1930 when the Anglicans broke ranks and allowed it (cf. J. Flader, *Question Time 4*, q. 559). And he knew that later that year Pope Pius XI had issued the encyclical *Casti Connubii* which stated that "any use of matrimony whatsoever in the exercise of which the act is deprived, by human interference, of its natural power to procreate life, is an offence against the law of God and of nature, and that those who commit it are guilty of grave sin" (*CC*

56). In short, the Church's age-old stand on contraception was part of its constant teaching and it could not be changed.

In many ways *Humanae vitae* was truly prophetic. In it Pope Paul warned of grave consequences that could follow the widespread use of contraception: the increase of marital infidelity and a general lowering of moral standards; the lack of respect of men towards women, seeing them as mere instruments for the satisfaction of their desires; and the recommendation or even imposition of contraceptive methods by governments on their people to solve the country's problems (cf. *HV* 17). It is no secret that all of these predictions have come to pass, with grave consequences.

Even more, in the last fifty years the fears of a population explosion have given way to the problems of demographic winter, with almost all the world's developed countries experiencing birth rates below replacement level. Japan's population is already falling and is expected to fall by a third in the next fifty years.

All in all, *Humanae vitae* was a momentous encyclical and it deserves to be read or reread by all, especially since Pope Paul VI has now been proclaimed a saint.

706 Why is contraception not permitted?

Now that we are commemorating the fiftieth anniversary of Pope Paul VI's encyclical Humanae vitae, can you remind me why contraception is not permitted?

The easiest way to understand why contraception is not permitted is from nature itself. As with other species in the animal kingdom, God created humans male and female and he formed their bodies in such a way that males could unite with females in order to bring offspring into the world. This is obviously the primary purpose of sexuality in God's plan.

In the case of humans, however, we are not simply animals destined to live on the planet for a time and then disappear altogether.

We are made in the image and likeness of God, with an immortal soul destined to be with God forever in heaven. God told our first parents to "be fruitful and multiply and fill the earth" (cf. *Gen* 1:28). He wants there to be many souls with him in heaven for all eternity and he gave us sexuality in order to bring that about.

To engage in sexual acts while preventing those acts from bringing forth new life thus goes against God's plan, against nature. In simple terms, as well as being an expression of love, the purpose of sex is procreation, cooperation with God in the creation of a new human being, a child of God. It is an awesome gift and responsibility. In the scriptures, children are always regarded as a blessing and sterility as a misfortune. Therefore, to use any means to render a person or an act intentionally sterile is contrary to God's plan for the continuation of the human race.

In *Humanae vitae* Pope Paul VI explains it like this: "That teaching, often set forth by the Magisterium, is founded upon the inseparable connection, willed by God and unable to be broken by man on his own initiative, between the two meanings of the conjugal act: the unitive meaning and the procreative meaning. Indeed, by its intimate structure, the conjugal act, while most closely uniting husband and wife, capacitates them for the generation of new lives, according to laws inscribed in the very being of man and of woman. By safeguarding both these essential aspects, the unitive and the procreative, the conjugal act preserves in its fullness the sense of true mutual love and its ordination towards man's most high calling to parenthood" (*HV* 12). In other words, the one-flesh union of husband and wife (the unitive aspect), must always be open to life (the procreative aspect).

What is more, an act of sexual union closed off to life is not an act of true love, no matter what the spouses may say. True love is a total self-giving of two persons to each other, holding nothing back. They do not love up to a point, subject to certain conditions, but totally, unconditionally. Their model is Christ himself, who, "having loved his own who were in the world, loved them to the end" (*Jn* 13:1). Indeed, Christ, so to speak, consummated his nuptial union with his spouse the Church by his death on the Cross, giving himself to the end, to the last drop of his blood and water, saying "It is consummated", "It is finished" (*Jn* 19:30).

If a couple use contraception they do not give themselves totally. They give their bodies but withhold their fertility, using a physical or chemical barrier to prevent the conception of a child. Not only is this contrary to God's plan for the use of sexuality, it is not true love. Pope St John Paul II in his Apostolic Exhortation *Familiaris consortio* (1981) explains that "the innate language that expresses the total reciprocal self-giving of husband and wife is overlaid, through contraception, by an objectively contradictory language, namely, that of not giving oneself totally to the other. This leads not only to a positive refusal to be open to life but also to a falsification of the inner truth of conjugal love, which is called upon to give itself in personal totality" (*FC* 32).

Couples who have been using contraception and later give themselves completely to one another without any barriers appreciate the difference keenly. If they have a serious reason to avoid a child for the time being or indefinitely, they can use natural family planning, abstaining from marital acts by mutual agreement during the fertile period each month. Those who use this method often find that their love for each other actually grows, as do their respect for each other and their self-mastery.

Would that more people were aware of this reasoning and lived in accordance with it.

707 Condoms and HIV

In a class of Studies of Religion one of my students asked whether the Church has a ruling on married couples using a condom to prevent the transmission of HIV. I didn't know the answer. Can you help me?

To my knowledge the Church has made no official pronouncement on this question. But theologians have written at length about it, especially after Professor Martin Rhonheimer of the Pontifical University of the Holy Cross in Rome published an article in *The Tablet* in 2004 arguing that it would be acceptable for a married couple to use a condom to prevent the transmission of HIV. The article gave rise to a flurry of responses from theologians around the world, some in favour and some against.

It should be said that the theologians on both sides of the question were highly regarded from the point of view both of professional expertise and of fidelity to traditional Church teaching.

In February 2011 William Newton published an online article in the *Linacre Quarterly* summarising the arguments on both sides, and I will draw on that article here. The issues are very technical, revolving around defining the moral object chosen by the couple in using a condom for the purpose of avoiding transmission of HIV, and I can't possibly explain all the subtleties in this column.

Newton begins by describing Fr Rhonheimer as a "highly respected and doctrinally orthodox moral philosopher", so his view cannot be dismissed out of hand, even if other theologians disagreed with him. Newton acknowledges that the moralists on both sides support the teaching of Pope St Paul VI's encyclical *Humanae vitae*.

In his article Rhonheimer stated that "the moral norm condemning contraception as intrinsically evil does not apply" to the case of married couples who use condoms to prevent the transmission of HIV. The reason he gives, in simple terms, is that the couple are not using the condom as a contraceptive, to avoid pregnancy, but rather as a means of avoiding infecting the other spouse with a potentially fatal virus.

While the physical description of their act is sexual intercourse with a condom, which in other circumstances would be contraceptive and therefore wrong, the moral description is engaging in sexual intercourse in such a way as to avoid infection. The fact that the condom will be contraceptive is not directly intended but is rather, in Rhonheimer's terms, *praeter intentionem,* outside or beyond the intention of the couple.

He uses the example of a knowingly sterile couple in which one spouse is HIV-infected who use a condom to prevent infection, obviously without it being used for contraception. He also draws support from the situation of a woman using a contraceptive pill for therapeutic reasons, for example for heavy bleeding or endometriosis, who is not choosing to contracept when engaging in sexual intercourse with her husband.

Other moralists, including Janet Smith, Benedict Guevin and Stephen Long disagree with Rhonheimer, maintaining that although the contraceptive effect of the condom is not directly intended, it is nonetheless "embedded" and must be included in the moral evaluation of the act.

Where does this leave a couple today, one of whom is HIV infected and does not want to infect the other spouse?

First, one can follow the traditional teaching that where reputable theologians disagree on a particular question and the Church has not given an official teaching on it a person can follow either course of action. It may be that the Church may one day give an official teaching but until then one is free to follow either course.

Nonetheless, given that condoms can sometimes be defective or slip off, some couples may choose to refrain altogether from marital relations in order to avoid exposing the wife to the man's seminal fluid and hence to HIV. This would be difficult but certainly the safest option. God will always give these couples his grace to be faithful, and to express their love in other ways.

In any case, a report on the HIV.gov website in March 2019 stated that people living with HIV who take HIV medication daily as prescribed and get and keep an undetectable level of the virus have effectively no risk of sexually transmitting HIV to their HIV-negative partners.

708 Politicians and legislation against the moral law

In recent years we have seen legislation passed which allows such practices as same-sex "marriage", euthanasia and abortion. Can a Catholic politician in good conscience vote for legislation of this sort?

This has become a very important question in recent times and the Church has spoken out on it. Pope St John Paul II in his encyclical

Evangelium vitae (1995) and the Vatican's Congregation for the Doctrine of the Faith in its "Doctrinal Note on Some Questions Regarding the Participation of Catholics in Political Life" (2002) have given criterion to guide politicians.

The Doctrinal Note situates the question within the culture of relativism, which "sanctions the decadence and disintegration of reason and the principles of the natural moral law. Furthermore, it is not unusual to hear the opinion expressed in the public sphere that such ethical pluralism is the very condition for democracy. As a result, citizens claim complete autonomy with regard to their moral choices, and lawmakers maintain that they are respecting this freedom of choice by enacting laws which ignore the principles of natural ethics and yield to ephemeral cultural and moral trends, as if every possible outlook on life were of equal value" (n. 2).

Catholic lawmakers cannot ignore the principles of natural ethics, the natural law, when they vote on moral issues like the ones you mention. In a democratic society they are free, and indeed as Catholics required, to be guided by the principles of the natural law as taught by the Church in their deliberations: "Democracy must be based on the true and solid foundation of non-negotiable ethical principles, which are the underpinning of life in society" (n. 3).

The Doctrinal Note adds that "while democracy is the best expression of the direct participation of citizens in political choices, it succeeds only to the extent that it is based on a correct understanding of the human person. Catholic involvement in political life cannot compromise on this principle, for otherwise the witness of the Christian faith in the world, as well as the unity and interior coherence of the faithful, would be non-existent" (n. 3).

Therefore, "Catholics, in this difficult situation, have the right and the duty to recall society to a deeper understanding of human life and to the responsibility of everyone in this regard. John Paul II, continuing the constant teaching of the Church, has reiterated many times that those who are directly involved in lawmaking bodies have a 'grave and clear obligation to oppose' any law that attacks human life. For them, as for every Catholic, it is impossible to promote such laws or to vote for them" (n. 4; John Paul II, Enc. *Evangelium vitae*, n.73). This could not be more clear.

In recent times it has been heartening to see courageous parliamentarians, Catholics and those of other faiths, stand up for the defence of human life in voting against the decriminalisation of abortion and euthanasia. At the same time, it is sad to see others who by their background should uphold these principles cave in, saying they don't want to impose their personal views on the wider community.

St John Paul comments that in this case "the original and inalienable right to life is questioned or denied on the basis of a parliamentary vote or the will of one part of the people – even if it is the majority. This is the sinister result of a relativism which reigns unopposed: the 'right' ceases to be such, because it is no longer firmly founded on the inviolable dignity of the person, but is made subject to the will of the stronger part. In this way democracy, contradicting its own principles, effectively moves towards a form of totalitarianism" (*EV* n. 20).

He goes on to say: "Really, what we have here is only the tragic caricature of legality; the democratic ideal, which is only truly such when it acknowledges and safeguards the dignity of every human person, is betrayed in its very foundations: 'How is it still possible to speak of the dignity of every human person when the killing of the weakest and most innocent is permitted? In the name of what justice is the most unjust of discriminations practised: some individuals are held to be deserving of defence and others are denied that dignity?' (John Paul II, Address, 18 December 1987). When this happens, the process leading to the breakdown of a genuinely human co-existence and the disintegration of the State itself has already begun" (*EV* 20).

709 Voting for a "less bad" law

With the abortion issue to be voted on shortly in our parliament, wouldn't it be better for a parliamentarian to vote for an amended bill which restricts access to abortion than to let it pass without these amendments?

You ask a very good question, which has in fact been answered by Pope St John Paul II in his encyclical *Evangelium vitae, The Gospel of Life*, in 1995. The idea behind your question is that, while in an ideal world we shouldn't vote for any bill that allows abortion, which is a horrendous attack on the innocent life of the baby in the womb, in the real world it may be better to vote for amendments to a bill which restrict access to abortion to some degree rather than let the bill be passed without these restrictions. In other words, to vote for a bill which is less bad.

What Pope John Paul wrote is the following: "It is precisely from obedience to God – to whom alone is due that fear which is acknowledgment of his absolute sovereignty – that the strength and the courage to resist unjust human laws are born. It is the strength and the courage of those prepared even to be imprisoned or put to the sword, in the certainty that this is what makes for 'the endurance and faith of the saints' (*Rev* 13:10). In the case of an intrinsically unjust law, such as a law permitting abortion or euthanasia, it is therefore never licit to obey it, or to 'take part in a propaganda campaign in favour of such a law, or vote for it'" (CDF, *Declaration on Procured Abortion*, 18 November 1974, n. 22; *EV* n. 73).

This would seem to forbid altogether voting for a law in any form which allows abortion. Nonetheless, Pope John Paul goes on to clarify the matter in a paragraph which answers your question: "A particular problem of conscience can arise in cases where a legislative vote would be decisive for the passage of a more restrictive law, aimed at limiting the number of authorised abortions, in place of a more permissive law already passed or ready to be voted on. Such cases are not infrequent. It is a fact that while in some parts of the world there continue to be campaigns to introduce laws favouring abortion, often supported by powerful international organisations, in other nations – particularly those which have already experienced the bitter fruits of such permissive legislation – there are growing signs of a rethinking in this matter. In a case like the one just mentioned, when it is not possible to overturn or completely abrogate a pro-abortion law, an elected official, whose absolute personal opposition to procured abortion was well known, could licitly support proposals aimed at limiting the harm done by such a law and at lessening its negative consequences at the level of general opinion and public morality. This does not in fact represent an illicit cooperation with an unjust law, but rather a legitimate and proper attempt to limit its evil aspects" (*EV* n. 73).

What this means in practice is that a parliamentarian, faced with a bill which will inevitably be passed in spite of his or her opposition to it, can and should fight to have amendments introduced which restrict access to abortion in some way. The amendments might, for example, restrict abortion to a certain number of weeks of gestation, require the assent of physicians who say that if the abortion were not carried out the mother's physical or mental health would be endangered, ban abortions motivated by the sex of the baby, etc. Naturally, parliamentarians should first do all in their power to convince their fellow-parliamentarians not to allow abortion at all, since it is nothing short of a crime against humanity.

It is interesting to note that a number of American states have recently passed legislation greatly restricting access to abortion. In May 2019 the state of Alabama outlawed abortions in all cases except when the mother's life was at risk. Also in May, the state of Missouri banned abortion after eight weeks of pregnancy and also abortions motivated solely by the sex or race of the foetus or by a diagnosis of Down Syndrome. Sadly, a federal judge in that state on 27 August blocked the state from enforcing the ban after the eighth week of pregnancy, although he did allow the ban on abortions because of the sex or race of the foetus, or because of Down Syndrome. Perhaps the tide is turning in favour of life, at least in some places.

710 Politicians and excommunication

I am disturbed by the fact that some Catholic politicians have voted for the legalisation of abortion in this country. For me, this is a great scandal. Could or should they be excommunicated for doing this?

We can begin by looking at what the Church teaches regarding the denial of Holy Communion in certain circumstances. Canon 915 of the *Code of Canon Law* reads: "Those ... who obstinately persist in manifest grave sin, are not to be admitted to Holy Communion." Can it be said that a person who publicly expresses support for the legalisation of abortion and who votes for such legislation is obstinately persisting in manifest grave sin? There would seem to be no doubt that this is the case. The Church has repeatedly taught that abortion is a grave sin. For example, the *Catechism of the Catholic Church* teaches: "Since the first century the Church has affirmed the moral evil of every procured abortion. This teaching has not changed and remains unchangeable. Direct abortion, that is to say, abortion willed either as an end or a means, is gravely contrary to the moral law" (*CCC* 2271).

Therefore, to deny publicly, to contradict openly a teaching as clear and fundamental as this is clearly a grave sin. It can be argued that someone who has not been taught the faith properly and does not understand the Church's clear position on this issue might not be guilty before God of a formal sin. But at the same time, since abortion is manifestly the ending of the life of an innocent human being in the womb of its mother, it should be clear to everyone that this practice is gravely contrary to the natural law. And at this stage of history virtually everyone, non-Catholics included, knows where the Catholic Church stands on the issue. It is therefore a scandal for a Catholic politician to support the legalisation of abortion and to vote for it.

Moreover, to deny a fundamental teaching like that on abortion is really to fall into the sin of heresy, defined in the Catechism as "the obstinate post-baptismal denial of some truth which must be believed with divine and catholic faith" (*CCC* 2089; Can. 751). The word "obstinate" is important. There may be Catholics who simply do not know what the Church teaches on a particular issue and who, once informed, accept the teaching. They are not heretics. But if someone has been warned that what they are advocating is contrary to Church teaching and they obstinately persist in their belief, they are guilty of heresy.

What is more, someone who persists in heresy automatically incurs a *latae sententiae* excommunication; that is, the person is excommunicated by the law itself (cf. Can. 1364). Since it is often not clear exactly who is guilty of heresy and is therefore excommunicated, the local bishop, after a proper investigation, may choose to declare publicly that the person is excommunicated.

So, in answer to your question, politicians who are known to be Catholics and who vote for legislation like the legalisation of abortion may be excommunicated. Whether the local bishop considers this to be the best way to proceed, however, is another matter.

One approach he may take, after speaking personally with the politician and warning him or her of the scandal they are causing, is to ask the person not to present himself or herself for Communion in any Masses they attend in his diocese. This is not the same as excommunication, which prevents the person from receiving any sacrament in the Church until such time as the person repents and has been absolved of the excommunication.

This approach was taken, for example, in 2008 by Archbishop Joseph Naumann of Kansas City against Kathleen Sebelius, Governor of Kansas, who had vetoed a bill passed by both houses of the state legislature greatly restricting access to abortion. After speaking personally several times with Governor Sebelius about her action, the Archbishop asked Sebelius not to present herself for Holy Communion until such time as she amended her life and publicly repudiated her previous actions. Other American Archbishops who have done this include John Myers and Raymond Burke.

In many cases this may be the best pastoral approach to a difficult problem. If the politician is not normally attending Mass and receiving Communion anyway, it still stands as a warning and a clarification to the faithful of the diocese.

711 Yoga and Christianity

My uncle is a yoga instructor and a practising Catholic. I thought yoga was somehow not compatible with our faith. Can you enlighten me on this?

I will answer your question making ample use of Brother Max Sculley DLS' excellent book *Yoga, Tai Chi, Reiki – A Guide for Christians* published by Modotti Press. The author makes clear that, although many Catholic groups are recommending and teaching yoga, the practice poses a real danger to our faith. I will summarise what he has to say, and for a fuller understanding I recommend reading the book itself.

Yoga is not merely a series of relaxation exercises to relieve stress and promote spiritual and physical well-being. It is intimately bound up with Hindu philosophy. Although there are many different forms of yoga, most involve assuming a series of postures, slowing down one's breathing, focusing the mind on the body and the breathing and repeating a mantra. All of this is intended to absorb prana, or divine energy, from the air and circulate it through the body so as to enter into an altered state of consciousness.

The practitioner learns to feel the prana and direct it to seven different chakras, or energy centres, which start in the groin and end in the crown of the head. The peak comes when the mind becomes void for extended periods of time and the person enters a state of self-realisation and enlightenment, aware that he or she is now divine and at one with the cosmos.

To be one with the divine is to be one, according to Hindus, with

Brahman, the impersonal, infinite energy which is the creator of the universe. The universe in turn is but an extension of Brahman, following the Hindu pantheistic belief that all of nature is somehow divine. It is understandable that yoga should be so popular with devotees of the New Age.

According to yoga theory, as the divine energy rises through the various chakras the person receives psychic powers appropriate to each level. These include the ability to read another's mind, to be aware of past lives, to communicate with the spirit world including the souls of the dead, and the powers of clairvoyance, levitation, and healing.

The rising of the prana through the body is symbolised by Kundalini, a Hindu goddess represented by a coiled snake sleeping at the base of the spine, which rises up and is finally united at the crown chakra with her consort, the Hindu god Shiva.

So why is yoga dangerous to one's Christian faith? As is clear from what we have seen, the whole belief in "divine energy" in the cosmos that one channels into the body, enabling the person to become somehow divine, at one with God, is completely contrary to Christian belief. So is the pantheistic belief that God is somehow identified with nature.

Even if one envisions this "energy" as God's grace or the Holy Spirit, our faith tells us that it is God who gives us this grace and the Holy Spirit, and he does it when and how he chooses. We cannot channel grace or the Holy Spirit into ourselves simply by willing it.

What is more, the altered state of consciousness as the goal of yoga where the mind is still and supposedly at one with the cosmos can open the person to the demonic. There are numerous cases of people who innocently went along to yoga classes and ended up needing to be delivered from various forms of demonic influence. And many ended up with psychiatric illnesses.

Even to seek peace and consolation of spirit, no matter how desirable they are, is not the Christian approach. In prayer we focus on

God and his glory, not on ourselves. And in some cases, especially that of saints like St Mother Teresa of Calcutta, their prayer may not result in consolation and peace at all, but rather in spiritual dryness in which God can seem to be distant.

And whereas the god of yoga is impersonal energy, the God of Christians is the incarnate Jesus Christ, who loves us so much that he died on the cross for us and remains with us in the Blessed Sacrament.

All in all, if a person wants peace of mind, it is better to go into a chapel, be still and meditate on the love of God present in the tabernacle. We don't need yoga.

712 Tai Chi and Christianity

I know a number of people, including fervent Catholics, who practise Tai Chi. Is there anything in this Chinese practice that would make it unsuitable for Christians?

As in my previous answer to a question on yoga, I will use Brother Max Sculley's book *Yoga, Tai Chi, Reiki – A Guide for Christians*. The author gives a comprehensive treatment of Tai Chi with numerous examples of people who have been adversely affected by it.

At the outset let me say that in Tai Chi one can distinguish between the physical exercise involved, which has merit in its own right, and the theory and practice which follow the Chinese Taoist understanding of medicine, in which there can be dangers. I know good Catholics who use Tai Chi simply as an exercise, which they say helps relax them and strengthen their muscles.

But first, what is Tai Chi? Tai Chi comes from China and is based on Taoist philosophy and religion. It involves slow gentle balanced movements with retarded, rhythmic breathing while focusing the mind on the breathing and visualising the movements.

The word Chi refers to energy within the body which, according to Chinese medical theory, is transmitted throughout the body along fourteen energy channels called meridians. Chi is supposedly stored in energy centres just below the navel, near the heart and between the eyebrows, from which it radiates out along the meridians to every cell in the body.

In a healthy person, according to the theory, Chi flows harmoniously to all parts of the body. However, most people have blockages to this flow and the exercise of Tai Chi clears them. As the exercises release tension in the different parts of the body, the channels are re-opened and the flow of Chi is re-established.

The place of the mind is important in each movement, since one of the chief aims of Tai Chi is to bring about balance between mind and body. This begins even before the movements, when the person focuses the mind on the slow, rhythmic, abdominal breathing. During the exercises, the mind visualises the body doing the movement. Ideally, this keeps the mind focused solely on the bodily movements and gradually lessens the stream of consciousness, inducing a sense of deep relaxation and an altered state of consciousness. In Taoist philosophy this is referred to as emptying the mind, allowing the unconscious mind to become highly receptive to cosmic Chi.

All created things are considered to be divine manifestations of Chi and so the ultimate purpose of Tai Chi is to enable the person to reach enlightenment, to become divine, and to find inner peace. As the person becomes more adept in controlling the flow of Chi, he or she acquires a range of gifts, the most prominent being superhuman powers of strength and the ability to heal oneself and others.

Tai Chi can also be practised as a martial art. In his book Brother Sculley relates the experience of a woman from Canberra who was watching a demonstration of Tai Chi as a martial art in a mall, when the man doing the demonstration seemed to follow her. Frightened, she entered a shoe shop where she was suddenly struck by a powerful force in her back through to her chest which made her lose balance, fall and feel decidedly unwell. She was in no doubt that this force had somehow come from the man doing the demonstration, even though he was some distance away. After she found out more about Tai Chi she observed that some of the people who practise it become more aggressive and strike out in a variety of ways at others.

Brother Sculley also relates something seen on nationwide television in the U.S. in 1993, where a ninety year-old Tai Chi master sent an entire line of his students falling to the ground merely by hurling Chi at them from a distance of some six metres. The students later revealed that they felt forced down by a mysterious and irresistible power, the power they themselves were seeking through the practice of Tai Chi.

As is clear, there are definite dangers in practising Tai Chi if one follows the philosophy behind it in its entirety. The philosophy is not at all compatible with Christianity.

IV. CHRISTIAN PRAYER

713 The value of the rosary

Although I love the rosary I know many Catholics who have problems with it. They say it is too repetitive, a prayer for children, out of date, etc. How can I answer them?

Years ago I came across an article on the rosary by Cardinal Albino Luciani, the future Pope John Paul I, which addressed some of the objections you raise (*Soul Magazine*, Sept-Oct. 1984). He began with an interesting observation: "The crisis of the rosary does not come first; what comes first is the crisis in prayer in general. Today people are all taken up in material interests; they think little about the soul. Then, noise invades our existence… For the interior life, and for the *dulcis sermocinatio*, or the tender colloquy with God, it is too tiring to find a few minutes of time. What a pity! What a pity!"

The first objection you mention is that the rosary is repetitive. With its recitation of the *Hail Mary* ten times in each mystery, no one can deny that. But do not people in love repeat the same words over and over again? "I love you." "I love you too". If we loved Our Lady more we would not get tired of repeating the *Hail Marys*.

Some words of St Josemaría Escrivá are relevant here: "'Immaculate Virgin, I know very well that I am only a miserable wretch, and all I do is increase each day the number of my sins.' You told me the other day that was how you spoke to Our Mother… And I was confident in advising you, with assurance, to pray the Holy Rosary. Blessed be that monotony of *Hail Marys* which purifies the monotony of your sins!" (*Furrow*, 475)

We should remember too that if we meditate on the mysteries while saying the rosary, our mind focuses on the mystery and does not notice the passing of the *Hail Marys*. Some words from a simple poem from A. Royo Marin's *The Virgin Mary*, published in Madrid in 1968 are helpful: "You who tire and are slow to pray/ because the same words we always say/ have little understanding what it is to be/ in love forever as I and she."

Some say that the rosary is a prayer for children. But didn't Our Lord say: "Unless you become again as little children, you cannot enter the kingdom of Heaven"? (*Mt* 18:3)

St Josemaría, in the introduction to his book *Holy Rosary*, addresses those who consider themselves "adult Christians": "I must tell these men a secret which may very well be the beginning of the road Christ wants them to follow. My friend: if you want to be great, become little. To be little you have to believe as children believe, to love as children love, to abandon yourself as children do..., to pray as children pray."

And Cardinal Luciani adds: "When people today speak of 'adult Christians' in prayer, sometimes they exaggerate. Personally, when I speak alone with God, and with Our Lady, more than as a grown-up, I prefer to feel myself a child... And I abandon myself to the spontaneous tenderness that a child has for his mama and papa... The Rosary, a simple and easy prayer, helps me to be a child again; and I am not ashamed of it at all."

Another objection is that the rosary is out of date and ought to be replaced by more modern forms of prayer and devotion. While every age can give rise to new forms of piety, and our own age certainly has, there are some devotions which will never be out of date. The *Apostles' Creed*, the *Our Father*, the *Hail Mary*, the *Glory be* and the *Hail, Holy Queen* which make up the Rosary will never be old-fashioned. Nor will meditating on the life of Christ and Our Lady, as is done in the Rosary. These will always be part of the life of true Christians.

Sr Lucy of Fatima comments in a letter published in the Portuguese weekly *A Ordem* in 1978: "As regards the repetition of the *Hail Marys*, it is not something old-fashioned, as some would have us believe. Everything which exists and has been made by God is maintained and preserved through the continuous repetition of the same acts. No one would think of calling the sun, the moon, the stars, the birds, the animals, the plants, etc., old-fashioned just because they are born, live and develop always in the same way. And to be sure these things are much older than the rosary. For God, nothing is old."

In any case, since Our Lady herself has asked us to say the rosary – she prayed the rosary with St Bernadette at Lourdes, she explicitly requested it at Fatima, etc. – let us please our Mother by continuing to say the rosary with love.

714 The rosary and the battle of Lepanto

I have read that victory in the battle of Lepanto in the sixteenth century has been attributed to the saying of the rosary. Can this be possible?

It is most certainly the case. Victory in the battle of Lepanto in 1571 undoubtedly changed the course of history, ending the Ottoman Turks' domination of the Mediterranean, and it has always been attributed to the saying of the rosary.

As we may recall, in 1453 the Ottoman Turks captured Constantinople, the Eastern centre of the Church, and later they took much of the Balkans, Hungary and Romania. In 1566 Selim II became Sultan of the Turks and he set out to achieve what his great-grandfather had vowed to do: capture Rome and stable his horses beneath the dome of St Peter's basilica. He captured Nicosia in Cyprus in 1570 and raided the islands off Venice in 1571, getting ever closer to Rome. This moved Pope St Pius V to call for an army to defeat the Turks. The army and fleet came largely from Spain and Venice and were under the command of the 24-year-old Don Juan of Austria, son of the Emperor Charles V.

Don Juan gave instructions that there was to be no blasphemy on the ships and all the men were to fast for three days. There were priests on the ships to say Mass and hear confessions and all the men were given a rosary. Before setting sail all the men prayed the rosary, led by Don Juan himself. The fleet finally sailed out of Messina in Sicily on 16 September 1571.

Meanwhile in Rome Pope St Pius V, who had standardised the rosary in its present form in 1569 and was very devoted to it, asked for churches to remain open day and night so that the faithful could pray the rosary for the success of the campaign. The people of Rome and the surrounding area heeded the request, as did those in the monasteries and convents of religious.

On the evening of 6 October 1571, which was in fact the eve of the decisive battle, Pope Pius himself led the rosary in the Dominican convent of Santa Maria Sopra Minerva in Rome, entrusting this most important cause to the powerful intercession of Our Lady.

On the following day, October 7, the Christian fleet encountered the Turkish fleet in the Gulf of Patrakas off the coast of Greece near the city of Lepanto. The fleet of the Holy League, as it was called, was heavily outnumbered by the Turks. Estimates vary considerably but the Turkish fleet had close to three hundred vessels and the Christians something over two hundred. The Turks had around 100,000 soldiers and sailors while the Holy League had some 70,000. It should be known that naval battles at that time were fought largely by the opposing ships ramming each other and the soldiers then fighting hand-to-hand on the decks.

The battle lasted some five hours and its outcome was decided when the flagships of both fleets engaged each other, Ali Pasha's *Sultana* ramming Don Juan's *Real*. In the ensuing battle on the decks of both ships Ali Pasha was killed and the *Sultana* was taken in tow by the *Real*. The Holy League sank or burned some 50 Turkish galleys and captured another 117 along with many thousands of men. They liberated some 15,000 Christians who were galley slaves on the Turkish ships. In turn they lost 12 galleys and had some 8,000 wounded, among them Miguel de Cervantes, the author of *Don Quixote*. After that decisive battle the Turkish fleet was no longer a threat on the Mediterranean.

On the very evening of the battle Pope Pius was in a meeting in Rome when he suddenly got up, looked out the window and had a vision that the battle had been fought and won. He turned around and exclaimed "Victory! Victory!" Two weeks later a courier arrived from

Venice with the official news of the victory.

The Pope attributed the victory to the rosary and instituted the feast of Our Lady of Victory, to be celebrated on October 7. In 1573 his successor Pope Gregory XIII changed the name of the feast to Our Lady of the Rosary. In Venice, the Senate commissioned the construction of a chapel dedicated to Our Lady of the Rosary. An inscription on the wall of the chapel read: "Neither valour, nor arms, nor armies, but Our Lady of the Rosary gave us victory!"

So yes, there is every reason to attribute that great victory to the rosary.

715 The rosary and more battles

I read somewhere that the rosary has been credited with victory not only in the battle of Lepanto but in other battles as well. Is this true?

It is most certainly true. Although the Ottoman Turks had been defeated in the naval battle of Lepanto in 1571, they maintained their goal of spreading Islam into Europe and ultimately of taking Rome.

In August 1716 they began an invasion of Hungary with an army of 160,000 soldiers. They were met at Peterwardein by a much smaller Christian force consisting of 91,000 Austrians, Serbs, Croatians, and Hungarians led by Prince Eugene of Savoy. The Christian army outflanked the Turks with their cavalry and driving home their advantage, routed them, leaving over 110,000 dead. The battle ended on August 5, the feast of Our Lady of the Snows.

After that victory, Prince Eugene marched east and made a series of further conquests, most notably at Temesvar in Hungary. There on August 31 his troops laid siege to the Turkish-held fortress and bombarded it repeatedly until on October 12 the Turks surrendered. That day is the feast of Our Lady of Pilar, celebrated especially in Saragossa, Spain. With that victory Hungary was freed from the threat of Turkish domination.

In August of that same year another Turkish force tried to lay siege to what was considered the bastion of western civilisation, the Venetian-held island of Corfu in the Ionian Sea off the coast of Greece. The Turks had over 33,000 soldiers while the Christian army defending the island had only some 8,000. The siege began on July 19 and, after several assaults and a severe storm on August 9 which resulted in many Turkish casualties and which the defenders attributed to Corfu's patron saint, St Spyridon, the siege was broken on August 11. The last Ottoman forces withdrew on August 20 and once again the Christians were victorious.

All of Christendom attributed the victories at Peterwardein, Temesvar and Corfu to the power of the rosary. To understand why, it is important to know that after the battle of Peterwardein the reigning Pope Clement XI declared the feast of Our Lady of the Rosary a universal feast for the entire Church.

Until then the feast, first called Our Lady of Victory by Pope Pius V after the battle of Lepanto in 1571 and then renamed Our Lady of the Rosary by his successor Pope Gregory XIII in 1573, was only allowed to be celebrated in churches that had an altar dedicated to the rosary. The only exception was Spain, where the feast could be celebrated in any church, owing to Spain's important contribution to the fleet that was victorious at Lepanto.

So after the victory at Peterwardein in August 1716, the following October was the first time that all of Christendom was celebrating the universal feast of Our Lady of the Rosary. For this reason, and because people all over the world were praying the rosary, victory in these battles was attributed to the rosary.

In the nineteenth century Pope Leo XIII affirmed this in two separate encyclicals. In 1883, in his encyclical *Supremi Apostolatus Officio*, declaring October the month of the rosary, he wrote: "Important successes were in the last century gained over the Turks at Temesvar, in Pannonia [Hungary], and at Corfu; and in both cases these engagements coincided with feasts of the Blessed Virgin and with the conclusion of public devotions of the rosary."

And in 1897, in the encyclical *Augustissimae Virginis Mariae*, he wrote: "The history of the Church bears testimony to the power and efficacy of this form of prayer [the rosary], recording as it does the rout of the Turkish forces at the naval battle of Lepanto, and the victories gained over the same in the last century at Temesvar in Hungary and in the island of Corfu."

Coincidentally, St Louis de Montfort, who had done so much to preach and write about the rosary, urging people everywhere to pray it, died earlier in 1716 on April 28. He too would have rejoiced over these victories and the establishment of the universal feast of the rosary.

Once again, we see how the rosary is a powerful prayer.

716 The Infant of Prague

My auntie has great devotion to the Infant of Prague and she has a little statue of the Infant in her lounge room which I have always liked but not really understood. What is the origin of this devotion, and what does it have to do with Prague?

Devotion to the Child Jesus under the title Infant of Prague owes its origin, as one can imagine, to the city of Prague, in what is today the Czech Republic. It seems that the statue first appeared in 1556 in Spain, when Maria Maximiliana Manriquez de Lara y Mendoza received it as a wedding present and took it to Bohemia on the occasion of her marriage to Czech nobleman Vratislav of Perstyn. An old legend has it that Maria's mother Doña Isabella had been given the statute by St Teresa of Avila. Maria in turn gave it to her daughter Princess Polyxena of Lobkowitz as a wedding gift.

The statue is about half a metre in height, of wood, wax, and cloth, with the infant Jesus dressed in royal robes and wearing a king's crown. In his left hand he holds a globe with a cross on top and his right hand is raised as if giving a blessing.

After the death of her husband, Princess Polyxena devoted herself to works of charity and was particularly helpful to the Carmelite Friars in Prague. In 1628, when the Carmelite Monastery was reduced to poverty owing to the ravages of war, the princess gave the statue of the Child Jesus to the friars, telling them: "I give you what I prize most highly in the world. Honour and respect the Child Jesus and you shall never be in want."

The Carmelites placed the statue in their oratory and conducted special devotions to the Child Jesus twice a day. The words of the princess proved prophetic, for as long as the Carmelites kept up their devotion to the Divine Infant of Prague, everything went well for them. In 1630 the Carmelites were forced to flee the city during the Thirty Years War and, in the confusion which reigned, they left the statue behind. The Swedish army took possession of the city in 1631 and one of the soldiers threw the statue onto a pile of rubbish behind the altar of the chapel.

In 1637 peace once again came to Prague and the Carmelites returned. One of the friars, Father Cyril, who had previously received great spiritual help through his devotion to the Infant of Prague, searched for the statue and eventually found it in the midst of the rubbish. Overjoyed, he placed it back where it had been in the oratory. Then he knelt down to pray before it and contemplated the great event of the Incarnation of the Son of God as man. He was filled with awe and wonder as he prayed to the God who had become a child out of love for mankind.

Suddenly the statue spoke to him. Father Cyril was stunned as he heard these words: "Have mercy on me and I will have mercy on you. Give me hands and I will give you peace. The more you honour me, the more I will bless you." Startled, Father Cyril examined the statue and, on drawing aside the mantle covering it, found that both hands were broken off. The hands were later restored through the generosity of a devotee of the Divine Child.

For almost four centuries the promise of peace and blessing has inspired worldwide devotion to the miraculous Infant Jesus of Prague. Among the most well-known devotees was St Therese of Lisieux, the Little Flower. The original statue is still preserved in the church of Our Lady of Victory in Prague.

Pope Leo XIII approved devotion to the image in 1896 and instituted a sodality in its honour. In 1913 Pope St Pius X established the Confraternity of the Infant Jesus of Prague under the care of the Carmelites and in 1924 Pope Pius XI granted its first canonical coronation. Pope Benedict XVI crowned the image for the second time during a visit to the Czech Republic in 2009. On that occasion he donated a golden crown with eight shells and numerous pearls and garnets which has adorned the statue ever since.

Today, replicas of the small statue are venerated all over the world and the list of blessings, favours and miraculous healings attributed to the devotion is endless.

717 Our Lady of Good Success

A friend recently told me about devotion surrounding a statue in Ecuador known as Our Lady of Good Success and about a seventeenth century nun associated with it who had revelations about the twentieth century which have proved very accurate. Can you tell me about this?

I hadn't heard about this devotion or the nun until you sent me the question and I have found the whole matter quite fascinating. I will write about the image and the nun in this column and reserve the revelations for the next one.

The image has its origin around 1606 in Spain when two Brothers of the newly-founded Order of Minims for the Service of the Sick were on their way to Rome to ask the Pope for official approval of their Order. When they were near the Catalonian town of Traigueras a fierce storm broke out and they feared for their lives. They prayed to Our Lady for help and then saw a soft light in the mountains and headed toward it. They found a cave with the fragrance of flowers that surrounded a beautiful statue of Our Lady. She had Jesus in her left arm, a scepter in her right and a precious crown on her head. They fell on their knees in veneration, wondering how the statue came to be in that remote place.

The next day they inquired of the local people about the cave and the statue but no one knew anything about them. The Brothers then took the statue with them to Rome. They told Pope Paul V what had happened and he not only acknowledged the supernatural character of the discovery but also approved the new Order, placing it under the protection of Our Lady, to whom he gave the name Our Lady of Good Success. It should be understood that the word "suceso" in Spanish does not mean success, but rather "event" or "happening".

Back in Spain the statue was placed in the Royal Hospital of Madrid and it soon became famous when numerous favours were attributed to it. In 1641 King Philip III ordered the construction of a beautiful shrine for it in the Puerta del Sol in Madrid. But how did the devotion reach Ecuador? The answer is to be found with the nun, Mother Mariana de Jesus Torres.

She was born Mariana Francisca Cadiz in the Spanish province of Vizcaya in 1563. On the day of her first Communion at the age of nine, Our Lady appeared to her and told her she would be a religious of her Immaculate Conception in the new world. In 1577, at the age of thirteen, Mariana left Spain in the company of her aunt, Mother Maria de Jesus Taboada and four other Sisters, to found a Royal Convent of the Order of the Immaculate Conception in Quito, Ecuador. Mariana joined the Order and over the years was the Abbess three times.

On 2 February 1610 Our Lady appeared to her and asked that a statue be made of her under the title Mary of Good Success of the Purification. The statue, similar to the one in Madrid, was to be placed above the Abbess' chair in the choir because Our Lady wanted to be the one to govern and watch over the convent. The statue was commissioned and it was blessed on 2 February 1611. The feast of Our Lady of Good Success, both in Spain and in Ecuador, is celebrated on 2 February.

One of the most extraordinary aspects of Mother Mariana's life was the fact that she "died" three times, as attested to by records in the archives of the convent and the diocese. The first time was in 1582, when she was only eighteen or nineteen. Standing before the judgment seat of God, she was given the choice of remaining in heaven or returning to earth to suffer as an expiatory victim for the sins of the twentieth century. She chose the latter.

Her second death was on Good Friday in 1588 after an apparition in which she saw the terrible abuses and heresies that would exist in the Church in our own times. She arose two days later on Easter Sunday morning. She finally died on 16 January 1635. Miracles through her intercession immediately followed and when her body was exhumed in 1906 during the remodelling of the convent it was found to be incorrupt. It is preserved there today. Her process of canonisation is open and she has been declared Venerable.

718 Our Lady of Good Success and prophecies about our times

I have a friend from Ecuador who says some nun from there made some extraordinary prophecies four centuries ago about situations today like the attack on marriage, the sexual abuse crisis and the decline in religious practice. Do you know anything about this?

I believe the prophecies to which you refer are those of the Venerable Mother Mariana de Jesus Torres, who was born in Spain in 1563 and went to Ecuador at the age of thirteen. There she joined the Order of the Immaculate Conception in Quito and became the abbess three times.

After her death on 16 January 1635, her process of canonisation was opened and she has been declared Venerable. From time to time she had revelations from Our Lord and Our Lady which are the source of the prophecies, later found to be "authentic, untampered with, and worthy of belief".

One of the most remarkable prophecies came on 8 December 1634, when Our Lady told Mother Mariana that "pontifical infallibility will be declared a dogma of the faith by the same Pope chosen to proclaim the dogma of the mystery of my Immaculate Conception. He will be persecuted and imprisoned in the Vatican by the unjust usurpation of the Pontifical States through the iniquity, envy and avarice of an earthly monarch." All of this came to pass two centuries later during the pontificate of Blessed Pope Pius IX.

Our Lady told Mother Mariana that at the end of the nineteenth century and especially in the twentieth, Satan would reign almost completely. She said: "As for the sacrament of Matrimony, which symbolises the union of Christ with his Church, it will be attacked and profaned in the fullest sense of the word. Masonry, which will then be in power, will enact iniquitous laws with the objective of doing away with this sacrament, making it easy for everyone to live in sin, encouraging the procreation of illegitimate children born without the blessing of the Church. The Christian spirit will rapidly decay, extinguishing the precious light of faith until it reaches the point that there will be an almost total and general corruption of customs. The effects of secular education will increase, which will be one reason for the lack of priestly and religious vocations..." It goes without saying that all of this has been borne out in our times.

As regards the priesthood, Our Lady said: "The sacred sacrament of Holy Orders will be ridiculed, oppressed and despised. ...The demon will try to persecute the ministers of the Lord in every possible way and he will labour with cruel and subtle astuteness to deviate them from the spirit of their vocation, corrupting many of them. These corrupted priests, who will scandalise the Christian people, will incite the hatred of the bad Christians and the enemies of the Roman, Catholic and Apostolic Church to fall upon all priests. This apparent triumph of Satan will bring enormous sufferings to the good pastors of the Church...." Again, we see this verified today, among other ways in the widespread clerical sexual abuse crisis.

"Moreover, in these unhappy times, there will be unbridled impurity which, acting thus to snare the rest into sin, will conquer innumerable frivolous souls who will be lost. Innocence will almost no longer be found in children, nor modesty in women. In this supreme moment of need of the Church, those who should speak will fall silent." This too has been a lamentable feature of our times with the widespread use of pornography, the lack of modesty and other sins against chastity.

These prophecies, given four centuries ago in considerable detail, are a clear manifestation of the grace of God in this remarkable nun.

Seasons and Feasts

719 Advent and penance

Our priest recently encouraged us to do special penances in Advent. I had never thought of Advent as a season of penance. Is this a proper way to live the season?

While the documents of the Church at present speak more of hope and expectation at the two comings of Christ – in Bethlehem two thousand years ago and at the end of time – historically Advent has always been a season of penance. The Church has traditionally prepared for all the great feasts by seasons and days of penance, so that Easter, for example, is preceded by forty days of penance in Lent. Advent too, historically, was a season of special penance to prepare for the birth of our Saviour, and it still is today, seen in the purple colour of the vestments.

Fr Francis Weiser SJ, in his *Handbook of Christian Feasts and Customs* (Harcourt, Brace 1958) describes the history of Advent in great detail and what follows is taken largely from that book.

As preparation for Christmas, the season of Advent began to be observed when the feast of Christmas came to be celebrated, in the fourth century in Rome and in the fifth in Gaul and Spain. From the beginning, penance was part of this preparation. Bishop Perpetuus of Tours (490) issued a regulation that there should be three days of fasting each week from the feast of St Martin of Tours (November 11) to Christmas. At that time the name Advent was not yet in use and the season was called *Quadragesima Sancti Martini,* the Forty Days of St Martin.

The practice of living a season of penance before Christmas soon spread throughout France, Spain and later Germany. The fast started on different days, among them September 24, November 1, 11 or 14, and December 1. It is interesting that for Mass on the weekdays of Advent the Church in Gaul used the texts for the Masses of Lent.

In Rome the celebration of Advent began in the sixth century without the penitential aspect. It was a festive and joyful time of preparation for Christmas and it began four or five Sundays before Christmas. In the eighth century the Church in France adopted the Roman liturgy with its shorter, non-penitential celebration of Advent. However, after a few centuries there emerged in both Rome and France a final structure of Advent which combined the shorter four weeks' duration of Rome with the fasting and penitential aspect of France. Since the thirteenth century this structure has remained practically unchanged.

The law of fast was never as strict as that of Lent and it varied considerably from place to place, both in content and in duration. In most places people were to fast three days a week and to abstain from certain foods. As regards the latter, Bishop Burchard of Worms in 1025 ordered abstinence from wine, ale, honey-beer, meat, fat, cheese and fat fish. In addition, people were to abstain from weddings, amusements, travel for pleasure and even, on days of fasting, from conjugal relations.

In later centuries papal indults gradually reduced the obligation of fasting to two days a week. These days were, for example, Friday and Saturday in Italy and Wednesday and Friday in Austria. The *Code of Canon Law* of 1917 did away with the requirement of fasting, except for the fast of Ember week and of the Christmas vigil.

The Orthodox Churches do not have a liturgical preparation for Christmas but ever since the eighth century they do observe a fast. It extends from November 15 to Christmas and is known as St Philip's Fast, since it begins on the day after the feast of St Philip, November 14 in their calendar. Different Eastern Churches have different lengths of this fast and many of them celebrate the birth of Christ on the feast of Epiphany.

Fr Weiser sums up the spirit of Advent: "By a spirit of humble penance and contrition we should prepare ourselves for a worthy and fruitful celebration of the feast of the Nativity. This penance is not as harsh as that of Lent – there is no prescribed fast – and the joyful note of the season helps people to perform penitential exercises in a mood of happy spiritual toil, to 'make ready the way of the Lord'" (*Mt* 3, 3; pp. 53-54). In short, it is up to each one to decide what to do but, as always in the matter of penance, the more the better.

720 Advent in the Eastern tradition

I was talking recently with a Maronite Catholic about how his Eastern Rite celebrates Advent and was surprised to learn how much penance they do. Is this something common to other Eastern rites?

As we have seen, in Orthodox tradition, ever since the eighth century Advent has been lived as a period of fasting extending from November 15 to Christmas or to the feast of Epiphany.

This early tradition of Advent as a season of penance and particularly of fasting has been observed up to our own day in the Eastern rites of the Catholic Church. Catholic Churches of the Byzantine Rite, among them the Ukrainian, Melkite and Romanian, follow most closely the Orthodox Advent observance. Like the Orthodox, they begin on the day after the feast of St Philip on November 14 and so call it St Philip's Fast. The Melkite Catholic Church begins the fast on December 10.

While the exact way of living it varies from one rite to another, the fast generally lasts for forty days. During this time the faithful abstain from such foods as meat, fish, dairy or other animal products and wine or oil on Mondays, Wednesdays and Fridays. They live a lesser abstinence from meat, fish and dairy or animal products on Tuesdays and Thursdays. They are allowed to eat fish on Saturdays and Sundays, but they abstain from all other animal products. Christmas Eve, December 24, is generally lived as a day of strict fast in which no solid food is eaten until evening. Although this Advent fast is very strict, it is somewhat less rigorous than that of Lent.

For the Maronites, about whom you asked, the days and manner of fasting in Advent can vary from place to place and from person to person. Advent for the Maronites begins on the sixth Sunday before Christmas. Fasting usually consists in not eating anything from midnight until noon. Abstinence consists in abstaining from all animal products, usually meat, but in some cases also dairy and eggs. They may also abstain from fish, sea products and alcohol.

In the early centuries the Advent Maronite fast began on November 15 and ended on December 24, Christmas Eve. Over the centuries various synods reduced the length of the fast so that it began variously on December 5 and December 13.

In general, all the Eastern Catholic rites observe a period of penance in Advent. While this is not required in the Latin rite, we would do well to choose some particular penance to do in Advent as a way of detaching ourselves from the world and its comforts and of cleaning out the stable of our soul so that Christ finds a warm welcome there at Christmas.

721 History of the celebration of Christmas

I am always intrigued by how our present-day celebration of feasts came to be and now I would like to ask about Christmas. When was this feast first celebrated and how did it develop over time?

I take much of my answer from the *Handbook of Christian Feasts and Customs* by F.X. Weiser, SJ.

First, why do we celebrate Christmas on December 25? I wrote about two possible explanations for the choice of the date in *Question Time 1*, q. 141. In any case, it is certain that by the second half of the fourth century the date was firmly fixed as December 25.

In that century writers from East and West such as St Ambrose, St Basil, St Gregory of Nazianzus and St John Chrysostom all wrote about the celebration of Christmas. And it is well known that Charlemagne was crowned emperor of the western Christian empire on Christmas Day, December 25, in 800 AD.

As Fr Weiser relates, from the fifth century on the celebration of

Christmas was regarded as so important that it marked the beginning of the ecclesiastical year. After the tenth century, however, Advent came to form an integral part of the Christmas cycle and so the beginning of the year was advanced to the first Sunday of Advent, where it is today.

The celebration of Christmas soon came to have consequences in secular life as well. In 425 Emperor Theodosius forbade holding the cruel circus games on Christmas Day, and in 529 Emperor Justinian prohibited work and business by declaring Christmas Day a public holiday.

In the spiritual realm the Council of Agde (506) urged all Christians to receive Holy Communion on the feast, and the Council of Tours (567) established the duty of Advent fasting in preparation for the feast and proclaimed the twelve days from Christmas to Epiphany as a sacred and festive season. The Council of Braga (563) forbade fasting on Christmas Day. All of this laid the foundation for a joyful celebration of Our Lord's birth in both church and home.

Little by little, as more countries of Europe became Christianised, the missionaries took the celebration of Christmas to them. Thus, in the fifth century St Patrick took it to Ireland and in the sixth St Augustine of Canterbury took it to England, where on Christmas Day in 598 he baptised more than ten thousand Britons. In the seventh century Saints Columban and Gall took the celebration to Switzerland and in the eighth St Boniface took it to Germany. In the ninth century St Ansgar took the celebration to the Scandinavians and the brothers Saints Cyril and Methodius to the Slavic nations. In the following century St Adalbert took Christmas to Hungary.

By about the year 1100 Christmas was being celebrated everywhere in Europe with great devotion and joy. The next four centuries saw the peak of the celebration of Christmas, with inspiring and colourful religious services held all over. During this time many Christmas carols and plays were written and customs were developed in each country.

With the Reformation in the sixteenth century things changed dramatically. Wherever Protestantism prevailed celebration of the sacrifice of the Mass was forbidden as was the liturgy of the Divine Office. Processions, the veneration of the Blessed Virgin Mary and of the saints were also banned. All that remained in many places was a prayer service and a sermon on Christmas Day. On the other hand some groups, like the Lutherans in Germany, maintained a tender devotion to the Christ Child and celebrated Christmas in a very spiritual way.

In England and later in America, the Puritans banned every form of celebration of Christmas, both as a religious and as a popular feast, since they believed that no feast of human institution should outrank the celebration of the Sabbath. They published pamphlets denouncing Christmas as pagan, calling it "antichrist-Mass, idolatry and abomination" and declaring any observance of it sinful. When they came to political power, in 1642 they forbade church services and civic festivities on Christmas Day, and two years later they declared Christmas Day a day of fast and penance.

Finally, with the restoration of the English monarchy in 1660, Christmas came once again to be celebrated as a feast, as it was in America especially in the second half of the nineteenth century. Today, Christmas is celebrated all over with great joy and religious fervour.

722 Christmas Names and Masses

Can you tell me something about the name Christmas and also the meaning of names like Yule and Noel? Also, why there are three different Mass texts for Christmas?

The original Latin names for Christmas were *Festum Nativitatis Domini Nostri Jesu Christi* (Feast of the Nativity of Our Lord Jesus Christ) and *Dies Natalis Domini* (Birthday of the Lord). These Latin names gave rise to the name for Christmas in many languages. For example, in Italy it is *Natale*, in southern France *Nadal*, in Portugal *Natal* and in Spain *Navidad*. In most of the Slavic languages too the name means "Nativity".

Another common name for Christmas is Noël. F.X. Weiser, SJ,

in his *Handbook of Christian Feasts and Customs*, explains that the French name *Noël* possibly comes from the word *nowel* which means "news." There is an old English Christmas verse where an angel says: "I come from hevin to tell the best nowellis that ever befell."

The English word Christmas is based on the pattern of the old names for other feasts, where the suffix "mas", for "Mass", is added to the name of the feast. Thus, we have such feasts as Michaelmas, Martinmas, Candlemas, etc. Weiser says that the first mention of the name "Christes Maesse", or Mass of Christ, dates from the year 1038. The name reminds us that the most important part of the Christmas celebration is the sacrifice of the Mass.

A similar name for Christmas is found in the Dutch and German languages. In the Dutch it is *Kersmis* (Mass of Christ) and in German *Christmesse*. The present-day German name, however, is *Weihnacht* or, in the plural, *Weihnachten*, meaning "blessed, or holy, night". Slavic languages like Czech and Slovak have a similar term. The Lithuanian word for Christmas *Kaledos* is derived from the verb *Kaledoti*, meaning to beg or pray. Hence Christmas is the "Day of Prayer".

As for the word "Yule", its origin is disputed. Some scholars say it derives from the old Germanic word *Jol* (also *Iul* or *Giul*), meaning a turning wheel, which in this case would be the wheel of the sun rising after the winter solstice. A better explanation, however, would be the *Anglo*-Saxon word *geol*, meaning "feast". Since the greatest popular feast in pre-Christian times was the celebration of the winter solstice, the whole month of December was called *geola* (feast month). This name was preserved in both English and German and was later applied to the feast of Christmas. Hence "Yule", or "Yuletide", in English and "Jul" in German.

Fr Weiser makes an interesting comment on the greeting "Merry Christmas". He says that originally the word "merry" did not mean "joyful" or "happy" as it does today, but rather "blessed, peaceful, or pleasant". In this sense it expressed the wish for spiritual blessedness rather than earthly happiness. The Christmas carol "God rest ye merry, gentlemen" is an example of this original meaning. The comma after the word merry indicates that the word "merry" is not an adjective describing "gentlemen", but rather an adverb describing "rest". The meaning, therefore, is not "God rest you, joyful gentlemen", but rather "God rest you merrily, gentlemen".

The custom of the three Masses goes back to the early centuries, where it was reserved to the Pope alone, being extended to the universal Church around the end of the first millennium. The first Mass was celebrated around midnight by the Pope with a small congregation in the little chapel of the manger in the church of St Mary Major in Rome. There in the fifth century Pope Sixtus III erected a chapel with a manger, considered to be a faithful replica of the crib in Bethlehem.

The second Christmas Mass was celebrated by the Pope at dawn in the palace church of the Byzantine governor in honour of the martyr St Anastasia, whose body had been transferred from Constantinople to that church around 465. It was attended mainly by the Byzantines.

The public and official Mass was celebrated by the Pope on Christmas Day in the church of St Peter, attended by a large crowd. In the eleventh century this Mass was transferred to St Mary Major, which was closer to the Lateran Palace where the Pope resided.

At present the texts for these Masses are those for the Midnight Mass, the Mass at dawn, and the Mass during the day. Following the gospels for the three Masses, the first Mass came to be called the "Angels Mass", the second the "Shepherds Mass" and the third the "Mass of the Divine Word".

723 History of the feast of Epiphany

Can you tell me the meaning of the word Epiphany and something about the origin of the feast?

The Greek word *epiphaneia,* means "manifestation". In the ancient Greco-Roman world the term was used for the official state visit of a king or emperor to some city in his realm, during which he appeared publicly and thus showed himself to the people. The apostles applied this term to Christ manifesting himself as our divine saviour. For example, St John writes: "He manifested his glory, and his disciples believed in him" (*Jn* 2:11).

In the ancient pagan world people believed that gods, too, sometimes appeared on earth and manifested themselves in human form. They used the word *theophaneia*, or manifestation of a god, for these apparitions. The early Church took up this word in both East and West and often used the name Theophany for the feast of Epiphany.

The liturgical feast of Christ's manifestation had its origin in the East, in Egypt, as far back as the third century. It should be remembered that the feast of Christ's birth at Christmas on December 25 originated a century later. It seems that the date of January 6 was chosen for the feast because the Egyptians celebrated on that day the great festival of the winter solstice in honour of the sun god. Their calendar was twelve days behind the Julian calendar used in the West, hence the late date for the solstice. The Church in Egypt replaced this pagan festival with the feast of the manifestation of the true Divine Saviour King at his birth.

It is interesting to note that the heretical Gnostics celebrated the feast of Epiphany as also the feast of Christ's Baptism, since they believed that Christ was only human until he became divine when the divinity united itself with his humanity at his Baptism in the Jordan. They claimed that the first truly divine manifestation of Christ could not take place at his birth but only at his Baptism.

The feast of Epiphany, which started as a feast of the manifestation of Christ's divinity at his birth, also came to include the commemoration of the visit and adoration of the Magi. In Egypt, and a century later in the whole Eastern Roman Empire, a commemoration of Christ's Baptism was added to emphasise the true character of this manifestation against the error of the Gnostics.

From the East the feast of Epiphany came to the West during

the fourth century, about the time when the new feast of Christmas came to be celebrated. In many places, among them Spain, Gaul and northern Italy, Epiphany was established first. In Milan it was observed as early as 353 AD, commemorating mainly the birth of Christ. By the end of the fourth century, the birth of Christ at Christmas was celebrated on December 25 throughout the West and soon in the East as well.

As can be imagined, this would have created confusion, with two feasts commemorating Christ's birth. The problem was resolved in the West with Christ's birth being celebrated on December 25, and the feast of Epiphany on January 6 commemorating mainly the adoration of the Magi. The Baptism of Christ and the miracle of Cana, other manifestations of Christ's divinity, were also commemorated on Epiphany, although in a subordinate way. In the East the visit of the Magi came to be celebrated along with Christ's birth on December 25 while Epiphany commemorated Christ's Baptism.

From the beginning Epiphany was one of the greatest feasts of the liturgical year. As early as the year 400 Emperors Honorius in the West and Arcadius in the East forbade horse races and circus games on January 6 in order to allow the people to attend the religious service. In 565 Emperor Justinian made Epiphany a full public holiday.

At the end of the fourth century Aetheria, a pilgrim to the Holy Land, described in her diary the joyful splendour and fervent devotion of the Christian community in Bethlehem and Jerusalem in celebrating Epiphany on January 6 and during the octave that followed.

During the Middle Ages the feast had a vigil with fast and abstinence and it was followed by a liturgical octave. The octave was abolished by Pope Pius XII in 1955 for the Latin Church. In the *Code of Canon Law* of 1983 Epiphany is still a holyday of obligation although in many places, including Australia, the feast is celebrated on the nearest Sunday.

724 Generosity in Lent

Some people I know are doing penances in Lent that I find quite extraordinary and others are doing very little. They say the Church doesn't require us to do more. How should I face this question myself?

Let me begin by looking at what the Church has lived over the centuries. Fr Francis Weiser SJ tells us in his *Handbook of Christian Feasts and Customs* that from the time of the apostles every Friday was a day of fast in honour of Christ's death on that day, and in addition many Christians lived a strict fast on Good Friday and Holy Saturday, not eating or drinking anything on those two days. This "Passion Fast" was based on Our Lord's words: "The days will come, when the bridegroom is taken away from them, and then they will fast in that day" (*Mk* 2:20).

Eventually a longer period of fasting was introduced in preparation for Easter, although its observance varied widely in the early centuries. In some places it was only during Holy Week while in others it lasted two or three weeks, with Sundays always excepted. In the third and fourth centuries a fast of forty days was gradually adopted in imitation of Christ's forty days of fasting before beginning his public ministry (cf. *Lk* 4:2). St Athanasius, Patriarch of Alexandria, who had travelled to Rome and throughout Europe, wrote in the year 339 that "the whole world" fasted for forty days at that time (Letter quoted by St Jerome, PL 22, 773).

The exact form of the fast varied but it gradually became unified. In a letter to St Augustine of Canterbury around the year 600, Pope St Gregory the Great wrote: "We abstain from flesh meat and from all things that come from flesh, such as milk, cheese, eggs" (*Epist. ad Augustinum*, PL 77, 1351). At that time, fish too was usually forbidden. This remained the norm for almost a thousand years, and it still is the practice in the Orthodox Churches.

In addition to abstinence from these foods, the early practice of fasting in the strict sense consisted of eating only one meal a day, towards evening. After the eighth century this meal was advanced to the hour of None in the Divine Office, around three in the afternoon, and in the fourteenth century it became customary to have it at midday, hence the word "noon".

Naturally, considerations of health exempted certain persons from this strict fast. St John Chrysostom wrote around the end of the fourth century: "If your body is not strong enough to continue fasting all day, no wise man will reprove you; for we serve a gentle and merciful Lord who expects nothing of us beyond our strength" (*Gen. Hom.*, X, 1; PG 53, 82).

In the ninth century the Benedictine monks, who worked hard in the fields, began to have a little piece of bread and something to drink in the evening, and it gradually became the custom for everyone to have a light meal in the evening. The practice of breaking the fast with breakfast in the morning is of recent origin, dating to the early nineteenth century.

Before the Second Vatican Council adults fasted on all the forty days of Lent, eating only one full meal and two smaller meals, and they abstained from meat on Ash Wednesday and the Fridays of Lent, as they did on all Fridays of the year.

At present, all that is required by the Church is fasting and abstinence from meat on Ash Wednesday and Good Friday. Pope St John Paul II, in his Wednesday audience address on 7 March 1984, commented on this requirement, saying that it "should be considered the absolute minimum; a whole style of penance should accompany the living out of a life of faith and be made concrete in precise acts, the fruit of generosity."

And in an address to the clergy of Rome on 17 February 1994, he said: "I do not know whether our other brothers, even our Orthodox Eastern Brothers, are in a stronger, more consistent position on this point than we are. Not to mention the Muslims, who have their "Ramadan"; certainly the Jewish faith is very observant on this point, in this regard. Sometimes I think that we are lagging behind the others."

So it is up to each of us to decide what we will do in Lent, but let us be generous!

725 Sackcloth and ashes

In the scriptures we sometimes read about people putting on "sackcloth and ashes". What was the meaning of this practice and was it ever used in the Church?

First, let us look at several scriptural passages which mention sackcloth and ashes. In the book of Jonah, when Jonah preached that in forty days the city of Nineveh would be overthrown, "the people of Nineveh believed God; they proclaimed a fast, and put on sackcloth, from the greatest of them to the least of them. Then tidings reached the king of Nineveh, and he arose from his throne, removed his robe, and covered himself with sackcloth, and sat in ashes" (*Jon* 3:5-6).

Similarly, when the prophet Jeremiah passed on God's message that a people from the north would come to attack Jerusalem, he told the people to "put on sackcloth, and roll in ashes; make mourning as for an only son, most bitter lamentation; for suddenly the destroyer will come upon us" (*Jer* 6:26).

Jesus himself spoke of the practice: "Woe to you, Chorazin! Woe to you, Bethsaida! For if the mighty works done in you had been done in Tyre and Sidon, they would have repented long ago in sackcloth and ashes" (*Mt* 11:21).

As is clear in all these cases, sackcloth and ashes were used as a sign of repentance, sometimes to avoid an impending evil. The early Church embraced this Jewish custom, especially in Lent.

Fr Francis X. Weiser SJ relates in his *Handbook of Christian Feasts and Customs* how in Rome as early as the fourth century persons who had committed serious public sin and scandal were required to do public penance from Ash Wednesday to Holy Thursday. These people, who had confessed their sins shortly before Lent, were presented by the priests to the bishop on Ash Wednesday outside the cathedral. They stood barefoot, dressed in sackcloth, with their heads bowed in humility and contrition. The bishop, assisted by his canons, then assigned to each one particular acts of penance, depending on the gravity of their sins.

After this they entered the cathedral, the bishop leading the first one by the hand and the others following in single file, holding on to the hand of the one in front and behind. Before the altar they all recited the seven penitential psalms (Psalms 6, 31, 37, 50, 101, 129 and 142), led by the bishop and the clergy.

Then, as each person approached, the bishop laid his hands on him, sprinkled him with holy water, put blessed ashes on his head and invested him with the sackcloth tunic. At the conclusion of the ceremony the penitents were led out of the cathedral and were forbidden to re-enter it until Holy Thursday. Since this was a period of forty days it was called "quarantine", or forty. The word later became accepted into general use to refer to a period of separation from human contact in the case of infectious diseases.

During this time the penitents would spend Lent apart from their families in a monastery or other suitable place, where they occupied themselves in prayer, manual labour and works of charity. They had to remain barefoot, they were forbidden to speak with others, they slept on the ground or on a bed of straw and they were not allowed to bathe or cut their hair.

On Holy Thursday the penitents would bathe, shave, cut their hair and put on clean clothes before presenting themselves in the cathedral for the absolution of their sins. After they had been absolved they would attend the Mass of Remission celebrated by the bishop, during which they would receive Holy Communion.

This was the first of three Masses celebrated by the bishop on that day. It was followed by the Mass of the Chrism, in which the holy oils were blessed, and finally in the evening the Mass of the Last Supper, commemorating the institution of the Eucharist. Since Holy Thursday was not a day of fast, the faithful could eat their customary meals and still receive Communion in the evening Mass. On other days, they had to fast from midnight before receiving Communion.

726 Passiontide

I know that the last two weeks of Lent are special and was wondering how this came about. I can understand Holy Week being different but am curious about the week preceding it.

You are right in saying that the last two weeks of Lent are special and they even have a special name: Passiontide. Passiontide begins on the fifth Sunday of Lent, which has been called Passion Sunday since the ninth century. The season is reflected in the liturgy of the Mass in that after Passion Sunday the two Prefaces of the Passion are used on weekdays instead of the Prefaces of Lent. Passiontide is even older than Lent, having been a period of fasting as early as the third century.

On the eve of Passion Sunday it has been traditional to cover all crucifixes, statues and pictures in the church with a purple cloth as a sign of mourning. The only images not covered by a veil are those of the Stations of the Cross and any stained-glass windows. There are various explanations of the origin of the custom. One is that it originated in Rome, where in the early centuries the images in the Pope's chapel were covered by a veil when the deacon sang the concluding words of the Sunday Gospel, "Jesus hid himself and went out of the temple" (*Jn* 8:59).

Another explanation is that the custom derived from a practice in Germany in the ninth century of hanging a large cloth in front of the altar from the beginning of Lent. This cloth, known as the "Hungertuch" or hunger cloth, hid the altar from the view of the people until the reading of the Passion on Wednesday of Holy Week, at the words "the veil of the temple was rent in two."

Some say the custom was a remnant of the ancient practice of ritually expelling public penitents from the church at the beginning of Lent. After the custom of public penance fell into disuse and the entire congregation was symbolically incorporated into the order of penitents through the imposition of ashes on Ash Wednesday, it was no longer possible to expel the penitents from the church, and so instead the altar was shielded from view until the penitents were reconciled with God at Easter. Later in the Middle Ages crosses and the images of saints were also covered at the beginning of Lent. The custom of limiting this veiling to the last two weeks of Lent, appears in the Ceremonial of Bishops in the seventeenth century (cf. J. Flader, *Question Time 4*, q. 573).

The Gospel readings during Passiontide are taken mainly from the Gospel of St John and they follow the events in Our Lord's life in the last days before his passion and death.

For many centuries on the Friday after Passion Sunday the Church celebrated the feast of the Seven Sorrows of Our Lady, commemorating the suffering of Mary as recorded in the Gospels. This was a very popular devotion in medieval times. In 1423 a synod in Cologne introduced a Mass text and prescribed a feast in honour of the Seven Sorrows to be celebrated annually on the third Sunday after Easter. After 1600 the feast became popular in France, and it was celebrated there on Friday of the fifth week of Lent. In 1727 Pope Benedict XIII extended the feast to the whole Church with the title the Seven Sorrows of the Blessed Virgin Mary.

In 1668 a second feast of the seven sorrows came to be celebrated by the Order of the Servants of Mary, the Servites, on the third Sunday of September. It was incorporated into the universal calendar by Pope Pius VII in 1814. In 1913 Pope Pius X moved the feast to September 15, the day after the feast of the Triumph of the Holy Cross and it is still celebrated on that day. To eliminate the duplication of the feast, the earlier feast on Friday of the fifth week of Lent was removed when the liturgical calendar was revised in 1969.

When the persecutions ended in the fourth century the faithful in Jerusalem began to re-enact the solemn entry of Christ into the city on the Sunday before Easter, holding branches in their hands and singing the "Hosanna" (cf. *Mt* 21:1-11). This gave rise to the Palm Sunday celebration which continues today. The custom soon spread to Rome and was incorporated into the liturgy. At least from the beginning of the eighth century on, the rite of blessing of the palms took place and a procession of the clergy and laity would follow, beginning outside the town and proceeding to the cathedral or principal church, where Mass would be celebrated. The hymn "All glory, praise and honour", which is still used today, was composed in the ninth century for use on Palm Sunday.

727 The history of Holy Week

I have always been intrigued by the name "Holy Week", which seems to imply that there is something different and holy about the whole week, not just the Triduum from Holy Thursday to the Easter Vigil. Can you enlighten me?

In the early centuries the whole week was regarded as very holy and the faithful's life was to reflect that. Fr Francis Weiser, SJ offers a fascinating history of Holy Week in his book *Handbook of Christian Feasts and Customs*.

From the very beginning of the Church Holy Week was devoted to a special commemoration of Our Lord's passion and death through the practice of meditation, fasting and other forms of penance. When the persecutions ended in the fourth century, the Christian emperors of both East and West issued decrees forbidding not only amusements and games but also ordinary work in trade, business, the professions and the courts during that week. In this way the week was to be spent free from worldly occupations and devoted to spiritual exercises.

Following this custom even kings and rulers in medieval times withdrew from all secular activities during Holy Week in order to devote themselves to prayer, often in a monastery. Likewise, farmers and artisans downed their tools, public service offices were closed and the courts did not sit. Popular sentiment brought about a ban on music, dancing, secular singing, hunting and all kinds of sport. The week was thus truly quiet and holy, even in public life.

Throughout the Middle Ages the three days of the Sacred Triduum beginning on Holy Thursday were considered holydays of obligation, and since the faithful were not engaging in secular work they were able to attend the liturgical ceremonies. The holyday obligation was removed by Pope Urban VIII in 1642.

Holy Thursday is sometimes called Maundy Thursday from the Latin word *mandatum*, or commandment, taken from Our Lord's words during the Last Supper: "A new commandment I give you, that you love one another" (*Jn* 13:34) and also the command to wash each other's feet (cf. *Jn* 13:14-17). In the early centuries the bishop celebrated three Masses on this day: the first for the reconciliation of public sinners with the Church after their long period of penance, the second for the blessing of the holy oils, and the third in the evening in commemoration of the Last Supper and the institution of the Eucharist.

After the Mass of the Last Supper the Blessed Sacrament was taken to a side altar richly adorned with flowers where the faithful kept vigil throughout the night, accompanying Our Lord in the prayer in the garden. The altar was "denuded" of its altar cloths and candles to represent Christ stripped of his garments. Also, after the Mass the ancient rite of the Mandatum, or washing of the feet of twelve chosen men took place. As early as 694 the Synod of Toledo prescribed the rite for this ceremony.

The ceremonies of Good Friday too go back to the earliest centuries. In the fourth century the *Apostolic Constitutions* called it a "day of mourning, not a day of festive joy" and St Ambrose spoke of it as a "day of bitterness on which we fast." The ceremonies at that time were basically the same as those today, with the reading of the Passion of St John, the universal prayer for all classes of people, the adoration of the Cross and the Communion service.

728 The Easter Vigil

Our parish priest says that the Easter Vigil ceremony is very ancient. How old is it and what can you tell me about it?

The Easter Vigil ceremony is indeed ancient. From the fourth century on, after the sombre penitential season of Lent, the Easter Vigil was celebrated especially by lighting numerous lamps and candles so that churches were ablaze with light. The ceremony was called by such titles as the "Mother of All Holy Vigils", the "Great Service of Light", the "Night of Radiant Splendour" and the "Night of Illumination".

The Christian historian Eusebius says that the Emperor Constantine (331) "transformed the night of the sacred vigil into the brilliance of day by lighting throughout the whole city [Milan] pillars of wax, while burning lamps illuminated every house, so that this nocturnal celebration was rendered brighter than the brightest day" (*De Vita Constant.*, IV, 22). St Gregory of Nyssa (394) in one of his Easter sermons spoke of "this glowing night which links the splendour of burning lamps to the morning rays of the sun, thus producing continuous daylight without any darkness" (*Oratio IV in S. Pascha*).

In addition to the element of light, the early Christians also lived the vigil through prayer. Francis X. Weiser, in his *Handbook of Christian Feasts and Customs,* says that the custom of spending the Easter Vigil in prayer seems to date from the time of the apostles. In the third century Tertullian speaks of prayer *per noctem* (throughout the night) and even earlier writings indicate that the early Christians spent the night in prayer together.

In the early centuries the vigil service began with the lighting of the Paschal Candle, a symbol of Christ. The various hymns that accompanied the lighting of the candle were in use from the end of the fourth century. One of the best known, entitled *Inventor rutilis* and written by Prudentius (405), a layman and government official of the Roman Empire, says: "Eternal God, O Lord of Light, who have created day and night: the sun has set, and shadows deep, now over land and waters creep; but darkness must not reign today: grant us the light of Christ, we pray."

The hymn that is sung today before the Easter candle, the *Exultet*, is also of ancient origin, the earliest manuscript with the present text dating from the seventh or eighth century. After the blessing of the candle, a prayer service was held which included reading passages from the Bible, followed by the recitation of psalms, antiphons and prayers by the priests and people. The service was very long and could last all night.

Toward midnight the bishop and clergy went in procession to the baptismal font, a large basin built in a structure outside the church, where the baptismal water was blessed with the prayers and ceremonies we use today. Then the catechumens, who had been preparing for Baptism , took off their ornaments and jewellery and stepped into the water along with the bishop, who baptised them one by one. After being baptised they were anointed, as they are today. Then they put on flowing white linen garments which they wore for all the services throughout the week. Towards dawn on Easter Sunday the vigil concluded with the customary praying of the litanies and the celebration of the Sacrifice of the Mass, at the hour when Christ would have risen from the dead.

The lighting of the fire, with which the Easter vigil begins today, is of slightly later origin. The Germanic peoples had a popular tradition of lighting big bonfires at the beginning of Spring, but because the custom had a pagan symbolism it was forbidden by the Church. Nonetheless, the Irish bishops and monks who took the faith to the continent in the sixth and seventh centuries brought with them the custom instituted by St Patrick himself of lighting big bonfires outside the church on Holy Saturday as a symbol of Christ, the light of the world. In the eighth and ninth centuries the custom became so popular that during the latter part of the ninth century it was incorporated into the liturgy of Rome.

So, yes, the Easter Vigil is truly ancient, dating back to the early centuries of the Church.

729 The Octave of Easter

I once read that in the early Church the week after Easter was like one continuous feast. Can you tell me something about it?

The feast of Easter was, and always will be, the most important feast of the liturgical year. It is the Feast of Feasts and in the early Church the celebration lasted all week.

Although the practice varied from place to place, most people abstained from their usual work all week and attended church services every day. Many went to all three services that at the time of the Roman Empire were held each day at morning, noon and night. In France priests celebrated two Masses each day during Easter Week and a ninth century Spanish missal has three different Mass texts for each day of the octave.

Gradually the Church reduced the obligatory attendance at Mass to four days and in 1094 it was reduced to three. Since 1911 even Easter Monday is no longer a holyday of obligation, although it remains a public holiday in many parts of Europe, both Catholic and Protestant, as well as in other countries of Christian tradition.

Because those who were baptised in the Easter Vigil put on new white linen garments and wore them all week, Easter Week was called "White Week" in the West and "Week of New Garments" in the East. During the whole week the newly baptised, wearing their white garments, stood close to the altar at all the services. Every day the bishop would address them with special instructions after the others had left. It was, in a sense, the honeymoon of their new life as Christians, a week of great joy for them and their families.

On the Sunday after Easter the neophytes, as they were known, attended Mass clothed in their white baptismal robes for the last time. For this reason this Sunday was called Sunday *in albis,* in white garments, or "Sunday in White". At the end of the Mass the bishop solemnly dismissed the neophytes from their place in the sanctuary near the altar, and from then on they wore their ordinary clothes to Mass.

In English this Sunday was also called "Low Sunday". The name arises from the custom of counting the octave day as belonging to the feast, so that the celebration of Easter lasted eight days. The primary day, Easter Sunday itself, was called "high" and the octave "low".

Another feature of Easter Week is the use of the sequence *Victimae Paschali Laudes,* Praise to the Paschal Victim. Sequences originated in the tenth century and were recited before the Gospel in Mass. The sequence *Victimae Paschali Laudes* was written around the year 1030 by the priest Wipo, court chaplain of the Emperor Conrad. It soon became part of the official text of the Easter Mass and was used on each day of Easter Week. Today it is recited on Easter Sunday and its use on the weekdays of the octave is optional.

It is interesting to note that some lines of the sequence became the inspiration for the miracle plays that soon were being performed all over. The lines ask Our Lady what she saw after the Resurrection of Christ: "Tell us, Mary: say what thou didst see upon the way. The tomb the Living did enclose; I saw Christ's glory as he rose! The angels there attesting; shroud with grave-clothes resting. Christ, my hope, has risen: he goes before you into Galilee. That Christ is truly risen from the dead we know. Victorious king, thy mercy show!"

To these words were added other phrases from the Scriptures and the play was presented with great devotion before a shrine of the Holy Sepulchre on Easter Sunday morning. It was called the "Visit to the Tomb". The clergy dramatised the scene of the Gospel that tells of the visit of the holy women to the tomb, with two young clerics in white representing the angels who said: "He is not here. He has risen as he said. Go, tell his disciples that he is risen. Alleluia."

Finally, the weeklong celebration of Easter is seen in the antiphon "This is the day which was made by the Lord: let us rejoice and be glad, alleluia" from Psalm 118, which is recited in the Divine Office each day of the octave. So the octave of Easter was and continues to be special indeed.

730 Easter water

Can you please tell me the difference between Easter water and ordinary holy water?

To answer your question briefly, Easter water is the holy water blessed in the Easter Vigil ceremony. It is holy water like any other but it is blessed on this very special occasion. In the Easter Vigil the water is used for the Baptism of catechumens and for sprinkling on all those in the congregation as a reminder of their Baptism. The Easter Vigil ceremony is one of the oldest in the Church, going back to the early centuries, and the blessing of water for Baptism was always a part of it.

The long and rich prayer of blessing of this water recalls the many times water appears in the Scriptures: at creation when the Spirit hovered over the waters, at the flood, at the Israelites' passing through the Red Sea, at the Baptism of Christ and at his death, when water flowed from his side, and when he sent the apostles out to baptise. At the end of the blessing the priest immerses the Easter candle, which represents Christ the light of the world, three times into the water, symbolising his death and resurrection.

In the early Church, when people were baptised by immersion as they can still be today, the person was lowered into the water and raised up three times in this same way in the name of the Father and of the Son and of the Holy Spirit. The priest also breathes over the water, symbolising the Holy Spirit coming down upon it.

In some countries it is traditional for the people to take some of the Easter water home where they use it to bless both their homes and some of the special foods prepared for the Easter meal. In any case we can always take it home to use as holy water. Many families have holy water in their homes which they use to bless themselves on entering the house, to bless their children by making the sign of the cross with it on their forehead, to sprinkle it on their bed before retiring, etc.

Easter water thus has a long and meaningful history and it is good to make ample use of it.

731 The Easter Season

I always enjoy the Easter Season, with its expressions of joy and the many Alleluias in the Mass. Can you tell me more about it?

I think we all enjoy this joy-filled season, which covers the seven weeks between Easter Sunday and Pentecost Sunday. During this time the liturgical colour is festive white and the "Queen of heaven, rejoice" (cf. J. Flader, *Question Time 1*, q. 130) is said instead of the Angelus.

Easter Sunday is the greatest of all the feasts of the year. From the earliest times it has been called "the peak (*acropolis*) of all feasts" and the "Queen of all solemnities". St Gregory of Nazianzus wrote: "This highest feast and greatest of celebrations so much surpasses not only civic holidays but also the other feast days of the Lord that it is like the sun among the stars" (*Oratio in Pasch.*, 42).

The *Catechism of the Catholic Church* says: "Beginning with the Easter Triduum as its source of light, the new age of the Resurrection fills the whole liturgical year with its brilliance. Gradually, on either side of this source, the year is transfigured by the liturgy. It really is a 'year of the Lord's favour' (*Lk* 4:19). The economy of salvation is at work within the framework of time, but since its fulfillment in the Passover of Jesus and the outpouring of the Holy Spirit, the culmination of history is anticipated 'as a foretaste' and the kingdom of God enters into our time" (*CCC* 1168).

The Catechism goes on: "Therefore *Easter* is not simply one feast among others, but the 'Feast of feasts,' the 'Solemnity of solemnities,' just as the Eucharist is the 'Sacrament of sacraments' (the Great Sacrament). St Athanasius calls Easter 'the Great Sunday' (*ep. fest.* 1) and the Eastern Churches call Holy Week 'the Great Week'. The mystery of the Resurrection, in which Christ crushed death, permeates with its powerful energy our old time until all is subjected to him" (*CCC* 1169). During the Easter season the words "This is the day which was made by the Lord: let us rejoice and be glad, alleluia" of Psalm 118 are recited often in the Divine Office.

The celebration of Easter is prolonged not only during the Easter Season itself but on every Sunday of the year. Quoting the Second Vatican Council, the Catechism teaches: "'By a tradition handed down from the apostles which took its origin from the very day of Christ's Resurrection, the Church celebrates the Paschal mystery every seventh day, which day is appropriately called the Lord's Day or Sunday' (*SC* 106). The day of Christ's Resurrection is both the first day of the week, the memorial of the first day of creation, and the 'eighth day', on which Christ after his 'rest' on the great sabbath inaugurates the 'day that the Lord has made,' the 'day that knows no evening' (Byzantine liturgy). The Lord's Supper is its center, for there the whole community of the faithful encounters the risen Lord who invites them to his banquet" (cf. *Jn* 21:12; *Lk* 24:30; *CCC* 1166).

The Catechism goes on to quote St Jerome: "The Lord's day, the day of the Resurrection, the day of Christians, is our day. It is called the Lord's day because on it the Lord rose victorious to the Father. If pagans call it the 'day of the sun,' we willingly agree, for today the light of the world is raised, today is revealed the sun of justice with healing in his rays" (*Pasch.*: CCL 78, 550; *CCC* 1166). Sunday is sometimes called "a little Easter" and for this reason it is never a day of penance, as it is not even in Lent.

One of the requirements of this season is the precept of the Church to receive Holy Communion. The Catechism teaches: "The third precept ('You shall receive the sacrament of the Eucharist at least during the Easter season') guarantees as a minimum the reception of the Lord's Body and Blood in connection with the Paschal feasts, the origin and centre of the Christian liturgy" (*CCC* 2042). The precept dates back to the Fourth Lateran Council in 1215. It was not intended to bring in a new practice but rather to guarantee the minimum practice of an old tradition. Although in the beginning to fulfil the precept Communion was to be received on Easter Sunday itself, the Church gradually extended the period so that at present it is any time between Ash Wednesday and Trinity Sunday.

732 Feast of the Ascension

I am always interested in the origin of the feast days we celebrate today. For example, was the feast of the Ascension of Our Lord celebrated in the early centuries?

The feast was indeed celebrated early on, at least from the fourth century. Since the New Testament mentions that Our Lord appeared to his disciples during forty days before he ascended into heaven (cf. *Acts* 1:3) it is likely that the event was commemorated in some way on that day from the time of the apostles as were, for example, the celebrations of Our Lord's death and Resurrection.

Nonetheless, it seems that the Ascension was not celebrated as a separate feast in the liturgy of the Church for the first three centuries but rather was included in the celebration of the coming of the Holy Spirit at Pentecost.

The first person to mention the Ascension as an established and separate feast was Eusebius, bishop of Nicomedia, who incidentally baptised the emperor Constantine and died in 341 AD (*De Soll. Pasch.,* 5). By the end of the fourth century the Ascension was celebrated throughout the Roman Empire.

St Augustine attributed its origin to the apostles themselves, probably because by his time the feast ranked with the greatest liturgical celebrations. He mentions as "solemn anniversaries" of the Lord the "passion, resurrection and ascension, and the coming of the Holy Spirit" (*Epist. ad Inquis. Januarii*, 54, 1).

By the end of the fourth century the feast was well established in the East too, as seen in the fact that St Gregory of Nyssa (*In Ascens. Christi*) and St John Chrysostom (*Hom. in Ascens.,* 2) preached homilies on the feast of the Ascension.

From those early times until our own day, the feast of the Ascension was always a holyday of obligation, celebrated on the Thursday after the sixth Sunday of Easter, the fortieth day after Easter Sunday.

With the reform of the liturgical calendar after the Second Vatican Council, as indicated in the *Code of Canon Law* of 1983, the bishops' conference of each country was allowed to transfer the liturgical celebration of the Ascension to the following Sunday and, if they did not transfer it, they could suppress it as a holyday of obligation (cf. Can. 1246, §2). In Australia before the new Code, the Ascension was celebrated on the Thursday and it was a holyday of obligation. Later the feast was transferred to the Sunday to enable more people to participate in it. And, as always, Sunday "is to be observed in the universal Church as the primary holyday of obligation" (Can. 1246, §1).

Whereas most of the greatest feasts of the year are preceded by a vigil celebration on the day before, as they are today in the Divine Office, the feast of the Ascension did not have a vigil until well into the seventh century, when it was mentioned in some Roman lists of holydays. The reason for this was that a vigil always involved the observance of penance to prepare for the feast, and in the festive season between Easter and Pentecost penance was considered to be out of place.

In the ninth century the celebration of the vigil passed from Rome to the Frankish empire and thus it became established as a universal practice in the Latin Church. The Greek Church never observed the vigil. Even though vigils were observed as days of fasting in the early Church, the obligation of the fast before the Ascension was gradually lessened, especially in recent centuries. The *Code of Canon Law* of 1917 no longer listed the vigil of the Ascension as a day of obligatory fasting.

As with the other feasts of Our Lord, the early Church highlighted not so much the historical event of Christ's ascension into heaven as its theological and spiritual significance for the faithful. For example, St John Chrysostom said: "Through the mystery of the Ascension we, who seemed unworthy of God's earth, are taken up into heaven... Our very nature, against which Cherubim guarded the gates of Paradise, is enthroned today high above all Cherubim" (*Hom. in Ascens.*, 2)

So yes, the feast of the Ascension goes back to the early centuries.

733 Feast of Pentecost

Can you please tell me when the Church first began to celebrate the feast of Pentecost as a Christian feast? I know the Jews celebrated it as one of their great feasts.

As you say, Pentecost was a Jewish feast, as it remains today, going back to the time of Moses. It commemorated two events: the end of the harvest fifty days after the Passover, for which it was called the Festival of Weeks, and the Giving of the Torah, or Law, to Moses on Mt Sinai fifty days after the first Passover, when Moses led the Israelites out of Egypt. For this feast all males were to go up to Jerusalem, which explains why the *Acts of the Apostles* tell us that "there were dwelling in Jerusalem Jews, devout men from every nation under heaven" (*Acts* 2:5). For a fuller treatment of the origin and significance of the Jewish feast of Pentecost see my book *Question Time 3*, q. 434.

When Christians began to celebrate Pentecost to commemorate the coming of the Holy Spirit on the apostles on the very day of the Jewish feast, they kept the name Pentecost, from the Greek word meaning "fiftieth", because it came fifty days after Easter. In English the feast is also known as Whitsunday, or White Sunday, because on that day catechumens were baptised and wore white garments for the services.

It is not known whether or how Pentecost was celebrated by Christians in the first two centuries. But it is likely that it was celebrated in some way very early on, since it came fifty days after the Resurrection of Christ on Easter Sunday, and the liturgical celebration of the feasts of Our Lord began with Easter in apostolic times. The first mention of Pentecost as a Christian feast was made in the third century by Origen and Tertullian. Tertullian referred to it as a well-established feast and as the second day for the solemn Baptism of catechumens, following Easter Sunday (*De Bapt.*, 19).

In the fourth century the bishop historian Eusebius of Caesaria called it "all-blessed and all-holy, the feast of feasts" (*Vita Constantini*, IV, 64). And early in the fifth century St John Chrysostom in a sermon on Pentecost said: "Today we have arrived at the peak of all blessings, we have reached the capital [metropolis] of feasts, we have obtained the very fruit of our Lord's promise" (*In Pent. Hom.*, 2). At about the same time St Augustine called "solemn anniversaries" of the Lord the "passion, resurrection and ascension, and the coming of the Holy Spirit" (*Epist. ad Inquis. Januarii*, 54, 1).

In the early centuries only the day of Pentecost itself was celebrated in the Western Church. After the seventh century, however, the whole week following the feast, the octave, came to be celebrated in a festive way. Throughout the octave law courts did not sit and servile work was forbidden. Later the Council of Constance in 1094 limited this prohibition of work to three days. In 1771 Pope Clement XIV declared the Tuesday of the octave to be no longer a holyday and in 1911 Pope St Pius X abolished Monday as a holyday of obligation.

As early as the third century in the West the vigil service in the evening before Pentecost Sunday included a solemn rite of Baptism of new converts. The catechumens gathered in church on Saturday afternoon for prayers and preparation and the bishop blessed the baptismal water. The ceremonies followed closely those of the Easter Vigil.

In the West the vigil of Pentecost was a day of fasting in preparation for the great feast. The East observed the ancient tradition of celebrating the full fifty days from Easter to Pentecost without penance, although the Vesper service in the evening of the feast assumed a penitential character to atone for excesses committed during the Easter season.

In the Mass the ancient sequence *Veni Sancte Spiritus* (Come, Holy Spirit) was used on each day of the octave. It appeared first in liturgical books around the year 1200 and was ascribed variously to Pope Innocent III, King Robert of France, Pope St Gregory the Great and Cardinal Stephen Langton. The beautiful hymn *Veni Creator Spiritus*, probably written in the ninth century by Rabanus Maurus, Archbishop of Mainz, was used in the Divine Office from the end of the tenth century.

734 Feast of Mary, Mother of the Church

I was happy to attend Mass on the Monday after Pentecost this year and find that it was the new feast of Mary, Mother of the Church. What is the background of this feast? Does it have a long history?

As regards Mary's title as Mother of the Church, in a real sense it goes back to the moment when she conceived Jesus in her womb, thus becoming his mother. We should remember that the person of Jesus can be understood in two senses. On one hand he is the eternal Son of God and the Son of Man, the Son of Mary. But he can also be understood as the head of his Mystical Body, the Church. Christ cannot be separated from his body the Church any more than a human person can be separated from his body. So in conceiving Christ, Mary conceived the whole Church and so became Mother of the Church.

St Augustine was fond of referring to Christ and the Church as the *Christus totus*, the "total Christ". Pope John Paul II mentioned this in his Apostolic Letter on St Augustine *Augustinum Hipponensem*: "Because Christ, the only mediator and Redeemer of people, is head of the Church, Christ and the Church are one single mystical person, the total Christ" (II, 3).

If Christ and the Church are one single mystical person, then Mary, in becoming the mother of Christ, became at the same time the mother of the Church. The Second Vatican Council taught this in the Dogmatic Constitution on the Church: "The Virgin ... is 'clearly the mother of the members of Christ' ... since she has by her charity joined in bringing about the birth of believers in the Church, who are members of its head" (*LG* 53; cf. St Augustine, *De virg.* 6).

In view of this teaching, in an address on 21 November 1964 at the conclusion of the third session of the Second Vatican Council, Pope Paul VI proclaimed Our Lady Mother of the Church: "Meditating on the close relationships between Mary and the Church, for the glory of the Virgin Mary and for our own consolation, we proclaim the Most Blessed Virgin Mary Mother of the Church, that is to say of all the people of God, of the faithful as well as of the pastors, who call her the most loving Mother."

He said that this title was not new to Christian piety. Indeed the Decree establishing the new feast states: "In some ways this was already present in the mind of the Church from the premonitory words of Saint Augustine and Saint Leo the Great. In fact the former says that Mary is the mother of the members of Christ, because with charity she cooperated in the rebirth of the faithful into the Church, while the latter says that the birth of the Head is also the birth of the body, thus indicating that Mary is at once Mother of Christ, the Son of God, and mother of the members of his Mystical Body, which is the Church." The Decree goes on to say that the title was also used by spiritual authors and by Popes Benedict XIV and Leo XIII.

Following Pope Paul's proclamation of Mary as Mother of the Church, the Holy See in the Holy Year 1975 issued the text for a votive Mass in honour of Our Lady, Mother of the Church, which was later inserted into the Roman Missal. In 1980 the Vatican granted the faculty to add this title to the litany of Loreto, which is often said at the end of the Rosary. And on 7 December 1981 Pope John Paul II had a mosaic of Mary, Mother of the Church, placed on the wall of the papal apartments, where it can be seen from anywhere in St Peter's Square.

The Decree of the Congregation for Divine Worship establishing the new feast was dated 11 February 2018, the 160th anniversary of the first apparition of Our Lady at Lourdes. The new feast, to be celebrated on the Monday after Pentecost, has the rank of Memorial, meaning that the Mass is to be celebrated by priests throughout the world.

The Decree expresses the desire that "the promotion of this devotion might encourage the growth of the maternal sense of the Church in the pastors, religious and faithful, as well as a growth of genuine Marian piety". It goes on to say: "This celebration will help us to remember that growth in the Christian life must be anchored to the Mystery of the Cross, to the oblation of Christ in the Eucharistic Banquet and to the Mother of the Redeemer and Mother of the Redeemed, the Virgin who makes her offering to God."

We give thanks to Pope Francis for instituting this new feast of our spiritual mother.

735 Feast of the Annunciation

Can you tell me something about the origin of the feast of the Annunciation, celebrated on March 25? Why do we celebrate it on that particular day?

The feast of the Annunciation is celebrated as a feast of Our Lady since it commemorates the annunciation to Mary by the Archangel Gabriel that she was to bear a son who would be the Son of God and the Redeemer of mankind (cf. *Lk* 1:26-38). Our Lady's *fiat*, "let it be done", brought about the Incarnation of the Son of God, the conception of Jesus. For this reason in early medieval times the feast was called "The Annunciation of the Lord" or the "The Conception of Christ".

The reason for celebrating the feast on March 25 is simply that when the date for the celebration of the birth of Christ, Christmas, was fixed as December 25 in the fourth century (cf. J. Flader, *Question Time 1*, q. 141) the date for his conception was put nine months earlier, on March 25. As I explained in my answer to that question in *Question Time 1,* there was also an early theory that Christ had died on the cross on March 25 and had been conceived on that day too, so that he would have been born on December 25.

The origin of the feast of the Annunciation goes back to as early as the fifth century in the East, and to the sixth and seventh centuries in the West. In Spain the tenth Synod of Toledo, held in 656, mentions it as a feast already well known and universally celebrated. It was celebrated then on the same day, March 25, in both East and West. In many churches in Spain, however, it was celebrated each year on December 18. During the eleventh century the Church in Spain adopted the Roman date of March 25 but also retained its own, so Spain had two feasts of the Annunciation.

In the eighteenth century the Vatican replaced the December feast in Spain with a feast of the "Expectation of Birth of the Blessed Virgin". The Gospel for the new feast was that of the Annunciation.

In the Middle Ages the feast of the Annunciation was a holyday of obligation and also a public holiday. In Catholic countries it was celebrated as a holyday up to 1917, when the obligation of attending Mass and resting from unnecessary work was removed by the new Code of Canon Law. The 1983 Code does not include it in the list of ten holydays of obligation. But it is still a major feast of Our Lady, being celebrated as a liturgical solemnity, the highest rank of feast.

It was an ancient custom of the Roman Curia to start the new year on March 25 for all communications and documents, calling it the "Year of the Incarnation". The practice was also adopted by many civil governments for the legal dating of their documents. The feast of the Annunciation, called "Lady Day", marked the beginning of the legal year also in England, even after the Reformation, until 1752.

The name of the feast varies slightly from country to country. In the Greek Church it is called "Glad Tidings", among the Slavs of Eastern Rite "Glad Tidings of Mary", among Slavs of the Latin Rite "Message to Lady Mary", and among Arabic Christians "Feast of Good News".

A curious name for the feast in central Europe is "Feast of the Swallows" because there is a belief that the first swallows return from their migration on or around that day. An ancient saying in Austria reads: "When Gabriel does the message bring, return the swallows, comes the Spring". Thus swallows are called "God's birds" in Hungary and "Mary's birds" in Austria and Germany.

In the Middle Ages in the cathedrals of France, Italy, Germany and England, the "Golden Mass" (*Missa aurea*) was celebrated on this feast, with Our Lady and the Archangel Gabriel represented by deacons kneeling in the sanctuary and singing the Gospel of the Mass in Latin dialogue, and another deacon singing the part of the narrator. It is said that the Golden Mass was inaugurated at Tournay in Belgium in 1231.

736 Feast of the Transfiguration

Can you please tell me why in some years the feast of the Transfiguration of Our Lord on August 6 takes the place of the Sunday liturgy and also something about the history of the feast? Is this an old feast or a new one?

In answer to your first question, there are some feasts, especially of Our Lord, which are important enough to take the place of the Sunday liturgy, and the Transfiguration is one of them. When I say "feast" I am using the word in the strict liturgical sense, to distinguish it from a solemnity or a memorial. A solemnity is the highest ranked feast, among which are the Assumption of Our Lady, the Annunciation, the feast of St Joseph, etc., and these always take precedence over the Sunday liturgy. But even some of the second ranked celebrations known as feasts can also take precedence. It is interesting to note that when a liturgical feast is celebrated on a weekday it has only two readings, the first reading and the Gospel, but when it falls on a Sunday it has the customary three readings for Sundays.

The feast of the Transfiguration commemorates Our Lord's manifestation of his divinity on Mt Tabor before Peter, James and John, with Moses and Elijah also appearing. Christ's face shone like the sun and his garments became dazzlingly white. The voice of the Father was heard saying "This is my beloved Son, with whom I am well pleased; listen to him" (*Mt* 17:5). This event was important enough to be celebrated early on in both East and West. It is an especially important feast in the East, for both the Orthodox and the Eastern Catholic rites.

It is not certain when the feast was first celebrated. The *Catholic Encyclopedia* says that the Armenian bishop Gregory Arsharuni, around the year 690 ascribed the origin of the feast to St Gregory the Illuminator, who died around 337. He says St Gregory instituted the feast to take the place of a pagan feast of Aphrodite called Rose Flame and kept that name because Christ opened his glory like a rose on Mt Tabor. While this is not certain, the Encyclopedia says the feast probably originated in the fourth or fifth century somewhere in Asia, taking the place of some pagan nature feast.

In the Latin Church the Transfiguration is not mentioned before the year 850. In the tenth century it became part of the liturgy in many dioceses and was celebrated mainly on August 6, as it is today. What is certain is that in 1456 Pope Callixtus III extended the feast to the universal Church in memory of the ending of the siege of Belgrade by the Turks on August 6 that year. Pope Callixtus himself composed the Divine Office.

In 2002 Pope John Paul II included the Transfiguration among the five new Luminous Mysteries of the Rosary, giving some idea of the importance of the event.

The Transfiguration is numbered among the twelve Great Feasts in Orthodoxy, where it is celebrated with a vigil the day before and an octave after it. According to Orthodox understanding it is celebrated forty days before the feast of the Elevation of the Holy Cross on September 14 to show that the one who gave up his life on the cross was truly God. It is regarded as a feast not only of Christ but also of the Blessed Trinity, since all three divine Persons were present: the Father, whose voice was heard from heaven, the Son, who was transfigured, and the Holy Spirit in the form of the cloud. In this sense the Orthodox regard the Transfiguration as the Small Epiphany, the Great Epiphany being the Baptism of Christ where the three Persons of the Blessed Trinity also appeared. In Orthodoxy as well as in the Latin Church, the liturgy of the Transfiguration takes the place of the Sunday liturgy when it falls on a Sunday.

St Matthew relates that the Transfiguration took place six days after Christ told the apostles that he would have to go up to Jerusalem to suffer and be put to death, but that on the third day he would be raised up. He wanted to prepare them for his passion and death by showing them that he was truly God. He added that anyone who would be his disciple should take up his cross and follow him and that anyone who loses his life for him will find it (cf. *Mt* 16:21, 24-25).

On the feast of the Transfiguration we can ponder the great lesson that if we are willing to take up our own cross and follow Christ, we will see him glorified in heaven.

737 Feast of the Holy Name of Mary

I am now in my fifties and I love the feast of the Holy Name of Mary, apart from other reasons because my name is Mary. I can't remember celebrating this feast when I was young. Is it new, and when did it begin?

You are right in thinking that the feast is new, because it was reinstated in the liturgical calendar as recently as 2002 by St John Paul II. But it goes back many centuries.

The feast began in the year 1513 as a local celebration in Cuenca, Spain, on 15 September. In 1587 Pope Sixtus V moved the celebration to 17 September and in 1622 Pope Gregory XV extended it to the Archdiocese of Toledo.

In 1666 the Discalced Carmelites received permission to recite the Divine Office of the Holy Name of Mary four times a year. In 1671 the feast was extended to the whole Kingdom of Spain, and from there it spread to the Kingdom of Naples.

Then in 1684 Pope Innocent XI included it in the universal calendar of the Church to commemorate the victory of the Christian armies led by Polish king Jan Sobieski over the Ottoman Turks in the Battle of Vienna in 1683.

It will be recalled that when Vienna was besieged by the Turks, Pope Innocent XI asked the Church to pray the Rosary to Our Lady under the title Help of Christians. The battle against overwhelming odds began on September 8, when the Church celebrates the birth of Our Lady, and it ended successfully four days later, on September 12. Thereafter, the military might of the Turks was no longer a threat to Christendom.

The following year Pope Innocent instituted the feast, to be celebrated each year on the Sunday within the octave of the Nativity of Mary.

In the reform of the calendar by Pope St Pius X in 1911, which gave Sundays more prominence in their own right, the feast of the Holy Name of Mary was transferred to September 12. Then in the reform of 1969 under Pope St Paul VI, it was considered that the feast was something of a duplication of the feast of the Nativity of Our Lady on September 8 and it was omitted altogether.

The feast was restored to the calendar in 2002 by Pope St John Paul II, to be celebrated on September 12. Pope John Paul also restored the feast of the Holy Name of Jesus, celebrated on January 3, two days after the feast of the Divine Maternity of Mary, formerly of the Circumcision of Our Lord, when Jesus was given his name.

Significantly, the feast of the Holy Name of Mary comes just four days after the commemoration of her birth, around the time when Saints Joaquim and Anne would have given their daughter the name Mary.

Among the great promoters of devotion to the Holy Name of Mary were St Anthony of Padua, St Bernard of Clairvaux and St Alphonsus Maria Liguori. A number of religious orders, including the Cistercians, Carthusians, Silvestrine Benedictines and numerous congregations of religious sisters customarily give their monks and nuns the name Mary.

The name Mary is all powerful. In addition to the victory in the Battle of Vienna in 1683, some of the other significant events attributed to the invocation of Our Lady are the victory of the Christian navy over the Turks in the naval Battle of Lepanto in 1571, victories in 1716 over the Ottoman Turks at Peterwardein and Temesvar in Hungary and on the island of Corfu, and the freeing of Pope Pius VII by Napoleon Bonaparte in 1814 (cf J. Flader, *Question Time 1,* q. 129).

Not for nothing is Our Lady called *omnipotentia supplex,* "supplicating omnipotence". As the Mother, Daughter and Spouse of God Mary shares in God's omnipotence by her power of intercession.

For this reason we can invoke the Holy Name of Mary with great confidence for all our spiritual and temporal needs. Our Mother, as we have seen, is all powerful and, as Mother of the Church and of all mankind, she loves her children dearly and will not fail to intercede before God for all our intentions.

738 Holy days of obligation

My wife is from Spain and on All Saints Day she asked me why this feast is not a Holy Day of obligation in Australia as it is in Spain. Why are there differences from one country to another?

The matter of holydays has a long and interesting history. In the Middle Ages there were very many days on which attendance at Mass was obligatory apart from Sundays, and these were reduced in 1642 by Pope Urban VIII to thirty-six. Early in the twentieth century the number was reduced to eight by Pope Pius X, but it was raised again to ten in the 1917 Code of Canon Law. Nonetheless, individual bishops could decide how many of them to observe in their own dioceses.

The 1983 Code of Canon Law has kept the number at ten. They are the Nativity of Our Lord Jesus Christ, the Epiphany, the Ascension of Christ, the feast of the Body and Blood of Christ, the feast of Mary the Mother of God, her Immaculate Conception, her Assumption, the feast of St Joseph, the feast of the Apostles Saints Peter and Paul, and the feast of All Saints (cf. Can. 1246, §1). However, the Episcopal Conference may, with the prior approval of the Apostolic See, suppress certain holydays of obligation or transfer them to a Sunday (cf. Can. 1246, §2).

In view of this last paragraph we can explain the differences between one country and another. In the Vatican City itself, for example, although not in the rest of the diocese of Rome, and in the diocese of Lugano in Switzerland, all ten holydays are observed. In other countries the numbers are smaller and they vary considerably.

In Australia before the 1983 Code of Canon Law there were five holydays of obligation: Christmas, New Year's Day (at first the feast of the Circumcision of Our Lord, later the feast of Mary the Mother of God), the Ascension of Our Lord, the Assumption of Our Lady and All Saints' Day.

After the new Code came into force, the Australian Catholic Bishops Conference in 2001 reduced the number of holydays to two: Christmas and the Assumption of Our Lady (August 15).

In addition, the Australian bishops transferred some of the holydays listed in the Code of Canon Law to a Sunday: the feasts of the Epiphany, the Ascension and the Body and Blood of Christ (Corpus Christi), so that these feasts could be more easily celebrated by all the faithful.

In Spain, where your wife came from, there are seven holydays: Christmas, Mary the Mother of God, Epiphany, St Joseph, the Assumption of Our Lady, All Saints' Day and the Immaculate Conception of Our Lady.

In the United States there are six: Christmas, Mary the Mother of God, the Ascension, the Assumption of Our Lady, All Saints' Day and the Immaculate Conception.

In Italy there are also six: Christmas, Mary the Mother of God, the Epiphany, the Assumption of Our Lady, All Saints' Day and the Immaculate Conception of Our Lady.

In Ireland too there are six: Christmas, the Epiphany, St Patrick's Day, the Assumption of Our Lady, All Saints' Day and the Immaculate Conception.

Interestingly, in Malaysia and Singapore Ash Wednesday is a holyday of obligation.

In the Eastern Rite Catholic Churches the Code of Canons for the Eastern Churches stipulates that there are to be five holydays common to all the Churches: the Nativity of Our Lord, the Epiphany, the Ascension, the Dormition of Our Lady and the feast of Saints Peter and Paul (cf. *CCEO,* Can. 880). The Dormition of Our Lady celebrates her falling asleep, or death, and subsequent assumption, and it is celebrated on August 15.

A question many people ask is whether they are bound to observe the holydays of their country when they are travelling or living overseas. In the case of those travelling it would seem logical that they should endeavour to observe the holydays of their own country but they would not be bound by the holydays of the country in which they happen to be at the time. But when they have taken up residence in a new country, they are bound by the holydays of their new country.

Our Lady and the Saints

739 Why devotion to Mary?

I was recently discussing Catholic beliefs with a protestant friend at work and he challenged our devotion to Our Lady, asking why we had it when it takes away from our love for Jesus. How do I answer him?

There are many reasons why Catholics have devotion to Our Lady and they are solidly based on Scripture, which is what protestants rely on for their belief. Personally, I have always wondered why protestants don't have devotion to Mary.

The first reason for our devotion is simply that Mary is Jesus' mother and if we love Jesus, as all good protestants do, we will also love his mother. After all, even Muslims have devotion to Our Lady because she is the mother of Jesus, whom they consider a great prophet even if not God. Amongst our friends too, we respect and speak well of their mothers, and not to do so would be considered a lack of respect for the friends themselves.

Second, the Scriptures make clear that God himself honours Mary. When the archangel Gabriel appears to Our Lady in the Annunciation he begins by saying, "Hail, full of grace, the Lord is with you!" (*Lk* 1:28) Mary is indeed full of grace, highly favoured by God, and God is with her in a very special way. The angel goes on: "Do not be afraid, Mary, for you have found favour with God" (*Lk* 1:30). God looks on Mary in a special way for she has pleased him and has found favour with him.

Later, Mary's kinswoman Elizabeth, moved by the Holy Spirit, by God, proclaims: "Blessed are you among women" (*Lk* 1:42). Among all women, Mary is the most blessed. She is truly someone special, proclaimed as such by God through the lips of Elizabeth.

Third, Mary is not only the mother of Jesus as man, she is also the mother of God. This too comes from God through the archangel Gabriel in speaking of the child to be born of Mary: "He will be great, and will be called the Son of the Most High; and the Lord God will give to him the throne of his father David, and he will reign over the house of Jacob for ever; and of his kingdom there will be no end. ... therefore the child to be born will be called holy, the Son of God" (*Lk* 1:32-33, 35). Surely we will honour and have devotion to the mother of God!

Fourth, Mary is not only the mother of God, she is also our mother. Jesus himself gives her to us through St John from the cross: "Then he said to the disciple, 'Behold your mother!'" (*Jn* 19:26-27). Tradition has always seen in St John the whole Church, so that we have all been given Mary as our mother. The fourth commandment tells us to honour our father and our mother, so how could we not honour Mary, our heavenly mother? To refuse to honour the mother Jesus himself has given us would be to dishonour him.

Fifth, Mary herself says that all future generations would honour her. In her beautiful hymn the Magnificat she says: "For behold, henceforth all generations will call me blessed" (*Lk* 1:48). They would do this because of what God had done in her: "for he who is mighty has done great things for me, and holy is his name" (*Lk* 1:49).

Since Mary is God's greatest masterpiece, in honouring her we are honouring her Maker, just as in admiring Michelangelo's Pieta in St Peter's Basilica in Rome, we are honouring Michelangelo himself. In this way our devotion to Mary takes nothing away from our love for God, as your protestant friend suggests, but only honours him all the more.

In view of all this, from the earliest centuries Christians have had great devotion to Mary. There is an image of Mary with child on the wall of the catacomb of Priscilla in Rome from the early third century, and once the persecutions ended in the fourth century numerous churches began to be named after her. Today they fill the world. Truly no woman in history has been the object of more churches, hymns, artworks, poems and books than Our Lady. All generations have called her blessed. Not to have devotion to her would reveal an utter lack of love for Jesus.

Even the early protestant reformers had devotion to her. Martin Luther wrote on 1 September 1522 that "the veneration of Mary is inscribed in the very depths of the human heart", and towards the end of his life he said, "Without doubt, Mary is the mother of God... and in one word is contained every honour which can be given to Mary."

740 Do Catholics worship Mary?

My daughter is married to a born-again Christian who challenges our devotion to Mary, accusing us of worshiping her and thus taking away from our love and worship of God. How can we answer him?

We can say three things in answer to this question.

First, we Catholics and other Christians who have devotion to Mary do not worship her. Our devotion, more properly termed veneration, is not the worship due to God alone. The *Catechism of the Catholic Church* teaches, quoting the Second Vatican Council: "The Church rightly honours 'the Blessed Virgin with special devotion. From the most ancient times the Blessed Virgin has been honoured with the title of "Mother of God," to whose protection the faithful fly in all their dangers and needs.... This very special devotion ... differs essentially from the adoration which is given to the incarnate Word and equally to the Father and the Holy Spirit, and greatly fosters this adoration'" (*CCC* 971; *LG* 66).

Traditionally the Church has taught that there are three types of cult or veneration: *latria,* the worship due to God alone; *dulia,* the veneration of the saints; and *hyperdulia,* a higher form of veneration than that of the saints due to Our Lady, who is more exalted than the saints since she is the very Mother of God and Queen of all saints. The veneration of Mary, while higher than that of the saints, is not the worship due to God.

We have statues and images of Our Lady in our churches, shrines and homes but we do not genuflect in front of them, as we do before the tabernacle, which contains the Real Presence of Christ. We may bow our head as a sign of respect, but we do not genuflect as we do before God.

The Second Vatican Council clarifies this: "Following the study of Sacred Scripture, the Holy Fathers, the doctors and liturgy of the Church, and under the guidance of the Church's magisterium, let them [theologians and preachers] rightly illustrate the duties and privileges of the Blessed Virgin which always look to Christ, the source of all truth, sanctity and piety. Let them assiduously keep away from whatever, either by word or deed, could lead separated brethren or any other into error regarding the true doctrine of the Church. Let the faithful remember moreover that true devotion consists neither in sterile or transitory affection, nor in a certain vain credulity, but proceeds from true faith, by which we are led to know the excellence of the Mother of God, and we are moved to a filial love toward our mother and to the imitation of her virtues" (*LG* 67).

The second thing we say in answer to our separated brethren is that our devotion to Mary stems from what God has done for her and hence moves us to love God all the more. After all, it was God who chose Mary to be his Mother and filled her with all her privileges: her Immaculate Conception, perpetual virginity, sinlessness, Assumption into heaven, etc. To honour her is therefore to honour the God who made her what she is. Veneration to Mary does not take us away from God but rather leads us to love God all the more.

And third, Mary herself leads us to God. It was she who brought God to us by accepting the Second Person of the Blessed Trinity into her womb and giving birth to him in Bethlehem. She brought God into the world and she wants all souls to worship him, as the shepherds and wise men did in Bethlehem. She suffered with Christ at Calvary so that all might be saved and she ardently desires the salvation of all. She is the most powerful intercessor for souls, especially those most distant, in order to lead them to God.

One personal experience illustrates this point. Many years ago, when I was chaplain in a university residence, a student who had not been practising his faith for many years came and asked me to hear his confession. When he finished he asked where he could get a rosary. He explained that many years before he had lived in a boarding school where they prayed the rosary every day and he wanted to take up the custom again. It occurred to me that that day was a feast of Our Lady and I asked him if he was aware of it. He said he wasn't. I told him I thought Our Lady brought him back to God on her feast day because of his devotion to her years before.

So we don't worship Mary and our devotion to her only increases our love for Christ.

741 Is Our Lady Co-redemptrix?

I have heard of efforts to have the Church define a new dogma of Mary Co-redemptrix or Co-redeemer. What is behind this and do you think such a title is opportune?

First, a bit of background. Already in the Second Vatican Council (1962-65) some fifty council fathers requested that this title be applied to Our Lady, even though the Council did not choose to do so. A year after the Council ended, during a Mariological Congress in August 1966 in Czestochowa, Poland, a commission was established in response to a request from the Holy See to canvass the opinion of the scholars there as to whether it was opportune to define a fifth Marian dogma declaring Our Lady Co-redemptrix, Mediatrix and Advocate. The commission unanimously declared that such a definition was not opportune, voting 23-0 against it.

In 2000 the then Cardinal Joseph Ratzinger, in his book *God and the World* had this to say in answer to a question on the matter: "The formula 'Co-redemptrix' departs to too great an extent from the language of Scripture and of the Fathers and therefore gives rise to misunderstandings. Everything comes from Christ, as the Letter to the Ephesians and the Letter to the Colossians, in particular, tell us; Mary, too, is everything she is through Him. The word 'Co-redemptrix' would obscure this origin. A correct intention being expressed in the wrong way."

What then are the arguments in favour of declaring Mary Co-redemptrix? A starting point is the fact that Mary in the Annunciation accepted Jesus our Redeemer into her womb and into the world, thereby cooperating at least in a mediate or indirect way in our Redemption. Then too, when Mary and Joseph presented Jesus to the Father in the temple, they were offering him up to fulfil his mission, especially to bring about our Redemption. And at the Cross of Calvary Our Lady suffered unspeakably with Our Lord, uniting herself with his redemptive sacrifice.

The Second Vatican Council speaks of this cooperation of Mary in the work of her Son: "She conceived, brought forth, and nourished Christ, she presented him to the Father in the temple, shared her Son's sufferings as he died on the cross. Thus, in a wholly singular way she cooperated by her obedience, faith, hope and burning charity in the work of the Saviour in restoring supernatural life to souls" (*LG*, n. 61). This cooperation in the work of Redemption surely makes Our Lady a co-redeemer, a co-redemptrix.

St Bernard's disciple Arnold of Chartres, contemplating the sacrifice of Calvary, saw in the cross "two altars, one in the heart of Mary, the other in the body of Christ. Christ immolated his own flesh, Mary her own soul." "Both equally offered to God the same holocaust." In this way Mary "obtained with Christ the common goal of the salvation of the world." Without calling Mary specifically "co-redemptrix" Arnold was laying the foundation for this title.

While it is true that only Our Lord, as God, could redeem us and reconcile us with the Father, there is nothing to prevent him from allowing others to cooperate with him in this work, as he did with Our Lady. At the cross Our Lady cooperated in the work of *objective redemption*, suffering with Christ for the redemption of all mankind. But she, and indeed all the baptised, are called to cooperate in the work of *subjective redemption*, the application of the fruits of the cross to individual souls. We do this by praying for others and bringing them closer to God so that they can be baptised and saved. In this way not only Our Lady, in a special way by her intercession for souls in heaven, but all of us here on earth are called to be co-redeemers with Christ. In this sense St Paul writes that "we are God's fellow workers" (*1 Cor* 3:9).

So even if it is never defined as a dogma, Our Lady cooperated with Our Lord in the work of redemption, which would make her a co-redeemer. Pope Benedict XV expressed this truth in his Apostolic Letter *Inter sodalicia* (1918): "In such a way, together with her Son suffering and dying, she suffered and almost died; and in such a way, for the salvation of mankind, she abdicated the rights of a mother over her Son and she immolated him, insofar as it depended on her, to satisfy the justice of God, that it can rightly be said that she redeemed mankind along with Christ."

742 Blessed Imelda Lambertini

A friend, whose daughter is going to make her first Communion told me that she is praying to Blessed Imelda Lambertini, the patron saint of first communicants. I had never heard of her. Who is she?

Imelda Lambertini was born in 1322 in Bologna, Italy, the only child of Count Egano Lambertini and Castora Galuzzi. Her parents were devout Catholics, known for their charity and generosity towards the poor of Bologna. Her mother taught Imelda to cook and sew for the poor and she cultivated in her child an eagerness to perform the corporal works of mercy.

Even in her childhood Imelda showed unusual piety, taking delight in prayer and often going off to a quiet corner of the house, which she decorated with flowers and pictures to make it into a little oratory. She had a special love for the Eucharist and would often attend Mass and Compline (Night Prayer of the Divine Office) at a nearby Dominican church. On her fifth birthday Imelda asked to receive Holy Communion, but the custom at the time was for children not to make their first Holy Communion until at least the age of twelve.

When she was only nine her parents, both of whom were getting on in years, were surprised when Imelda asked permission to go to live with the Dominican nuns at the nearby monastery of Val di Pietra. As difficult as the decision was, her parents sensed the depth of their child's desire and entrusted her spiritual formation to the Dominicans.

Her pleasant disposition soon endeared her to all the nuns and her zeal to enter into the religious life of the convent edified them. It seems the nuns allowed her to wear the Dominican habit, to pray with them, including chanting the Divine Office, and to follow their way of life to the extent that it was possible for such a young girl.

Imelda had a special devotion to the Eucharistic presence of Our Lord in the Mass and the tabernacle and she ardently desired to receive Our Lord in Holy Communion. She repeatedly asked to be able to do so but the nuns had to tell her gently that she would need to wait until she was older and better prepared. Because of her burning desire to receive Our Lord she would ask: "Tell me, can anyone receive Jesus into his heart and not die?"

The saints, whose stories she had learned from her parents and from the nuns, became her "secret companions", and they probably had a role in nurturing her longing to receive Jesus in Holy Communion. And so Imelda continued, with the earnestness of a child, to get to know Jesus more deeply and to desire to receive him all the more.

When she was eleven, shortly before the feast of the Ascension Imelda asked once again, with great insistence, to make her first Communion. The nuns relayed this request to the chaplain, but he agreed with the nuns that she was still too young. Then on the Vigil of the Ascension, 12 May 1333, Imelda was present with the rest of the community at Mass, praying quietly while the nuns received Communion and longing to do so herself.

When the nuns had left the chapel, one of them was clearing the altar when she heard a noise and looked up to see Imelda kneeling before the tabernacle with a bright light above her head and a Sacred Host suspended in the light. The nun quickly called the priest and he hurried forward to see what was happening. Seeing that it was indeed a host which had somehow miraculously appeared, he realised that Jesus himself was making his desire known. After all, he had said "Let the little children come to me and do not stop them." The priest then gave Imelda her first Holy Communion.

The prioress allowed Imelda to remain for some time in thanksgiving, and then sent for her to go to breakfast. They found Imelda still kneeling where they had left her, a smile on her face. When they called her to come, she did not react. Her body was still. In fact, she had died of love and joy. She was now with Jesus whom she loved so much and whom she desired so ardently to receive.

Imelda was beatified by Pope Leo XII in 1826. Her remains are kept in Bologna at the Church of San Sigismondo, beneath a wax effigy of her likeness.

743 St Rose of Lima

A friend recently told me that St Rose of Lima did great penances in her lifetime. Is this true and can you tell me more about this saint?

St Rose was the first person from the Americas to be canonised a saint. She was from Lima, Peru, and was born Isabel Flores de Oliva on April 20, 1586. She was one of the many children of Gaspar Flores, born in Spain and a cavalryman in the Spanish army, and his wife, María de Oliva y Herrera, a native of Peru. When Isabel was confirmed in 1597 by the Archbishop of Lima, Toribio de Mogrovejo who would himself later be declared a saint, she took the name Rose.

As a child Rose was already known for her great piety and love for everything relating to God. She had a great devotion to the infant Jesus and his Blessed Mother, and spent hours in prayer before their altar. She was very obedient to her parents' instructions and was always busy, very attentive to her studies and to her work in the home, especially her needlework.

As you say, Rose was given over to great penances, and these began when she was still young. In imitation of St Catherine of Siena, when still a young girl she began to fast three times a week and she performed other severe penances in secret. When she became aware that men were admiring her for her beauty she cut off her hair and smeared pepper on her face. She began to wear clothing made of rough cloth and to roughen her hands by hard work. Against the objections of her parents and friends, who wanted her to marry, she rejected all those who sought her hand.

She spent many hours contemplating the Blessed Sacrament and she received Communion daily, an extremely rare practice at the time. When still young Rose was determined to take a vow of virginity, but since her parents were opposed to it she joined the Third Order of St Dominic, like St Catherine of Siena. Finally when she was nineteen, with her parents' permission, she took a vow of perpetual virginity and began to wear the habit of a Dominican tertiary. She continued to live at home, where her parents gave her a room to herself.

At that time she had strong temptations against chastity, faith and perseverance, which caused her considerable anguish and moved her to intensify her mortification. But Our Lord revealed himself to her frequently, strengthening her with the knowledge of his presence and consoling her with manifestations of his love. This filled her with such peace and joy that it left her in ecstasy for hours at a time.

Over time Rose began to fast everyday and then to abstain permanently from meat. She ended up eating only the coarsest food, just sufficient to stay alive. She allowed herself only two hours of sleep each night in order to devote more time to prayer. She wore a heavy crown made of silver, which had small spikes on the inside, concealed by roses, in imitation of the crown of thorns of Our Lord, and she had an iron chain around her waist.

She went whole days without food, save for a drink of gall mixed with bitter herbs. When she could no longer stand, she lay down on a bed she had made covered with broken glass, stone, potsherds and thorns. She admitted that the thought of lying down on it filled her with dread. She offered these penances in expiation for the many offences against Our Lord, for the idolatry of her country, for the conversion of sinners and for the souls in Purgatory.

Rose was very much given over to helping the sick and the hungry in the area and she often took them to her room to look after them. She loved sewing and sold her fine needlework, lace and embroidery, and the flowers she had grown to help her family and the poor. When her work allowed it, she retired to a small grotto she had built with the help of her brother in their small garden, where she would spend long hours in solitude and prayer, sometimes staying there overnight. With the consent of her confessor she became practically a recluse in the grotto, except for her visits to the Blessed Sacrament.

After eleven years of this rigorous life she died on 24 August 1617 at the age of just 31. It is said that she prophesied the date of her death. She was canonised in 1671 by Pope Clement X and her feast is celebrated in the universal calendar on August 23. She is often depicted with a crown of roses on her head.

744 St Nunzio Sulprizio

A friend told me that one of those canonised on 14 October 2018 by Pope Francis during the Synod of Bishops on youth was a boy who died in his teens. Who was he?

The new saint is Nunzio Sulprizio, an Italian who was born in Pescosansonesco in the province of Pescara in April of 1817. When he was only three his father died and his younger sister died a few months later. Two years later his mother married a much older man who treated Nunzio very harshly. Nunzio had a close relationship with his mother and also with his maternal grandmother.

Soon he began to attend the local school where he learned to read and write. From his childhood he attended Mass regularly and came to love Jesus Christ and the saints, whom he strove to imitate. A month before his sixth birthday Nunzio's mother died and he went to live with his grandmother, who was strong in the faith and took him to Mass regularly. But then she too passed away when Nunzio was turning nine.

He then went to live with his uncle, who took him on as an apprentice blacksmith but treated him cruelly, making him work long hours in the intense cold or heat and making him carry things that were far too heavy for him. He did not allow him to go to school, and he sometimes made him go without food and beat and cursed him if he was angry with him. Nunzio sought refuge in the tabernacle, where he kept Jesus company.

With all this abuse, when he was fourteen Nunzio contracted a serious illness after his uncle sent him on a long errand one morning in the winter. That evening his leg had swollen and he had a burning fever. He did not mention it to his uncle but the following morning he could not even stand up. The uncle was indifferent to his suffering. The leg was oozing puss which Nunzio cleaned regularly in a nearby stream, praying rosaries as he did so. He was later hospitalised and diagnosed as having gangrene in his leg. He bore the pain with patience and offered it to God.

In his suffering he would say such things as: "Jesus suffered so much for us and by his merits we await eternal life. If we suffer a little bit, we will taste the joy of paradise." "Jesus suffered a lot for me. Why should I not suffer for Him?" "I would die in order to convert even one sinner." When asked who was taking care of him, he would reply: "God's Providence".

While in hospital Nunzio met another uncle who introduced him to an army colonel who looked after him like a father and paid for his medical treatment. In 1835, when Nunzio was eighteen, the doctors had to amputate his leg but the pain continued. His condition worsened and his fever increased but Nunzio abandoned himself in the hands of God, aware that the end was near. He asked for a crucifix and received the sacraments before finally surrendering his soul to God in May 1836, at the age of nineteen. He died of bone cancer. One of the last things he told his colonel friend was, "Be cheerful. From heaven I will always be helping you."

Such was his fame of sanctity that his cause of beatification was opened in 1843, only seven years after his death. In 1891 Pope Leo XIII approved the decree on heroic virtues, declaring him Venerable and proposing Nunzio as a model for workers. Nunzio was beatified by Pope Paul VI in December 1963 and was fittingly canonised along with St Paul VI in October 2018. In that ceremony Pope Francis called Nunzio "the saintly, courageous, humble young man who encountered Jesus in his suffering, in silence and in the offering of himself."

In the beatification ceremony in 1963 Pope Paul VI had said: "Nunzio Sulprizio will tell you that the period of youth should not be considered the age of free passions, of inevitable falls, of invincible crises, of decadent pessimism, of harmful selfishness. Rather, he will tell you how being young is a grace... He will tell you that no other age than yours, young people, is as suitable for great ideals, for generous heroism, for the coherent demands of thought and action. He will teach you how you young people can regenerate the world in which Providence has called you to live, and how it is up to you first to consecrate yourselves for the salvation of a society that needs strong and fearless souls. He will teach you that the supreme word of Christ is to be the sacrifice, the cross, for our own salvation and that of the world. Young people understand this supreme vocation."

745 St Giuseppe Moscati

I am a medical student and a friend recently told me about St Giuseppe Moscati, an Italian physician and professor of medicine who was canonised by Pope John Paul II. I would like to pray to him for success in my studies. Can you tell me more about him?

Giuseppe Moscati (1880-1927) was a physician, professor of medicine, and a pioneer in the field of biochemistry. He was canonised by Pope John Paul II in 1987 during the synod of bishops on the laity.

Giuseppe was the seventh of nine children born into an aristocratic Italian family. His father's career as a magistrate led the family to settle in Naples. His father was very pious and even served Mass when the family was on holidays in his native region of Avellino.

Giuseppe's decision to study medicine rather than law came when his older brother Alberto, a lieutenant in the artillery, fell from a horse in 1893 and suffered an incurable head injury. For years Giuseppe helped care for his injured brother at home. When Giuseppe enrolled in medical school in 1897, the University of Naples had an openly agnostic, amoral, and anti-clerical atmosphere and so it was a difficult place for a young Catholic. But Giuseppe studied diligently and continued to practise his faith, gaining a doctoral degree with honours in 1903.

Dr Moscati practised medicine at the Hospital for Incurables in Naples and taught general medicine at the university. He soon became a hospital administrator. He demonstrated extraordinary skill in diagnosing his patients' ailments, attributed by some of his colleagues to his ability to combine traditional methods with the findings of the new science of biochemistry.

His approach was holistic, as seen in a letter he wrote to a young doctor who had been one of his students: "Remember that you must treat not only bodies, but also souls, with counsel that appeals to their minds and hearts rather than with cold prescriptions to be sent in to the pharmacist." In another letter, to a student, he wrote, "Not science, but charity has transformed the world."

A flock of interns would follow Dr Moscati when he made his rounds at the hospital, so as to learn his techniques. While dedicating the Church of St Giuseppe Moscati in the suburbs of Rome in 1993, Pope John Paul II described the doctor's approach: "In addition to the resources of his acclaimed skill, in caring for the sick he used the warmth of his humanity and the witness of his faith."

Giuseppe regarded his medical practice as a true apostolate, a ministry to the suffering. Before examining a patient or engaging in research he would place himself in the presence of God and he would encourage his patients, especially those who were about to undergo surgery, to receive the sacraments. He was very generous in attending to his patients' temporal needs, treating poor patients free of charge and often sending someone home with an envelope containing a prescription and a 50-lira note.

On occasion he risked his life to help others. When Mount Vesuvius erupted in April 1906, he voluntarily helped evacuate a nursing home in the endangered area, personally moving the frail and sick patients to safety minutes before the roof of the building collapsed under the weight of the ash. He also served beyond the call of duty during the 1911 cholera epidemic and he treated some 3,000 soldiers during World War I.

"The holy physician of Naples," as he was called, might have pursued a brilliant academic career, taken a professorial chair and devoted more time to research, but he preferred to continue working with patients and to train interns.

On Tuesday, 12 April 1927, Giuseppe went to Mass and received Holy Communion, as he did every day, and then made his rounds at the hospital. After a midday meal he felt weary, lay down, and died peacefully. He was not yet 47 years old.

Giuseppe was beatified in 1975 and declared a saint by Pope John Paul II on October 25, 1987. His feast day is November 16.

746 St Josephine Bakhita

On February 8 our priest celebrated the Mass of St Josephine Bakhita and told us she had once been a slave. Is this true and can you tell me more about her?

St Bakhita was indeed a slave and the story of her life is remarkable. She was born in Darfur, in western Sudan, around 1869. She had three brothers and three sisters and her father was a respected and prosperous brother of the village chief.

In 1877, when she was only seven or eight years old, Bakhita was seized by Arab slave traders, who had abducted her older sister two years earlier, and she was forced to walk barefoot some 960 kilometres to El-Obeid, having been sold and bought twice before she arrived there. Over the next twelve years she was sold three more times and then given away. It seems that the trauma of her abduction caused her to forget her name and so she took the name Bakhita given her by the slave traders. Bakhita in Arabic means lucky or fortunate.

In El-Obeid Bakhita was bought by a rich Arab who used her as a maid for his two daughters, who treated her well. But their brother got angry with her and beat and kicked her so badly that she was unable to get out of her straw bed for over a month. Her fourth owner was a Turkish general, who had her serve his wife and mother-in-law. They treated her cruelly, moving Bakhita to speak later of that time: "I do not recall a day that passed without some wound or other. When a wound from the whip began to heal, other blows would pour down on me."

In 1883 Bakhita was sold to the Italian Vice-Consul, Callisto Legnani, who treated her kindly. In 1885, when Legnani had to return to Italy, Bakhita begged to go with him. This was not possible but she did manage to travel to Italy with a friend of Legnani, Augusto Michieli. Legnani gave ownership of Bakhita to Michieli's wife and she lived with that family for the next three years, working as nanny to their infant daughter Mimmina.

In 1888, when Michieli acquired a hotel in the Sudan and went there to live, his wife wanted to accompany him and so she left Bakhita and Mimmina in the care of the Canossian Sisters in Venice. There the Sisters instructed Bakhita in the Catholic faith, introducing her to "that God who from childhood I had felt in my heart without knowing who he was," as she later wrote. She had a special love for Jesus Christ who, like her, had been scourged.

When Mrs Michieli returned to Italy to take Mimmina and

Bakhita to the Sudan, Bakhita refused to go with her. This led to legal proceedings which resulted in an Italian court ruling in 1889 that Bakhita was not legally a slave and so, free for the first time, she stayed with the Sisters.

On 9 January 1890 she was baptised with the names Josephine Margaret and Fortunata, the Latin translation of Bakhita. On the same day she was confirmed and received Holy Communion from Archbishop Giuseppe Sarto, the future Pope St Pius X. In 1893 she entered the Canossian Sisters and in 1896 she took her final vows. In 1902 she was assigned to the Canossian convent at Schio, where she spent the rest of her life, except for the years 1935-39, when she stayed at the Missionary Novitiate in Vimercate, helping prepare young Sisters for work in Africa.

During her 42 years in Schio Bakhita worked as a cook, sacristan and door keeper and she was known for her gentleness, calm voice and constant smile. During the Second World War the townspeople considered her a saint and they felt protected by her mere presence. In her last years she suffered much pain and sickness, and she died on Saturday, 8 February 1947. Her last words were "Our Lady, Our Lady." Thousands of people went to pay their respects before her body.

Such was her sanctity that when a student once asked Bakhita what she would do if she met her captors she replied immediately: "If I were to meet those who kidnapped me, and even those who tortured me, I would kneel and kiss their hands. For, if these things had not happened, I would not have been a Christian and a religious today."

St Bakhita was beatified by Pope St John Paul II on 17 May 1992 in the same ceremony as St Josemaría Escrivá, and she was canonised by the same Pope on 1 October 2000. Her feast day is February 8 and she is the patron saint of the Sudan and of victims of slavery and trafficking.

747 St Padre Pio

I was recently invited to attend a prayer group devoted to St Padre Pio and found this saint very inspiring. I have to say I knew little about him and would be grateful if you could tell me more about who he was and what made him such a popular saint.

Padre Pio, or more properly St Pio of Pietrelcina was a popular saint indeed, regarded widely as a saint already in his lifetime. Although he died as recently as 1968, he was canonised by Pope St John Paul II in 2002 and his feast day was quickly incorporated into the Roman missal to be celebrated by the universal Church. There are thousands of prayer groups devoted to him all over the world.

Padre Pio, born Francesco Forgione on 25 May 1887 in the Italian town of Pietrelcina in the south of Italy, was the fourth of eight children. His parents Grazio and Maria were peasant farmers and deeply religious, attending Mass daily, praying the rosary every night and abstaining from meat three days a week.

Padre Pio said that when he was five he had already decided to dedicate his whole life to God and that from his youth he experienced heavenly visions of Our Lord and Our Lady. When he was ten he felt drawn to the life of the Capuchin Franciscan friars but his parents were told that he should receive more education first. In 1903 at the age of fifteen Francesco entered the novitiate of the Capuchin friars at Morcone, near Pietrelcina, where he took the religious name of Fra Pio in honour of Pope Pius I, whose relic was venerated in the Santa Anna Chapel in Pietrelcina.

Despite suffering considerable ill health, he was ordained a priest in 1910. After six years living with his family because of his health, in 1916 Padre Pio was sent to the Capuchin friary in San Giovanni Rotondo, where he lived until his death in 1968 and where his remains are venerated.

Padre Pio was very devoted to the rosary and he recommended meditation and self- examination twice daily: in the morning to prepare for the day and in the evening to examine how it went. He also recommended weekly confession, which he compared to the weekly dusting of a house. His five rules for spiritual growth were weekly confession, daily Communion, spiritual reading, meditation and examination of conscience.

He led an austere life of fasting and penance, and he had the wounds of Christ, the stigmata, on his hands, feet and side from 1918 until his death fifty years later. He wore mittens or black coverings on his hands to hide the wounds, which bled and gave him intense pain, such as Christ would have felt on the Cross. The wounds gave off a pleasant smell, as of flowers.

Padre Pio was also known for such spiritual gifts as healing, bilocation, ecstasy, levitation and prophecy. He was especially known for his long hours in the confessional and for knowing aspects of a person's life he could not have known by human means. The devil attacked him both physically and spiritually, as he had St John Vianney, the Curé of Ars, another great confessor.

For a number of years Padre Pio was forbidden to say Mass in public and to hear confessions, something that cost him dearly but which he accepted as coming from the hands of his mother the Church. Finally, in 1933 Pope Pius XI ordered the ban to be lifted, saying that he had been badly informed about Padre Pio.

Padre Pio's health deteriorated in the 1960s but he kept up his spiritual work, especially hearing confessions. On 21 September 1968, the day after the fiftieth anniversary of his receiving the stigmata, he felt very tired. The following day he was supposed to offer a Solemn Mass, but because of his weakness he asked his superior if he might say a Low Mass instead. Due to the large number of pilgrims present the superior decided that he should say the Solemn Mass, which he did with great effort, appearing extremely weak and with a faint voice. This was to be his last Mass.

Early in the morning of 23 September, Padre Pio made his last confession and renewed his Franciscan vows. With the rosary in his hands he repeated the words "Jesus, Mary" until he finally breathed his last. Over 100,000 people attended his funeral on 26 September. He was beatified by Pope St John Paul II in 1999 and canonised in 2002. Some 300,000 people attended his canonisation ceremony in Rome. His feast is celebrated on 23 September.

748 Pope St Paul VI

I know that Pope Paul VI was canonised in 2018. I was born during the pontificate of St John Paul II and don't know much about Paul VI. For what should he be remembered?

Before answering your question, let me give you a brief overview of his life.

Pope Paul VI was born Giovanni Battista Montini in 1897 in Concesio in the province of Brescia, Italy. His father Giorgio was a lawyer, journalist, director of Catholic Action and a member of the Italian parliament. His mother Giudetta was from a family of rural nobility. He had two brothers, one of whom was a physician and the other a lawyer and politician.

Giovanni Battista was ordained priest in 1920 in Brescia and in the same year completed his studies in Milan for a doctorate in Canon Law. He did further studies in Rome and in 1922, at the age of twenty-five, he began work in the Vatican's Secretariat of State. After a posting in the nunciature in Poland beginning in 1923, he returned to Rome where he held several positions in the Vatican, especially in the Secretariat of State, where he also served as a personal assistant to Pope Pius XII. During the Second World War he coordinated assistance to thousands of refugees.

In 1954 Pope Pius XII appointed him Archbishop of Milan and in 1958 Pope John XXIII made him a cardinal. Following the death from cancer of Pope John XXIII early in June 1963, Cardinal Montini was elected Pope later that month, taking the name Paul VI.

Pope Paul VI will be remembered for a number of very important acts that had great repercussions on the universal Church. The first was his decision to continue the Second Vatican Council, which had begun in 1962 under Pope John XXIII. When a Pope dies during an Ecumenical Council, his successor must decide whether to continue the Council or declare it concluded. Fortunately Pope Paul VI chose the former and the result was the collection of documents produced by the Council, many of which had great significance for the life of the Church. Pope Paul closed the Council on 8 December 1965.

In July 1968 Pope Paul VI gave the Church what was undoubtedly his most important and controversial document: the encyclical *Humanae vitae*. Echoing the constant tradition of the Church, as articulated by Pope Pius XI in the encyclical *Casti connubii* (1930), he declared that no form of contraception was acceptable as a means of avoiding pregnancy. He knew the encyclical would meet with a negative response from many but, after much prayer and with considerable courage, he repeated the traditional teaching of the Church. As expected, the encyclical was applauded by many but also much criticised, both within and outside the Church.

Another important contribution of Paul VI was the establishment of the Synod of Bishops as a permanent advisory body to the Pope. The Synod is a periodic gathering of bishops from around the world to discuss issues proposed by the Pope. Several meetings of the Synod were held under Paul VI, including one on evangelisation which led to his important Apostolic Exhortation *Evangelii nuntiandi* in 1975.

The reform of the Roman Curia was another of Pope Paul VI's accomplishments. Having worked in the Curia for more than thirty years, he understood it well and, in a number of stages, he reduced its bureaucracy, streamlined the existing congregations and other bodies, and brought about a broader representation of non-Italians in it.

The reform of the liturgy was still another important contribution of Pope Paul VI, with the introduction of a new Roman Missal in 1969, with four Eucharistic Prayers instead of the former one. This was followed by a new Lectionary, with a much broader selection of readings from Scripture.

In addition to *Humanae vitae* Pope Paul VI wrote six other encyclicals, the most important of which were *Ecclesiam suam* (1964) on the Church, *Mysterium fidei* (1965) on the Eucharist, *Populorum progressio* (1967) on social development and *Sacerdotalis caelibatus* (1967) on priestly celibacy.

Every Pope bears the burden of the most important office in the world: that of the Vicar of Christ. He must be a leader by word and example both of the universal Church and of the family of nations. The work demanded of a Pope is extraordinarily heavy and Pope Paul VI devoted himself to all aspects of this task with great diligence and attentiveness. His secretaries testified that he worked for four hours straight every night, two hours with each secretary, going through one set of papers after another.

Pope St Paul VI travelled to many countries at his advanced age (including Australia in 1970), he met bishops and diplomats in the way the Roman Pontiff is expected to do as the head of the Church and as head of State of Vatican City, he met pilgrims coming to Rome, and he gave outstanding and enlightening addresses at his Wednesday audiences, written by himself.

As an evident sign of his holiness, some time after Paul VI died his secretary Bishop John Magee stated that the Pope had worn a hairshirt every Friday to atone for the sins of defecting priests.

Pope St Paul VI died on 6 August 1978, feast of the Transfiguration. He was canonised by Pope Francis on 14 October 2018 and his feast day is 29 May, the day of his priestly ordination.

Apparitions

749 Our Lady of Guadalupe

A friend recently returned from Mexico, where she visited the Basilica of Our Lady of Guadalupe in Mexico City. She told me the image venerated there has some remarkable features. Can you tell me something about the image?

To remind our readers, in December 1531 Our Lady appeared several times to an Aztec convert St Juan Diego and on December 12 she left a miraculous image of herself on Juan Diego's cactus fibre tilma or cloak, which is the one venerated in the basilica.

Among the most remarkable features of the image is the very preservation of the fabric itself. Normally a cactus fibre garment would disintegrate within some twenty to forty years, yet here the fabric is still intact after almost five centuries.

Another is the brightness of the image, which has remained virtually unchanged over all these years, in spite of the fact that for the first approximately 116 years the image was exposed to the humid air, to infrared and ultraviolet radiation and to the smoke of thousands of candles with no protective cover over it.

What is more, the image repaired itself after a nitric acid spill in 1791 that damaged it considerably. And an attempt to destroy the image completely by exploding a bomb on the altar immediately beneath it on 14 November 1921 left the image unharmed, even though a brass crucifix on the altar was bent double.

Perhaps the most extraordinary feature came to light when the image was photographed and then magnified 2500 times by ophthalmologist José Aste Tonsmann of the Mexican Center of Guadalupan Studies. In the partially closed eyes of Our Lady on the rough fabric there appeared the reflection of all those present when Juan Diego opened his tilma to give some flowers to the bishop. Visible are a seated Indian, who is looking up at the heavens; a balding, elderly man with a white beard, much like the portrait of Bishop Juan de Zumárraga; a younger man, who could be the interpreter Juan González; an Indian with a beard and moustache who unfolds his tilma before the bishop; a woman of dark complexion, possibly a slave who was in the bishop's service; a man with Spanish features who looks on, stroking his beard with his hand; and an Indian family made up of a woman, a man and several children. In all there are a total of thirteen people.

Also extraordinary and humanly inexplicable is the fact that the image was not painted by human hand. As early as the eighteenth century scientists showed that it was not possible to paint an image like that on a fabric of such rough texture. In 1936 biochemist Richard Kuhn, the 1938 Nobel Prize winner in chemistry, found that the image did not have any natural animal, vegetable or mineral colourings. Since there were no synthetic colourings in 1531 there is no human explanation for the image.

In 1979 Americans Philip Callahan, a biophysicist from the University of Florida, and Professor Jody B. Smith subjected the image to infrared photography and found that there was no trace of paint and that the fabric had not been treated with any kind of technique. They also showed how the image changes in colour slightly according to the angle of viewing, a phenomenon known as iridescence which cannot be reproduced by human means. In short, the image is an ongoing miracle, much like the image on the Shroud of Turin.

Other features regard the image's symbolism for the Aztecs. Mary's uncovered face shows that she is human, not a goddess, and she has a sash on her waist, indicating that she is carrying a child in her womb. The fact that she appears blocking out the rays of the sun behind her shows that she is more powerful than the sun itself, and her standing on a darkened crescent moon shows that she is trampling on the Aztecs' moon god. Yet with her hands folded in prayer she is praying to a God more powerful then herself. All of this, together with the fact that she appeared dressed as an Aztec princess, helped some eight to ten million people in Mexico and the neighbouring countries convert to the Catholic faith over the next ten years.

The feast of Our Lady of Guadalupe is celebrated on December 12.

750 Our Lady of Zeitoun

I have an Egyptian friend who says she saw Our Lady in an apparition above a Coptic Orthodox church in Cairo in the late 1960s. Has this apparition been approved and, even if not, can you tell me something about it?

I too know people who saw the apparitions in Cairo, in a district called Zeitoun. According to Coptic tradition, Zeitoun is believed to be one of the places where the Holy Family stayed during their flight into Egypt after the birth of Jesus. It is said that in 1918 Our Lady appeared in a dream to Khalil Ibrahim, who owned several plots of land in that part of Cairo, asking him to build a church there in her honour and telling him that a miracle would take place. The church of St Mary, a beautiful white Coptic Orthodox church with four small domes over the corners and one large one in the centre, was completed in 1924. It has been a shrine of the Holy Family ever since.

In 1968 when Our Lady began appearing, Christians were being persecuted in Egypt, with crosses painted on their front doors to identify them. On the evening of 2 April 1968 a 31 year-old Muslim named Farouk Mohammed Atwa, who worked across the street from St Mary's, saw what he thought was a woman dressed in white standing on the main dome of the church. He feared she was about to jump to her death and called out to her not to jump. The woman appeared to float effortlessly over the sloping roof of the church toward its cross, with her head bowed and her hands folded in prayer. Atwa pointed her out to the people standing nearby and they too saw her. They called the police, who arrived quickly, by which time a crowd had gathered.

A week later, on April 9, the woman in light appeared again for only a few minutes. After that the apparitions were more frequent, sometimes two or three times a week, gradually becoming less frequent until the last apparition in 1971. It became clear to all that the figure was indeed the Blessed Virgin Mary.

Sometimes she would be visible for only a short time and others for hours at a time. She always appeared to be praying, sometimes bowing toward the cross or blessing those watching on the streets below, sometimes remaining stationary and other times gliding across the church roof.

On many occasions she appeared as on the Miraculous Medal, with her arms extending down and forward. Sometimes there appeared around her what looked like doves of light.

Over the next few years many healings took place there. The first one involved Farouk Atwa himself, who the day after the first apparition went for a scheduled operation to amputate a finger which had developed gangrene only to discover that the finger had inexplicably healed. A blind Muslim was given back his sight and saw Our Lady during an apparition; a girl who had suffered from polio from the age of six months was able to walk without the aid of crutches; paralysed people were cured of their paralysis; a woman with breast cancer saw Our Lady beside her bed and the following day the cancer disappeared; some Muslims became Christians.

People were able to take photographs of the apparitions, and newspapers, including the *New York Times*, carried articles about them. The number of people who saw Our Lady grew greatly and on one occasion numbered nearly 250,000 of all faiths: Orthodox, Catholics, Jews and Muslims. Overall, it was estimated that between hundreds of thousands and millions of people saw Our Lady, making these the most widely viewed apparitions in history. Even the Egyptian President Gamal Abdel Nasser saw them, leading him to soften his stance against Christians.

The head of the Coptic Orthodox Church, Pope Kyrillos VI, appointed a commission of high-ranking bishops and priests to investigate the phenomenon and on 5 May 1968 he issued a statement confirming the authenticity of the apparitions.

The Egyptian government too conducted an investigation and, after not finding any human explanation for the apparitions or any evidence of a hoax, declared that "it has been considered an undeniable fact that the Blessed Virgin Mary has been appearing on Zeitoun Church in a clear and luminous body seen by all present in front of the church, whether Christian or Muslim."

Although Our Lady never spoke, people saw the apparitions as bringing a message of peace and hope. On 12 May 2018 the Coptic Church, led by Pope Tawadros II, celebrated the golden jubilee of the apparitions along with priests and lay faithful from all over Egypt.

INDEX

abortion, 3, 73, 80, 87, 158, 164-6, 177-83, 205-8, 220, 237, 239-43
Advent, 79, 109, 264-8
Alphonsus Liguori, St, 26, 300
Ambrose, St, 53-4, 104, 267, 281
Amoris laetitia, 86, 210, 212
Aquinas, St Thomas, 76, 112, 125, 177
Aristotle, 177
Ascension, feast of, 288-91, 301-2, 311
assisted suicide, 187-90, 192-3, 196-9
Athanasius, St, 52, 274, 287
Augustine, St, 54-5, 75-6, 82, 89, 112, 133, 177, 219, 268, 274

Basil the Great, St, 52
Benedict XVI, Pope, 73, 84, 91, 184, 211, 214, 259
Bernard of Clairvaux, St, 300, 309
blessings, 12, 84, 97-9, 103, 279, 281-2, 286, 291, 329
  blessing of gay couples, 151-3
  What can be blessed, 97-8
  Book of Blessings, 97-8

celibacy, priestly, 18, 130-1, 325
Ceremonies of the Modern Roman Rite, 108
Christ, Jesus, 24, 28ff

Did he act like God, 32-3
Did he know he was God, 30-1
historical evidence for, 28-9
Jesus as Messiah, 34-7
proof of his Resurrection, 38-40
Christmas, 267-70
Church, 41ff
  Apostolicity, 47-8
  catholicity, 45-6
  holiness, 43-4
  oneness, 41-2
Clement of Rome, St, 50
Communion, Holy, 107
  for Protestants, 113-4
  in nursing homes, 115-6
  kneeling, 111-2
Confession, 124-9
  seal of, 124-5
contraception, 231-4
  and HIV, 235-6
  and threat of rape, 81, 181
  Why not permitted, 233-4
Corfu, battle of, 256-7, 300
Cyprian, St, 57
Cyril of Alexandria, St, 52

Dead Sea Scrolls, 17-18
death penalty, 181-5
Declaration on Procured Abortion, 177, 240

INDEX

Didache, 58, 103, 115
Dignitas personae, 175
Doctors of the Church, 50
dogmas, 60-2
Donum veritatis, 74
Donum vitae, 179
double effect, principle of, 163-5

Easter, 274-87
   Octave of, 283-4
   Season of, 286-7
   Vigil of, 281-2
   Water, 285-6
Elliott, Bishop Peter, 108
embryo adoption, 174-6
ensoulment, 177
Ephesus, Council of, 13, 53, 56
Escrivá, St Josemaría, 251, 320
Essenes, 18-19
Eucharistic miracles, 117-23
   Amsterdam, 119-20
   Santarem, 117-8
   Tixtla, Mexico, 121-2
euthanasia, 73, 81, 166, 185-199, 206, 219, 237, 239-40
Evangelii gaudium, 86, 212
Evangelium vitae, 185, 187-9, 238-40
excommunication, 56, 126, 242-3

family, attack on, 216-22
Fathers of the Church, 49-59
   Apologists, 51
   Apostolic Fathers, 50

Cappadocian, 52
   Eastern, 51-2
   Pre-Nicene, 51
   Post-Nicene, 51
   Western, 53-7
Feasts, Jewish, 6-12
   Day of Atonement (Yom Kippur), 9-10
   Dedication of Temple (Hanukkah), 10
   New Moon, Day of, 11-12
   Passover, 6-7
   Pentecost, 7-8
   Purim, 11
   Sabbath, 11
   Tabernacles, 8
   Unleavened Bread, 7
First Vatican Council, 50, 61, 77
Fourth Lateran Council, 124, 288
Francis, Pope, 44, 63, 69, 74, 83-7, 90, 109-10, 113, 122, 137-9, 142, 182-4, 210-12, 294, 314, 316, 325
freedom and responsibility, 159-60
   Can it be diminished, 157-8
   emotions and, 161-2

Gaudete et Exsultate, 44
gender theory, 200-215
   European Union and, 206-7
   origins of, 200-1
   Pope Francis and, 210-11
   power of, 204-5

INDEX 333

Vatican document on, 212-3
Yogyakarta Principles of, 202-3
General Instruction of the Roman Missal, 109
Giuseppe Moscati, St, 316-7
Global Sexual Revolution, The, 200, 202, 205-6, 217-8, 221
God, 1ff
    as Father, 2-4
    gender-neutral?, 1-2
    natural disasters a punishment?, 3-5
Gregory of Nazianzus, St, 52, 267, 287
Gregory of Nyssa, St, 52, 158, 177, 282, 289
Gregory of Tours, St, 57
Gregory the Great, St, 49, 53, 55, 274, 292

Handbook of Christian Feasts and Customs, 264, 267, 270, 274, 276, 280, 282
Hasmoneans, 19
hell, 80, 88, 90-2, 165, 167
Hilary of Poitiers, St, 57
Hippolytus, St, 56-7
holy days of obligation, 301-3
Holy Week, 274, 278, 280, 287
Humanae vitae, 231-4, 236, 324-5

Ignatius of Antioch, St 45, 50, 59, 91, 108
Imelda Lambertini, Blessed 310-2

incense in the liturgy, 99-101
indirect voluntary, 167-9
Infant of Prague, 257-9
Inter insigniores, 135
International Theological Commission, 73-5, 77
Irenaeus, St, 43, 56, 58
Isidore of Seville, St, 49, 57

Jerome, St, 53-4, 75, 109, 274, 288
John Cassian, St, 57
John Chrysostom, St, 52-3, 267, 275, 289-91
John Damascene, St, 49, 53, 55
John Paul I, Pope, 251
John Paul II, Pope St, 26, 44, 61, 84, 131, 134-5, 170, 175, 184-7, 189, 193, 197, 232, 235, 237-40, 275, 293-4, 298-300, 316-8, 320-1, 323
Josephine Bakhita, St, 318-20
Josephus, Flavius, 13, 18, 28
Justin Martyr, St, 51, 59

Kuby, Gabriele, 200, 202, 205-6, 217-8, 220-1

laicisation, 132, 134
Laudato si', 86, 211
Lent, 91, 265-6, 274, 277-9
Leo XIII, Pope, 84, 256, 259, 316
Lepanto, battle of, 253-7, 300
Leuven Project, 62-3
Lucy of Fatima, Sr, 252

Mariana de Jesus Torres, Mother, 260-2
marriage, 137-48
  convalidation of, 139-40
  not celebrated in a church, 137-8
  same-sex, 145-8
Mary, Blessed Virgin, 304-9
  Annunciation, feast, 295-6
  Assumption, 53, 61, 172, 297, 301-3, 307
  Co-redemptrix, title, 308-9
  devotion to, 304-5
  Guadalupe, Our Lady of, 326-7
  Holy Name of, feast, 299-300
  Immaculate Conception, 61, 76, 261-2, 301-2, 307
  Mother of the Church, feast, 292-4
  Our Lady of Good Success, 259-61
  perpetual virginity, 76, 307
  Zeitoun, apparitions of, 328-9
Maximus the Confessor, St, 53
Michael the Archangel, St, 83-4
mortal sin, 89, 91, 112, 133, 165-7, 173
Mystici corporis, 82

New Testament, 6, 12-18, 20-1, 24, 28, 38, 55, 100, 135, 288
  accuracy of text, 12-13
  Archaeological evidence for, 14-16
Newman, St John Henry, 76
Nicaea, Council of, 51-2
Nunzio Sulprizio, St 314-5

Ordinatio sacerdotalis, 61, 134-5
Origen, 50, 291

Padre Pio, St, 321-2
Passiontide, 278-9
Pastores dabo vobis, 131
Pentecost, feast of, 8, 40, 45-6, 286, 289-92, 294
Peterwardein, battle of, 255-6, 300
Pharisees, 18-23, 32
Pius V, Pope St, 119, 253-4, 256
Pius IX, Pope, 61, 262
Pius X, Pope St, 259, 279, 292, 300-1, 320
Pius XI, 232, 259, 322, 324
Pius XII, Pope, 61, 82, 273, 323
Plenary Council, 2020 66, 68, 70, 72, 78
Pliny the Elder, 18, 29, 87
Pliny the Younger, 29
Polycarp, St, 50-1, 56
predestination, 88-90

Rhonheimer, Fr Martin, 235-7
rosary, 83-4, 97-8, 167, 251-7, 294, 298-9, 308, 321-2
Rose of Lima, St, 312-3

Sadducees, 18-21
Safe Schools program, 149, 201, 204-5, 208, 215, 217-8, 225-8
Salvifici doloris, 26
Sarah, Cardinal Robert, 112

scribes, 21-3, 32, 38
Sculley, Brother Max DLS, 244, 246-8
Second Vatican Council, 23, 41, 43-4, 61-2, 64, 73-4, 77, 89, 111, 114, 136, 213, 231, 275, 287, 289, 293, 306-9, 324
Seleucids, 19
Sensus fidei, 72, 74-9
Sensus fidelium, 72, 74
Seventh-Day Adventists, 79-81
Strobel, Lee, 14
Tacitus, 13, 29, 39
Tai Chi, 244, 246-8

Temesvar, battle of, 255-7, 300
Tertullian, 49-50, 56, 75, 95, 282, 291
The Case for Christ, 14
Transfiguration, feast of, 297-9, 325
Trent, Council of, 50, 61, 76, 130

Vincent of Lerins, St, 75

Ward, Roz, 208, 225
Weiser, Fr Francis S.J., 264-5, 267, 269-70, 274, 276, 280, 282

Yoga, 244-6

www.ingramcontent.com/pod-product-compliance
Lightning Source LLC
Chambersburg PA
CBHW051108230426
43667CB00014B/2493